MENU READER

For eating out in over 25 countries

Austria, Belgium, Czech Republic, Denmark, Finland, France, Germany, Greece, Hungary, Italy, Netherlands, Norway, Poland, Portugal, Russia, Slovakia, Spain, Sweden, Switzerland, and more

Berlitz Publishing / APA Publications GmbH & Co. Verlag KG, Singapore Branch, Singapore

How best to use this menu reader

What's for dinner? That's an easy enough question at home, but on a trip, the answer might not come as quickly. Dishes are often untranslatable and the waiter may be of little assistance. Berlitz has addressed this problem and the result is this handy glossary of local dishes and national cuisines which makes an invaluable companion for eating out across Europe.

● To make gastromonic experimentation more fun, we've organized this book into **15 language areas**. The sections on France, Germany, Holland, Italy, Portugal and Spain also include dishes from Belgium, Switzerland, Austria and Latin America—depending on the language.

● Each **food glossary** provides an easy look-up of any dish on the menu, with as much detail of ingredients as necessary to convey its appearance and taste.

● As a supplement to each section on food, a **drink section** includes descriptions of local wines, beers, spirits and non-alcoholic beverages.

● Each food and drink section is preceded by a **pronunciation guide** to help you order aloud. For the particular difficulties presented by Greek and Russian, a simplified **transliteration** is provided of all the dishes and terms.

● In addition, we've included some of the most **common expressions** you'll need in a restaurant or bar, from booking a table, ordering, paying and, should the need unfortunately arise, making a complaint.

● Consult the inside back cover for **conversion tables** if you're not sure of metric weights and measures, and the handy **tipping guide** (pp. 317–320) for the appropriate gratuity in the country of your visit.

Finally, if this Menu Reader whets your appetite for the language as well as the food, why not obtain a Berlitz phrase book, cassette pack or pocket dictionary to accompany you on your travels!
Bon appétit and *à votre santé*.

Contacting the Editors
Every effort has been made to provide accurate information in this publication, but changes are inevitable. The publisher cannot be responsible for any resulting loss, inconvenience or injury. We would appreciate it if readers would call our attention to any errors or outdated information by contacting Berlitz Publishing, 95 Progress Street, Union, NJ 07083, USA. Fax: 1-908-206-1103 email: comments@berlitzbooks.com

Reprinted 2003 Printed in Singapore by Insight Print Services

Contents

Czech

Guide to pronunciation

Letter **Consonants**	**Approximate pronunciation**
b, d, f, g, k, m, n, p, t, v, z	are pronounced as in English
c	like **ts** in ca**ts**
č	like **ch** in **ch**urch
d'	like **d** in **d**uty; for American speakers close to **j** in **j**am
g	like **g** in **g**ood
h	like **h** in **h**alf
ch	like **ch** in in Scottish lo**ch**
j	like **y** in **y**es
ň	like **nn** in a**nn**ual or **ny** in ca**ny**on
r	rolled (like a Scottish **r**)
ř	a sound unique to Czech; like a rolled **r** but flatten the tip of the tongue to make a short forceful buzz like **ž** below
s	like **s** in **s**et
š	like **sh** in **sh**ort
t'	like **t** in **t**une; for American speakers close to **ch** in **ch**urch

w	like **v** in van; found only in foreign words
ž	like **s** in pleasure

Notes

1) **ě** — the sign ˇ written over the letter **e** makes the preceding consonant soft. A similar effect is produced by pronouncing **y** as in **y**et.
2) Voiced consonants (**b, d, d', h, z, zh, v**) become voiceless (**p, t, t', kh, s, sh, f** respectively) at the beginning and end of a word, and before a voiceless consonant. Voiceless consonants within a word become voiced if followed by a voiced consonant (this involves particularly voiceless **k** becoming voiced **g**).

Vowels

Vowels in Czech can be either short (**a, e, i, o, u, y**) or long (**á, é, í, ó, ú, ů, ý**). The length of the vowel is an essential feature since it can differentiate meanings of words which are otherwise written with the same spelling.

a	between the **a** in c**a**t and the **u** in c**u**t
á	like **a** in f**a**ther
e	like **e** in m**e**t; this is always pronounced, even at the end of a word
é	similar to the **e** in b**e**d but longer
i	like **i** in b**i**t
í	like **ee** in s**ee**
o	like **o** in h**o**t
ó	like **o** in sh**o**rt, found only in foreign words
u	like **oo** in b**oo**k
ú	like **oo** in m**oo**n
ů	like **ú** above
y	like **i** above
ý	like **ee** in s**ee**

Diphthongs

au	like **ow** in c**ow**
ou	like **ow** in m**ow**, or the exclamation **oh**

Stressing of words

Stress in Czech falls always on the first syllable of a word, though it is weaker than in English. Prepositions in Czech are pronounced together with their object as a single word, so the stress falls on the preposition.

CZECH

Some useful expressions

Hungry?

I'm hungry/I'm thirsty.	**Mám hlad/Mám žízeň.**
Can you recommend a good restaurant?	**Můžete nám doporučit dobrou restauraci?**
Are there any inexpensive restaurants around here?	**Jsou tu blízko nějaké lacinější restaurace?**
I'd like to reserve a table for 4.	**Chci si zamluvit stůl pro 4.**
We'll come at 8.	**Přijdeme v 8 hodin.**
Could we have a table ...?	**Máte volný stůl...?**
in the corner	**v rohu**
by the window	**u okna**
outside	**venku**
on the terrace	**na terase**
in a non-smoking area	**v nekuřácké části**

Asking and ordering

I'd like ...	**Chtěl(a) bych ...**
Could we have a/an ..., please?	**Mohl[a] byste mi dát ...?**
ashtray	**popelník**
cup	**šálek**
fork	**vidličku**
glass	**skleničku**
knife	**nůž**
napkin (serviette)	**ubrousek**
plate	**talíř**
spoon	**lžíci**
May I have some ...?	**Přineste mi prosím...**
bread	**chleba**
butter	**máslo**
lemon	**citrón**
oil	**olej**
pepper	**pepř**
salt	**sůl**
seasoning	**koření**
sugar	**cukr**

baked	**pečené**
fried	**smažené**
grilled	**grilované**
marinated	**marinované**
poached	**do ztracena**
sautéed	**na másle**
smoked	**uzené**
steamed	**vařené v páře**
boiled	**vařené**
braised	**dušené**
fried	**smažené**
roast	**pečeně**
stewed	**dušené**
very rare	**na krvavo**
underdone (rare)	**lehce udělané**
medium	**středně udělané**
well-done	**dobře udělané**

I'd like a glass of ...	**Rád(a) bych sklenice ...**
Waiter/waitress, bring me another ..., please.	**Pane/paní vrchní, ještě ..., prosím.**
red	**červené**
white	**bilé**
rosé	**ružové**
sparkling	**šumivé**
dry	**suché**
sweet	**sladký**

Complaints

That's not what I ordered.	**To jsem si neobjednal(a).**
I asked for ...	**Já jsem chtěl(a)...**
May I change this?	**Můžu si to vyměnit?**
The meat is ...	**To maso je...**
overdone	**předělané**
underdone	**nedodělané**
too tough	**tvrdé**
This is too ...	**Tohle je moc...**
bitter/salty/sweet	**hořké/slané/sladké**
I don't like this.	**To mi nechutná.**

The food is cold.	**To jídlo je studené.**
This isn't fresh.	**Tohle není čerstvé.**
What's taking you so long?	**Proč vám to tak dlouho trvá?**
This isn't clean.	**Tohle není čisté.**
Would you ask the head waiter to come over?	**Zavolal[a] byste pana vrchního?**

The bill (check)

I'd like to pay.	**Platit, prosím.**
We'd like to pay separately.	**My budeme platit zvlášť'.**
I think there's a mistake in this bill.	**V tom učtu je asi chyba.**
What's this amount for?	**Za co je tohle?**
Is service included?	**Zahrnuje to služby?**
Do you accept traveller's cheques?	**Přijímáte cestovní šeky?**
Can I pay with this credit card?	**Mohu platit touto uvěrovou kartou?**
Keep the change.	**Nechte si drobné.**
That was delicious.	**To bylo vynikající.**
We enjoyed it, thank you.	**Moc nám to chutnalo, děkujeme.**

Numbers

0	**nula**	11	**jedenáct**
1	**jedna**	12	**dvanáct**
2	**dvě**	13	**třináct**
3	**tři**	14	**čtrnáct**
4	**čtyři**	15	**patnáct**
5	**pět**	16	**šestnáct**
6	**šest**	17	**sedmnáct**
7	**sedm**	18	**osmnáct**
8	**osm**	19	**devatenáct**
9	**devět**	20	**dvacet**
10	**deset**		

Food

Please note that the Czech alphabetical order is **a, á, b, c, č, d, d', e, é, f, g, h, ch, i, í, j, k, l, m, n, ň, o, ó, p, q, r, ř, s, š, t, t', u, ú, ů, v, w, x, y, ý, z, ž.**

ananas pineapple
angrešt gooseberries
aperitiv aperitif
arašídy peanuts
artyčok artichoke
aspik aspic
~ **maso v aspiku** meat in aspic
~ **šunka v aspiku** ham in aspic
~ **vejce v aspiku** egg in aspic
bažant pheasant
~ **na slanině** roast pheasant with bacon
~ **dušený na žampionech** pheasant casserole with mushrooms
bábovka sponge cake
baklažán aubergine
banán banana
bešamel white sauce
biftek beefsteak
bílé víno white vine
biskupský chlebíček fruit cake
bobkový list laurel
bochník loaf
bonbóny sweets (candy)
boršč borscht; vegetable soup with meat and sour cream; may be served hot or chilled
borůvky bilberries (US blueberries)
bramborák potato cakes made from raw potatoes
bramborová kaše mashed potatoes
bramborové škubánky potato pudding
bramborové omelety se špenátem potato omelettes with spinach
bramborové placky potato pancake
bramborové šišky small flour and potato dumplings
bramborové knedlíky potato dumplings
brambory potatoes
~ **na loupačku** skin boiled
~ **restované** fried, hashed-brown
~ **vařené** boiled
broskev peach
brynza sheep cheese
brzlík sweetbreads
bublanina sponge with cherries
buchty baked yeast dumplings filled with cottage cheese, jam, apples, poppy seeds or plums
bujón bouillon
burské oříšky peanuts
celer celery
celerový salát celeriac salad

CZECH

cena price
cibule onion
cikorka chicory (US endive)
citrón lemon
cukr sugar
~ **kostkový** lump
~ **krystal** granulated
~ **moučka** castor
cukroví cookies
čerstvý fresh
červená řepa beetroot
červený rybíz redcurrants
česnečka garlic soup
česnek garlic
čevabčiči minced meat grilled in rolled pieces, served with minced raw onion
čočka lentils
~ **čočka nakyselo** savoury lentils
čočková polévka lentil soup
čočkový salát lentil salad
čokoláda chocolate
~ **mléčná** milk chocolate bar
~ **na vaření** cooking chocolate
~ **oříšková** chocolate bar with hazelnuts
~ **s arašídý** chocolate bar with peanuts
~ **s rozinkami** with raisins
čufty meatballs
datle dates
džem jam
dezert dessert
dietní low calorie
divoký králík na česneku wild rabbit with garlic
divoký kanec wild boar
dobře propečeno well done
domácí šunka country ham
domácí homemade
~ **klobásy** homemade sausages
domažlické koláče a pie, patterned with stripes of cream cheese, plum cheese and poppy seed filling
dort z karlovarských oplatek "Carlsbad layer cake", made from thin wafers sandwiching a walnut and cocoa butter filling and topped with icing
dort cake
~ **čokoládový** chocolate cake
~ **punčový** frosted sponge cake sprinkled with rum
drůbež fowl
dršťková polévka tripe soup
dršťky tripe
dušená kachna s brusinkami braised duck with cranberries
dušené maso stew
~ **hovězí** beef
~ **kuřecí** stewed chicken
~ **telecí** veal
dušený braised
dukátové buchtičky tiny doughnuts
džuveč pork chop, rice and vegetables (all oven-baked)
dýně marrow (US zucchini)
ementál Swiss cheese
estragon tarragon
fazole dry beans
fazole na kyselo sour beans
fazolové lusky green beans
feferonky pimentos
fíky figs
filé fillet
granátové jablko pomegranate
grapefruit grapefruit
gril grill
~ **grilovat** to grill
~ **maso na grilu** a grilled meat
grilovací jehla skewer
grilovaný grilled

~ **vepřový kotlet** grilled pork chop
guláš goulash; a spicy meat stew
~ **bramborový** with potatoes
~ **hovězí** beef
~ **segedínský** with sauerkraut and onion
~ **telecí** veal
~ **vepřový** pork
guláš z daňčího masa venison goulash
guláš z hovězího masa na smetaně beef goulash with cream sauce
gulášová polévka Hungarian goulash soup made with beef chunks, potatoes, onions, tomatoes and peppers, richly spiced with paprika, caraway seeds and garlic
Harlekýn chocolate sponge cake with whipped cream
hlávkový salát green salad
hlemýždi snails
holub pigeon
hořčák bitter
hořčice mustard
hotová jídla short-order dishes, ready-to-serve dishes
houby mushrooms
hovězí beef
~ **tokáň** beef in a wine and tomato puree
~ **vývar s nudlemi** beef broth with noodles
~ **dušené na hříbkách** beef ragout with mushrooms
~ **na grilu** grilled beefsteak
~ **pečeně** roast beef
hrách dry peas
hrachová polévka s uzeným masem pea soup with smoked meat
hranolky chips (US french fries)
hrášek green peas
hroznové víno grapes
~ **bílé** green
~ **červené** red
hruška pear
hřebíček cloves
humr lobster
husí žaludky zadělávané goose stomach in white sauce
husí játra goose liver
~ **smažená** fried goose liver in bread crumbs
husí krky plněné stuffed goose neck
chřest asparagus
chlazeno chilled
chléb bread
~ **bílý** white
~ **celozrnný** wholemeal
~ **černy** black
chlebíček open sandwich
~ **s lososem** salmon
~ **s kaviárem** caviar
~ **s uherákem** Hungarian salami
~ **se sýrem** cheese
~ **se šunkou** ham
chlupaté knedlíky se zelím Bohemian potato dumplings with cabbage, made from raw grated potato, flour and egg
chobotnice octopus
chod course, dish
~ **hlavní** main course
jablečný štrůdl apple tart, pie
jablka v županu baked apples in pastry
jablko apple
jablkový závin apple pie
jahody strawberries
játra liver
~ **dušená** braised
~ **na roštu** grilled
~ **telecí** calf

játrová paštika liver pâté
jazyk tongue
~ **s omáčkou** tongue in gravy
jehněčí lamb
~ **kotleta** lamb chop
~ **hrudí** breast of lamb
~ **pečeně** roast of lamb
jelito blood sausage
ječmen barley
jemný drobenkový koláč cheese crumble pie
jeseter sturgeon
jídelní lístek menu
jídlo food
~ **z konzervy** tinned (canned) food
jitrnice white sausage
jogurt yoghurt
kachna duck
kadeřavá kapusta cabbage
kalmar squid
kandované ovoce candied fruit
kapary capers
kapie pickled sweet peppers
kapr carp
~ **na modro** carp cooked in stock with vine and spices served with butter
~ **na kmíně** carp baked with caraway seeds
~ **na černo** carp in a black sauce of peppercorns, prunes and dark beer
kapusta (růžičková) brussels sprouts
kapustová polévka cabbage soup
karabanátek hamburger
karamel caramel
kari curry
kaštanové pyré chestnut puree
~ **se šlehačkou** with whipped cream
kaštany chestnuts
kaviár caviar
kdoule quince
kedlubna kohlrabi; a green-leaf vegetable
kefír sour milk
keksy biscuits, cookies
kečup ketchup
klikva cranberries
klobásy sausages
~ **bílé** pork white
~ **domácí** home made
~ **opečené** fried
kmín caraway
kmínová polévka caraway seed soup
knedlíky dumplings
~ **bramborove** potato dumplings
~ **houskové** bread dumplings
~ **švestkové** plum dumplings
~ **meruňkové** apricot dumplings
kobliha doughnut
koření spices
kokos coconut
kokosky coconut meringues
kokosový ořech coconut
koláč cake
koláčky sweet buns
koleno knuckle
~ **ovarové** boiled pig's knuckle
~ **uzené** smoked pig's knuckle
kompot stewed fruit
~ **broskvový** stewed peaches
~ **hruškový** stewed pears
~ **jablkový** stewed apples
~ **mandarinkový** stewed tangerines
~ **meruňkový** stewed apricots
~ **míchaný** stewed fruit (mixed)
~ **švestkový** stewed plums

konzerva tin (US can)
kopr dill
koroptev partridge
koroptev pečená v červeném zelí roast partrige with red cabbage
kost bone
kotlet, kotleta cutlet
krabi crabs
~ **mořští** saltwater crawfish
~ **říční** freshwater crayfish
králík rabbit
krev blood
~ **husí** goose blood
krevetky scampi, prawns, shrimps
krocan turkey
~ **s kaštanovou nádivkou** roast turkey stuffed with chestnuts
krokety croquettes
krůta turkey
křen horseradish
křepelka quail
kuře na paprice stewed chicken with red peppers
kuře pečené s nádivkou roast chicken with chicken liver stuffing
kukuřice corn
~ **pečená kukuřice** roasted
~ **vařená kukuřice** boiled
kukuiné vloky corn flakes
kvasnice yeast
květák cauliflower
kyjevský kotlet boned breast of chicken stuffed with butter, breaded, then deep fried; Kiev style
kysané zelí sauerkraut
kyselá pickled
kyselé okurky gherkins
kyselý sour
kýta leg, haunch
langoše fried pastry coated in garlic
lanýž truffles
led ice
ledvinky kidneys
~ **ledvinky vepřové** tenderloin
~ **telecí** tenderloin of veal
lesní jahody wild strawberries
libovy lean
lilek aubergine
lískové oříšky hazelnuts
lívance fritters
losos salmon
majonéza mayonnaise
makaróny macaroni
~ **s masem** with meat
~ **se sýrem** with cheese
makový koláč poppy-seed cake
makrela mackerel
maliny raspberries
mandle almonds
marcipán marzipan
marinovaný marinated
marmeláda jam
marokánky macaroons
máslo butter
med honey
meloun melon, watermelon
menu menu
meruňkové knedlíky apricot dumplings, made from sweet based dough, filled with fruit, boiled and served with sugar and sour cream
meruňky apricots
míchaná vejce scrambled eggs
míchaná zmrzlina mixed ice-cream
míchaný mixed, assorted
místní speciality local specialities
mléko milk
~ **kyselé** sour milk

CZECH

mleté maso minced meat
Moravské uzené smoked ham
moravský salám Moravian salami
moravští vrabci "Moravian sparrows", roasted pieces of pork sprinkled with caraway seeds
mořské speciality seafood specialties
mouka flour
mozeček brains
mražená káva iced coffee
mrkev carrots
musaka layers of minced meat and either sliced potato or aubergine (eggplant), with a topping of eggs and sour milk; oven browned
na ztraceno poached (fish)
nadívané hrudí stuffed breast
nadívaný stuffed
nádivka stuffing
nakládačka gherkin
nakládané houby pickled mushrooms
nakládané papriky pickled peppers
nákyp pudding
nedopečené maso rare meat
nízkokalorický low calorie
nudle noodles
nudličky small noodles
obalovaný breaded
oběd lunch
občerstvení snack, generally with drink
obilné klíčky barley groats
obložená masová mísa assorted meat, cold cuts
obloženy chléb sandwich
obloha with vegetable garnish
ocet vinegar
okoun bass
okurka cucumber
olej oil
oliheň squid
olivový olej olive oil
olivy olives
omáčka sauce, gravy
omeleta omelet
~ **přírodní** plain
~ **se sýrem** cheese
~ **se šunkou** ham
opepřený peppery, hot
oplatky waffle
ostružiny blackberries
ostrý hot, spicy
ovarová polévka ze zabíjačky a rich pork soup flavoured with garlic and marjoram and served with boiled barley or rice; has a special place in carnival week
ovarová hlava brawn (US headcheese)
ovesná kaše porridge
ovesné vločky oats
ovčí sýr sheep's milk cheese
ovoce fruit
~ **kandované** candied
ovocný salát fruit cocktail
ovocný protlak puree
~ **broskvový** peach
~ **hruškový** pear
~ **jablkový** apple
~ **meruňkový** apricot
pařísky řízek veal cutlet dipped in egg and flour
pažitka chives
palačinky pancakes
~ **s džemem** with jam
~ **s tvarohem** with cream cheese
~ **s vaječným koňakem** with egg brandy
paprikový salát green pepper salad

CZECH

párek v rohlíku hot dog
parenica a tasty hard cheese from sheep's milk; mild if young, slightly sharp if aged
paprika green pepper
párky frankfurters
párky sausages
parmazán Parmesan cheese
parmice red mullet
pastiňák parsley
paštika pâté
~ **drůbeží** fowl
~ **játrová** liver
předkrm appetizer
~ **studený** cold
~ **teplý** warm
pečeně roast
~ **hovězí** beef
~ **jehněčí** lamb
~ **telecí** veal joint
~ **vepřová** pork
pečená husí játra s mandlemi goose liver with almonds
pepř pepper
~ **černý** black
perkelt chopped pork or lamb braised with onion; sour cream added
perník gingerbread cookie made with honey, almonds and spices
petržel parsley
piškot sponge finger (US ladyfinger)
piškotová roláda Swiss roll served with redcurrant jam and whipped cream
piškotový dort sponge cake
pivní sýr beer cheese
platýz plaice, halibut
plecko pork shoulder
plísňový sýr blue cheese
plněné papriky stuffed pepper
~ **v rajčatové omáčce** stuffed peppers in tomato sauce
podle jídelního lístku à la carte
podmáslí sour milk
polévka soup
~ **hovězí** beef
~ **bramborová** potato
~ **fazolová** butter bean (US navy-bean)
~ **houbová** mushroom
~ **kuřecí** chicken
~ **rybí** fish
~ **zeleninová** vegetable
pomeranč orange
porce portion
pórek leek
pórková polévka leek soup
pražená kukuřice popcorn
pražské telecí hrudí Prague-style breast of veal, stuffed with a mixture of eggs, ham, peas and whipped cream, roasted with butter
pražská pečeně na smetaně a tasty cut of beef in a special sour cream and spice sauce
prejt black pudding
prošpikovaný larded
prorostlá slanina bacon with strips of meat
prsíčka breast
~ **nadívaná** stuffed
přírodní řízek breaded hamburger
pstruh trout
~ **říční** river trout
~ **na másle** grilled trout with herb butter
pudink custard cream (US pudding)
punčový dort frosted sponge cake sprinkled with rum
pusinky small mounds of meringue

ragú stew
rajčatový salát tomato salad
rajče tomato
rajská polévka tomato soup
rajská omáčka tomato sauce
rakvičky meringue with whipped cream
ramínko pork shoulder
ravioli ravioli, dough envelopes
ražniči chunks of veal or pork grilled on a skewer
rebarbora rhubarb
rizoto casserole of rice, meat and vegetables
rohlík roll
rohlíčky crescent-shaped cookies, often made with nuts
roláda roll-shaped cake
~ **roláda** roll-shaped meat
roštěnky na pivě carbonade, a stew of beef and onion cooked in beer
rozinky raisins
ryba fish
~ **čerstvá** fish, kept in the restaurant's aquarium
~ **mořská** saltwater fish
~ **říční** freshwater fish
rybí filé fish fillet
rybí polévka fish soup
rybí polévka z kapra carp soup
ryngle greengages
rýže rice
rýžový nákyp rice pudding
ředkvička radish
řepa turnip
řeřicha watercress
s ledem with ice
s křenem with horseradish
sádlo lard
salám salami
salát salad
~ **bramborový** potato
~ **fazolový** bean
~ **francouzský** diced vegetables with mayonnaise
~ **okurkový** cucumber
~ **rybí** fish salad with mayonnaise
~ **srbský** tomato, green pepper and onion
~ **šopský** tomato salad with onions, pimentos and grated white cheese
~ **zeleninový** mixed vegetables salad
~ **z červené řepy** beetroot
~ **z červeného zelí** red cabbage salad
~ **z kyselého zelí** sauerkraut
sardinky pilchard
segedínský with sauerkraut and onion
~ **telecí** veal
~ **vepřový** pork
sekaná pork and beef minced loaf
sele sucking pig
~ **na rožni** roast suckling pig
sirup syrup
skořice cinnamon
skopové mutton
sůl salt
sladkosti sweets (US candy)
slaneček herring
slanina bacon
~ **prorostlá** with strips of meat
~ **anglická** smoked
slaný salted
slepice na paprice stewed fowl
slepičí polévka chicken consomme
slepičí vývar s nudlemi chicken broth with vermicelli
slívy greengages
smažené brambůrky fried potatoes

smažené rybí filé fried fillet of fish
smažené květákové nočky fried cauliflower dumplings
smažené sýrové knedlíčky se smetanou fried cheese dumplings
smažený sýr v těstíčku cheese fried in butter
smaženy řízek breaded chop
~ **telecí** veal
~ **vepřový** pork
smažený karbanátek fried burger
smaženy sýr fried cheese in bread crumbs
smaženy fried
smetana cream
smetanový creamed
snídaně breakfast
srdce heart
Staročeská (plzeňská) pivní polévka old Czech or Pilsen style beer soup, based on a light beer, thickened with bread cubes and egg yolks
středně propečeno medium rare
stehýnko leg of fowl
~ **kuřecí** chicken leg
~ **křidéko** wing of fowl
~ **bílé maso** white meat of fowl
strava meal, food
strouhaný grated
studené předkrmy cold appetizers
studený nářez cold cuts
suchar rusks (US zwieback)
sušené ovoce dried fruit
sušené švestky prunes
sušenky biscuits, cookies
sumec sheat-fish
šípek rosehip
šlehačka whipped cream
šlehaný bílek beaten egg white and sugar
škraloup skin of boiled milk
škubánky s mákem potato dumplings with poppy seeds and sugar cookies
škvarky crackling
špagety spaghetti
~ **s masem** with meat
~ **se sýrem** with cheese
špekáčky wieners
špenát spinach
špenátové smaženky s houbami spinach rissoles with mushrooms
špíz mixed grilled meat
štika pickerel, pike
štrůdl paper-thin layers of pastry filled with fruit
šunka boiled ham
~ **po staročesku** old-Bohemian style boiled ham, with a sauce of plums, prunes, walnuts and wine
šunkové flíčky noodles with sliced ham
~ **šunka s vejci** ham and eggs
švestkové knedlíky plum dumplings
švestkový koláč na plech plum pie with crumble
sýr cheese
~ **odtučněný** fat free
~ **ovčí** from sheep's milk
syrečky beer cheese
sýrové pavézky cheese cutlets
talíř plate
tatarský biftek steak tartare
tavený sýr cheese spread
telecí veal
~ **pečeně** roasted veal joint
~ **brzlík** veal sweetbreads
~ **guláš** veal stew
~ **párek** veal sausage

~ **maso na víně** veal braised with wine
~ **řízek** breaded veal cutlet
~ **játra** calf's liver
těsto dough
těstoviny pasta
tlačenka collared pork
toust toast
treska cod
trubičky se šlehačkou puff pastry cream cornets
třešně cherries
tuňák tuna
tučný fatty, oily
tvarohový závin a rolled flaky pastry with a cream cheese filling; strudel
tvaroh cottage cheese
~ **měkký** cream cheese
tvarohové palačinky cottage cheese pancakes
tykev pumpkin, marrow, squash
tymián thyme
uherský salám Hungarian salami
uzená krkovička smoked neck of pork
uzená šunka smoked ham
uzený smoked
~ **jazyk** smoked tongue
úhoř eel
ústřice oysters
vařené boiled
~ **brambory** boiled potatoes
~ **hovězí** boiled beef
vařené hovězí boiled beef
~ **s křenem** with horseradish
vařené jídlo cooked meal
vařené maso boiled meat
vafle waffle
vaječný koňak egg brandy
vanilka vanilla
vánočka sugary loaf confection of a special shape, made with raisins and almonds, originally prepared only for Christmas
ve vlastní sťávě in brine
večeře dinner
vegetaríanská strava vegetarian food
vejce eggs
~ **míchaná** scrambled
~ **na divoko** devilled
~ **nakládaná** pickled
~ **na měkko** soft boiled
~ **na tvrdo** hard-boiled
~ **ruské** egg salad
~ **smažená** scrambled
~ **volská oka** fried
~ **ztracená** poached
vepřová krkovička po selsku neck of pork, rubbed with garlic and roasted with onions
vepřová pečeně pork roast
vepřové žebírko stewed rib of pork
vepřové koleno pork knuckles
vepřové kotlety na pivě pork chops in beer
vepřové klobásy pork sausages
vepřový kotlet pork chop
vepřový guláš se zelím pork goulash with sauerkraut
vídeňsky řízek wienerschnitzel cutlet
višně Morello cherries
vinný střik wine diluted with water
vlašské ořechy nuts, walnuts
věneček cream puff
větrník cream puff
vuřt sausage
vývar broth
zadělávaný květák se sýrem cauliflower with cream sauce and cheese
zajíc hare
~ **na divoko** larded hare

cooked with onion and vegetables in red wine
~ **na smetaně** hare in cream sauce
~ **na černo** stewed hare in thick, dark, sweet sauce
zakysaná smetana sour cream
zákusek piece of cake
závin paper-thin layers of pastry filled with fruit, strudel
~ **jablkový** with apples
zavináče rollmops
zelenina vegetables
zeleninová polévka vegetable soup
zeleninové karbanátky fried vegetable rissoles in bread crumbs
zeleninový salát mixed salad
zelí cabbage
zelná polévka s klobásou cabbage soup with smoked sausage
zmrzlina ice-cream
~ **borůvková** blueberry
~ **citrónová** lemon
~ **čokoládová** chocolate
~ **jahodová** strawberry
~ **míchaná** assorted
~ **oříšková** with nuts
~ **vanilková** vanilla
zmrzlinový pohár sundae
znojemská pečeně slices of roast beef in a gherkin sauce
znojemská roštěná sirloin à la Znojmo, fried then stewed with onions
ztracená poached
zvěřina venison
žabí stehýnka frog's legs
žaludek tripe
žebírko ribs
želé jelly, aspic
žemle roll, bun
žemlovka bread and butter pudding
živáňská pečeně grilled meat, generally outdoors
žloutek egg yolk

Drink

absint absint liqueur
Becherovka a kind of liqueur made from herbs
Bohemia Czech sparling wine
brandy brandy
Budvar well rounded lager brewed in Ceské Budějovice (Budweis), with a depth of spicy-sweet maltiness
Cabernet full bodied red wine (southern Moravia)
chlazený chilled
cola cola drink
čaj tea
~ **bylinkový** herb
~ **ovocný** fruit
~ **s citrónem** lemon
~ **s mlékem** with milk
červené víno red wine
České Budějovice a town in southern Bohemia, formerly named Budweis, home of the world's most famous style of beer
desertní víno dessert wine
džus juice

CZECH

~ **ananasový** pineapple
~ **broskvový** peach
~ **grapefruitový** grapefruit
~ **meruňkový** apricot
~ **ovocný** fruit
~ **pomerančový** orange
Flekovské pivo strong, special dark beer brewed in a historical brewery in Prague
gin gin
~ **a tonic** gin and tonic
griotka cherry liqueur
grog rum punch
Hubert Czech sparkling wine
jablečné víno cider
jablečný mošt apple juice
kakao hot chocolate
káva coffee
~ **bílá** white
~ **espresso** espresso
~ **turecká** strong turkish style
~ **vídeňská** with whipped cream, Viennese style
koňak brandy, cognac
kofola soft drink in the cola style
láhvové pivo bottled beer
lánev bottle
led ice
likér liquor
limonáda lemonade
meruňkovice apricot brandy
minerálka mineral water
mléko milk
~ **studené** cold milk
~ **svareňě** boiled milk
mléčný koktail milk shake
nápoj drink
nápoje drinks
~ **alkoholické** alkoholic drinks
~ **nealkoholické** soft drinks
nasládlé víno slightly sweet wine
oranžada orangeade
ovocné víno fruit wine to which sugar has been added to increase the alcoholic content
ovocný džus fruit juice
přírodní víno natural wine
pivo pro diabetiky low-calorie beer
pivo beer
~ **černé** dark
~ **ležák** lager
~ **světlé** lager
~ **výčepní** draft; Czech beer is world famous, based on a brewing tradition over one thousand years old
Plzeň a town in western Bohemia, home of the world's most widely produced style of beer: Pilsner or Pils
Plzeňský Prazdroj the original pilsner lager, exported as Pilsner Urquell; a dry and golden lager with an aromatic, hoppy flavour and drinkability
rajčatová šť'áva tomato juice
růzové víno rose wine
rum rum
ryzlink dry white wine
slivovice plum brandy
sodová voda soda water
speciální pivo extra strong beer
Stará myslivecká Czech brandy
Starobrno a soft, light lager from the brewery in Brno
Staropramen a soft, sweetish, light beer from the largest brewery in Prague
studený cold
suché (víno) dry (wine)
svareňě víno mulled wine with water and sugar added
světlé pivo light beer
šumivé sparkling

šumivé víno sparkling wine
točené pivo draught beer
tonik tonic water
vaječný koňak egg brandy
vermut vermouth
vinný střik wine mixed with soda water
vinný lístek wine list
víno wine; there are many home-grown wines in the Czech and Slovak republics, though the amount that is exported is small. Southern Moravia and southern Slovakia produce excellent white wines and there are many cellars you can visit. Wines to look out for are the popular whites: *Vlašský ryzlink*, *Rulandské bílé*, *Müller-Thurgau*, *Veltlínské zelené* and *Ryzlink rýnský*; the reds: *Kláštorné červené and Rulandské červené*, as well as *Sekt Cremant Rose*, a red champagne.
voda water
~ **minerálka** mineral water
~ **sodovka** soda water
vodka vodka
whisky whisky
~ **se sodou** whisky and soda
Zlatý Bažant "Golden Pheasant", the fresh, dry and most famous Slovak beer
Zubrovka vodka flavoured with a herb extract

Danish

Guide to pronunciation

Letter	Approximate pronunciation
Consonants	
b, c, f, h, l, m, n, v	as in English
d	1) when at the end of the word, or between two vowels, like **th** in **th**is 2) otherwise, as in English
g	1) at the beginning of a word or syllable, as in **g**o 2) when at the end of a word after a long vowel or before unstressed **e,** like **ch** in Scottish lo**ch,** but weaker and voiced 3) usually mute after **i, y** and sometimes mute after **a, e, o**
j, hj	like **y** in **y**et
hv	like **v** in **v**iew
k, p, t	1) when at the beginning of a word, as in **k**ite, **p**ill and **t**o 2) otherwise, like **g, b, d** in **g**o, **b**it and **d**o

l	always as in **l**eaf, never as in be**ll**
r	pronounced in the back of the throat
s	always as in **s**ee
sj	like **sh** in **sh**eet
w	for Danes this is the same as **v**
z	like **s** in **s**o

Vowels

A vowel is generally long in stressesd syllables when it's the final letter or followed by only one consonant. If followed by two or more consonants, or in unstressed syllables, the vowel is generally short.

a	1) when long, like **a** in c**a**r; it can also be pronounced like **a** in b**a**d, but longer 2) when short, like long **a**
e	1) when long, the same quality as **a** in pl**a**te, but longer, and a pure vowel, not a diphthong 2) when short, somewhere between the **a** in pl**a**te and the **i** in h**i**t 3) when short, also like **e** in m**e**t 4) when unstressed, like **a** in **a**bout
i	1) when long, like **ee** in b**ee** 2) when short, like **ee** in m**ee**t
o	1) when long, like **aw** in s**aw**, but with the tongue higher in the mouth; quite like **u** in p**u**t 2) when short, more or less the same quality of sound 3) when short, also like **o** in l**o**t
u	1) when long, like **oo** in p**oo**l 2) when short, like **oo** in l**oo**t
y	put your tongue in the position for the **ee** of b**ee**, but round your lips as for the **oo** of p**oo**l; the vowel you pronounce like this should be more or less correct
æ	1) when long, like the first part of the word **air** 2) when short, like **e** in g**e**t, but next to **r** it sounds more like the **a** of h**a**t
å	1) when long, like **aw** in s**aw** 2) when short, like **o** in **o**n
ø	like **ur** in f**ur**, but with the lips rounded; can be long or short

DANISH

Diphthongs

av	like **ow** in n**ow**
ej	like **igh** in s**igh**
ev	like **e** in g**e**t followed by a short **u** as in p**u**t
ou	like **o** in g**o**t followed by a short **u** as in p**u**t
øi	like **oi** in **oi**l
øv	like **ur** in h**ur**t followed by a short **u** as in p**u**t

Note

1. Many Danish speakers put a glottal stop in or after vowels (like the Cockney pronunciation of **t** in *wa'er*). Although it has a certain distinctive role, you'll be understood perfectly well if you don't use it.
2. **dd** and **gg** between vowels are pronounced like **d** in **d**o and **g** in **g**o.
3. The letter **d** isn't pronounced in **nd** and **ld** at the end of a word or syllable or before unstressed **e** or before **t** or **s** in the same syllable.

Some useful expressions

Hungry

I'm hungry/I'm thirsty.	**Jeg er sulten/Jeg er tørstig.**
Can you recommend a good restaurant?	**Kan De anbefale en god restaurant?**
Are there any good, cheap restaurants around here?	**Er der en god, billig restaurant i nærheden?**
I'd like to reserve a table for ... people.	**Jeg vil gerne reservere et bord til ... personer.**
We'll come at ... o'clock.	**Vi er der klokken ...**

Asking

Good evening. I'd like a table for ... people.	**Godaften. Jeg vil gerne have et bord til ... personer.**
Could we have a table...?	**Kan vi få et bord...?**
in the corner	**i hjørnet**
by the window	**ved vinduet**
outside	**udenfor**
on the terrace	**på terrassen**

May I please have the menu?	**Må jeg få spisekortet?**
What's this?	**Hvad er dette?**
Do you have…?	**Har De …?**
a set menu	**en fast menu**
local dishes	**specialiteter fra egnen**
a children's menu	**en ret til børn**
Waiter/Waitress!	**Tjener/Frøken!**
What do you recommend?	**Hvad kan De anbefale?**
Could I have (a/an)… please?	**Må jeg få …?**
ashtray	**et askebæger**
another chair	**en ekstra stol**
finger bowl	**en skylleskål**
fork	**en gaffel**
glass	**et glas**
knife	**en kniv**
napkin	**en serviet**
plate	**en tallerken**
pepper mill	**en peberkværn**
serviette	**en serviet**
spoon	**en ske**
toothpick	**en tandstikker**

Ordering

I'd like a/an/some…	**Jeg vil gerne have …**
aperitif	**en aperitif**
appetizer	**en appetitvækker**
beer	**en øl**
bread	**noget brød**
butter	**noget smør**
cheese	**ost**
chips	**pommes frites**
coffee	**kaffe**
dessert	**en dessert**
fish	**fisk**
french fries	**pommes frites**
fruit	**frugt**
game	**vildt**
ice-cream	**is**

lemon	**citron**
lettuce	**grøn salat**
meat	**kød**
mineral water	**en mineralvand**
milk	**mælk**
mustard	**sennep**
noodles	**nudler**
oil	**olie**
olive oil	**olivenolie**
pepper	**peber**
potatoes	**kartofler**
poultry	**fjerkræ**
rice	**ris**
rolls	**rundstykker**
saccharin	**sødetabletter**
salad	**salat**
salt	**salt**
sandwich	**en sandwich**
seafood	**skaldyr**
seasoning	**krydderier**
soup	**suppe**
starter	**en forret**
sugar	**sukker**
tea	**te**
vegetables	**grønsager**
vinegar	**eddike**
(iced) water	**(is)vand**
wine	**vin**

VELBEKOMME!
ENJOY YOUR MEAL!

baked	**bagt**
baked in parchment	**bagt i folie**
boiled	**kogt**
braised	**grydestegt**
cured	**lagret**
fried	**stegt på panden**
grilled	**grillstegt**
marinated	**marineret**

poached	**pocheret**
roasted	**ovnstegt**
sautéed	**sauteret**
smoked	**røget**
steamed	**dampkogt**
stewed	**kogt over svag ild**
underdone (rare)	**rødstegt**
medium	**mellemstegt**
well-done	**gennemstegt**

SKÅL!
CHEERS!

glass	**et glas**
bottle	**en flaske**
red	**rød**
white	**hvid**
rosé	**rosé**
very dry	**meget tør**
dry	**tør**
sweet	**sød**
light	**let**
full-bodied	**fyldig**
sparkling	**mousserende**
neat (straight)	**tør**
on the rocks	**med isterninger**

The bill

I'd like to pay.	**Jeg vil gerne betale.**
We'd like to pay separately.	**Vi vil gerne betale hver for sig.**
You've made a mistake in this bill, I think.	**Jeg tror, De har lavet en fejl i regningen.**
What's this amount for?	**Hvad dækker dette beløb?**
Is service included?	**Er det med betjening?**
Is everything included?	**Er alt inkluderet?**
Do you accept traveller's cheques?	**Tager De imod rejsechecks?**

Thank you. This is for you.	**Mange tak, dette er til Dem.**
Keep the change.	**Behold småpengene.**
That was a very good meal.	**Det var et dejligt måltid.**
We enjoyed it, thank you.	**Vi har nydt det.**

Complaints

That's not what I ordered. I asked for…	**Det er ikke det, jeg bestilte. Jeg har bestilt …**
May I change this?	**Kan jeg få noget andet?**
The meat is…	**Kødet er …**
overdone	**stegt for meget**
underdone	**stegt for lidt**
too rare	**for råt**
too tough	**for sejt**
This is too…	**Dette er for …**
bitter/salty/sweet	**bittert/salt/sødt**
The food is cold.	**Maden er kold.**
This isn't fresh.	**Dette er ikke friskt.**
What's taking you so long?	**Hvorfor varer det så længe?**
Where are our drinks?	**Hvor bliver vore drinks af?**
This isn't clean.	**Dette er ikke rent.**
Would you ask the head waiter to come over?	**Vil De kalde på overtjeneren?**

Numbers

1	**en, et**	11	**elleve**
2	**to**	12	**tolv**
3	**tre**	13	**tretten**
4	**fire**	14	**fjorten**
5	**fem**	15	**femten**
6	**seks**	16	**seksten**
7	**syv**	17	**sytten**
8	**otte**	18	**atten**
9	**ni**	19	**nitten**
10	**ti**	20	**tyve**

Food

Please note that Danish alphabetical order is **a-z, æ, ø, å.**

aborre perch
abrikos apricot
aftensmad dinner
agerhøne partridge
agurk cucumber
agurkesalat sliced cucumber in vinegar dressing
ananas pineapple
and duck
ansjos 1) marinated sprat 2) anchovy
appelsin orange
artiskok artichoke
asie kind of large cucumber, seeded and pickled
asparges asparagus
bagt kartoffel baked potato
banan banana
bankekød beef stew
benløse fugle thin slices of veal or beef wrapped around a stuffing of bacon, parsley and chopped onions
betjening iberegnet service included
biksemad diced meat fried with potatoes and onions
blodpølse black pudding (US blood sausage)
blomkål cauliflower
blomme plum
blødkogt æg soft-boiled egg
blåbær bilberry (US blueberry)
bolle 1) bun 2) meat or fish ball
bondepige med slør dessert made from stewed apples, rye-bread crumbs toasted in butter and sugar, topped with whipped cream
brasede kartofler sliced, sautéed potatoes
brisler sweetbreads
brombær blackberry
brun kage brown, spicy biscuit (US cookie)
brunede kartofler boiled, caramelized potatoes
brunet smør browned butter sauce
brød bread
budding pudding
bøf (beef) steak
~**sandwich** hamburger
~**tatar** steak tartare; finely chopped raw beef, served on rye bread with egg-yolk, onion horse-radish and capers
bønne bean
børnemenu children's menu
chalotteløg shallot
champignon mushroom
citron lemon
~**fromage** lemon blancmange mousse (pudding)
daddelblomme persimmon
dadler dates

dagens middag set menu
dagens ret day's special
dampet steamed
Danablue Danish blue cheese
Danbo mild, firm cheese, sometimes flavoured with caraway seed
dild dill
diætmad diet food
due pigeon (US squab)
dyrekølle haunch of venison
dyresteg roast venison
eddike white vinegar
Elbo cheese with mild flavour
engelsk bøf steak and onions
Esrom mild, slightly aromatic cheese
fasan pheasant
fersken peach
fisk fish
fiskefilet fillet of fish (usually plaice)
fiskefrikadelle fried fishball, served hot, or cold on *smørrebrød*
fjerkræ fowl
flamberet flamed
flute kind of French bread
flæskesteg roast pork with crackling
flæskeæggekage thick omelet with fried bacon, tomatoes and chives, served with rye bread
fløde cream
 ~**kage** pastry topped with whipped cream
 ~**ost** cream cheese
 ~**skum** whipped cream
forloren hare type of meatloaf of pork and veal, served with apple halves filled with redcurrant jelly, together with potatoes and red cabbage
forret first course, starter
forårsrulle (Chinese) spring roll, egg roll
franskbrød white bread
frikadelle meatball of minced pork and veal
frisk fresh
friturekogt, -stegt deep fried
frokost lunch
 ~**bord** buffet of cold and hot specialities to make your own *smørrebrød*
 ~**platte** hot and cold specialities to make your own *smørrebrød*, served on a tray
fromage blancmange, mousse (pudding)
frugt fruit
frølår frogs' legs
fyld stuffing
fyldt stuffed
 ~ **hvidkål** cabbage stuffed with minced pork and veal
Fynbo mild, rich cheese similar to *Samsø*
fårekød mutton
gedde pike
gennemstegt well-done
grapefrugt grapefruit
gratin baked casserole
gravad laks, gravlaks salt and dill-cured salmon, served with a creamy mustard sauce
grillstegt grilled
gryderet stew of meat and vegetables
grydestegt braised
grøn bønne French bean (US green bean)
grøn salat lettuce
grønlangkål creamed kale
grøn(t)sager vegetables
grønært green pea
grønærtesuppe pea soup
gule ærter med flæsk split-pea

soup served with boiled, salt pork and sausages
gulerødder carrots
gås goose
gåselever(postej) goose liver (paté)
gåsesteg roast goose
~ **med æbler og svesker** stuffed with apples and prunes
hakkebøf med løg hamburger steak served with fried onions
hakket chopped, minced
halv, halvdel half
hamburgerryg slightly smoked loin of pork
haresteg roast hare
hasselnød hazelnut
Havarti semi-hard cheese with a piquant flavour
havregrød oatmeal
helleflynder halibut
helstegt roasted whole
hindbær raspberry
hjemmelavet home-made
hjerte heart
hjerter i flødesovs hearts, usually of pork, served in a cream sauce
honning honey
hornfisk garfish
hovedret main dish
hummer lobster
hvidkål cabbage
hvidløg garlic
hytteost cottage cheese
høne hen
hønsebryst chicken breast
hønsekødsuppe chicken broth
hårdkogt æg hard-boiled egg
ingefær ginger
~**brød** gingerbread
is ice-cream, ice
italiensk salat mayonnaise mixed with peas, chopped carrots and asparagus, served with ham on *smørrebrød*
jomfruhummer Norway lobster
jordbær strawberry
~**grød** kind of strawberry purée, served with cream
julesalat chicory (US endive)
kage cake
kalkun turkey
kalvebrisler sweetbreads
kalvekød veal
kantarel chanterelle mushroom
kapers capers
karamelrand caramel custard
karbonade breaded minced steak of pork or veal
karpe carp
karry curry
karse cress
kartoffel potato
~**mos** mashed potatoes
~**salat** potato salad (hot or cold)
kastanie chestnut
kaviar caviar
kiks biscuit (US cookie)
kirsebær cherry
klar suppe consommé, clear soup
~ **med boller og grønsager** consommé with meat balls and vegetables
klipfisk dried salt cod
kogt boiled
~ **torsk (med sennepssovs)** steamed cod (with mustard sauce)
kold cold
koldt bord a wide variety of open sandwiches, small warm dishes, salads and cheeses
kotelet cutlet, chop
krabbe crab
kransekage pyramid of almond macaroons

DANISH

krebs freshwater crayfish
kringle variety of Danish pastry
krydder toasted bun
krydderi spice
kryddersild pickled herring
kryddersmør herb butter
kræmmerhus med flødeskum pastry cone filled with whipped cream and topped with jam
kuvertbrød (French) roll
kvæde quince
kylling chicken
kærnemælkskoldskål chilled buttermilk soup, served with rusks (US zwieback)
kød meat
~**bolle** meatball
~**fars** forcemeat, stuffing
kørvelsuppe chervil soup
kål cabbage
labskovs lobscouse; casserole of potatoes, meat and vegetables
lagkage layer cake, usually filled with whipped cream, jam, fruit purée or custard
laks salmon
lammebov shoulder of lamb
lammebryst breast of lamb
lammekød lamb
lammekølle leg of lamb
legeret suppe cream soup
lever liver
~**postej** liver pâté
linse 1) lentil 2) custard pastry
løg onion
majs maize (US corn)
~**kolbe** corn on the cob
makrel mackerel
makron macaroon
mandel almond
Maribo soft, mild cheese
marineret marinated
~ **sild** marinated herring
medisterpølse pork sausage
melbolle dumpling
mellemstegt medium (done)
millionbøf minced meat in cream sauce
Molbo a yellow, pressed cheese similar to Edam
morgencomplet continental breakfast
morgenmad breakfast
musling mussel
Mycella cheese similar to Danish blue, but milder
mørbrad fillet of meat (US tenderloin)
~**bøf** small round pork fillet
~**steg** porterhouse steak
måltid meal
nye kartofler new potatoes
nyre kidney
nød nut
oksebryst brisket of beef
oksefilet fillet of beef (US tenderloin)
oksehalesuppe oxtail soup
oksekød beef
~**suppe** broth, consommé
oksemørbrad fillet of beef
oksesteg roast beef
olie oil
oliven olive
omelet med kyllingelever chicken liver omelet
ost cheese
osteanretning cheese board
Othellokage layer cake filled with custard, topped with chocolate sauce and whipped cream
ovnbagt baked
ovnstegt roasted
pandekage pancake
paneret breaded
pariserbøf hamburger on toast with egg-yolk, chopped onions and capers

parisertoast toasted ham-and-cheese sandwich
pattegris suck(l)ing pig
peber black pepper
~**bøf** (beef)steak with pepper-corns
~**frugt** pimiento
~**rod** horse-radish
persille parsley
pighvar turbot
pillede rejer shelled shrimps
pocheret poached
pommes frites chips (US French fries)
porre leek
purløg chive
pære pear
pølse sausage
pålæg cold meat, sausage, salad, fish or cheese as a garnish for *smørrebrød*
rabarber rhubarb
radise radish
regning bill (US check)
reje shrimp
remoulade mayonnaise flavoured with finely chopped pickles, capers, onions and mustard
ribbenssteg rib-roast of pork with crackling, often served with red cabbage
~ **med æbler og svesker** rib-roast of pork stuffed with apples and prunes
ribs currant (red or white)
~**gelé** redcurrant jelly
ris rice
~ **à l'amande** rice pudding with grated almonds, served with hot cherry sauce
risengrød rice boiled in milk, served with cinnamon and butter
rosenkål brussels sprouts
rosin raisin
roulade 1) meat roll 2) Swiss roll
rugbrød rye bread
rullepølse kind of sausage made of rolled veal and pork, sliced and served on *smørrebrød*
rundstykke poppy-seed roll
rødbede beetroot
rødgrød kind of thickened red fruit juice, served with cream
rødkål red cabbage
rødspætte plaice
~**filet** fillet of plaice
rødstegt underdone (US rare)
røget smoked
~ **sild** smoked herring on rye bread garnished with chopped hardboiled eggs, onions, radishes and chives
rørt smør creamed butter
røræg scrambled eggs
rå raw
~**kost** uncooked vegetables or fruit
salat 1) salad 2) lettuce
saltet salted, cured
sammenkogt ret stew of meat and vegetables
Samsø mild, firm cheese with a sweet flavour
selleri celery
sennep mustard
sigtebrød bread made of rye and wheat flour
sild herring
sildesalat herring and beetroot salad
skaldyr shellfish
skinke ham
~ **med spejlæg** ham and eggs
skipperlabskovs lobscouse; thick stew of beef, carrots and onions
skive slice

skrubbe flounder
slankekost low calorie food
smeltet smør melted butter
smør butter
smørrebrød slices of buttered rye (or wheat) bread with any of a variety of garnishes, such as shrimps, herring, ham, roast beef, cheese and salads
småkage biscuit (US cookie)
snittebønne sliced French bean
solbær blackcurrant
sovs sauce
spegepølse kind of raw sausage, salami
spejlæg fried egg
spinat spinach
spisekort menu, bill of fare
steg joint of meat, roast
stegt fried, roasted
stikkelsbær gooseberry
stuvet creamed
sukker sugar
suppe soup
surkål sauerkraut
sursød sweet-and-sour
sveske prune
svinekam med svesker roast loin of pork stuffed with prunes
svinekød pork
svinemørbrad fillet of pork (US tenderloin)
sylte brawn (US head cheese)
syltede agurker gherkins (US pickles)
syltetøj jam
sød sweet
søtunge sole
tatar see *bøftatar*
tebirkes type of bun with poppy seeds
timian thyme
tomatsuppe tomato soup
torsk cod
torskerogn cod roe
tranebær cranberry
tunfisk tunny (US tuna)
tunge tongue
tykmælk kind of junket, thin yoghurt
tyttebær mountain cranberry, red whortleberry
tærte cake, tart
vaffel wafer, waffle
vagtel quail
valnød walnut
vandmelon watermelon
varm warm
vildand wild duck
vildt game
vindrue grape
vinkort wine list
wienerbrød Danish pastry
ymer kind of sour milk
æble apple
~**flæsk** fried apples and bacon
~**grød** stewed apples
~**kage** kind of apple charlotte
~**mos** apple sauce
~**skive** kind of fritter, served with jam
æg egg(s)
æggeblomme egg-yolk
ært pea
ørred trout
østers oyster
ål eel
~ **i gelé** jellied

Drink

akvavit aquavit, spirits distilled from potatoes or grain, often flavoured with aromatic seeds and spices
alkoholfri non-alcoholic
appelsinjuice orange juice
appelsinvand orangeade
bordvin table wine
Carlsberg a renowned Danish brewery
Cherry Heering see *Peter Heering*
chokolade hot chocolate (drink)
citronvand lemonade
danskvand soda water
dessertvin dessert wine
elefantøl also known as *exportøl* or *luksusøl:* beer with a high alcoholic content
fadøl draught (US draft) beer
fløde cream
frugtjuice fruit juice
gløgg mulled wine (Christmas speciality)
hedvin fortified wine
husets vin open wine
hvidvin white wine
irsk kaffe Irish coffee
kaffe coffee
~ **med fløde** with cream
~ **med mælk** with milk
kærnemælk buttermilk
lagerøl dark lager
letmælk partially skimmed milk
likør liqueur, cordial
lyst øl light beer
mineralvand mineral water
mousserende vin sparkling wine
mælk milk
mørkt øl dark beer
Peter Heering a renowned Danish cherry liqueur
pilsner lager; light beer
porter stout
portvin port (wine)
påskebryg beer with a high alcoholic content, brewed at Easter
rom rum
rødvin red wine
saft juice
saftevand squash (US fruit drink)
skummetmælk skim milk
snaps see *akvavit*
sodavand fruit-flavoured soda water
sødmælk full milk
te tea
~ **med citron** with lemon
~ **med mælk** with milk
Tuborg a renowned Danish brewery
vand water
varm mælk hot milk
vin wine
æblemost apple juice
øl beer

Dutch

Guide to pronunciation

Letter	Approximate pronunciation
Consonants	
c, f, h, k, l, m, n, p, q, t, v, y, z	as in English
b	as in English, but when at the end of a word, like **p** in cu**p**
ch	1) generally like **ch** in Scottish lo**ch** 2) in words of French origin like **sh** in **sh**ut
chtj	like Dutch **ch** followed by Dutch **j**
d	as in English, but when at the end of a word like **t** in hi**t**
g	1) generally like **ch** in Scottish lo**ch**, but often slightly softer and voiced 2) in a few words of French origin, like **s** in plea**s**ure
j	like **y** in **y**es
nj	like **ni** in o**ni**on
r	always trilled, either in the front or the back of the mouth

s	always like **s** in **s**it
sj, stj	like **sh** in **sh**ut
sch	like **s** followed by a Dutch **ch**
th	like **t**
tj	like **ty** in hi**t y**ou
w	something like **v**, but with the bottom lip raised a little higher

Vowels

In Dutch a vowel is *short* when followed by two consonants or by one consonant at the end of a word. It's *long* when it's at the end of a word, before a consonant followed by a vowel or when written double.

a	1) when short, between **a** in c**a**rt and **u** in c**u**t 2) when long, like **a** in c**a**rt
e	1) when short, like **e** in b**e**d 2) when long, like **a** in l**a**te, but a pure vowel 3) in unstressed syllables, like **a** in **a**bove
eu	long, like **eu** in French f**eu**; approximately like **u** in f**u**r, said with rounded lips
i	1) when short, like **i** in b**i**t 2) when long (also spelt **ie**), like **ee** in b**ee** 3) sometimes, in unstressed syllables, like **a** in **a**bove
ij	sometimes, in unstressed syllables, like **a** in **a**bove
o	1) when short, like a very short version of **aw** in l**aw**n 2) when long, something like **oa** in r**oa**d, but a pure vowel and with more rounded lips
oe	long, like **oo** in m**oo**n and well rounded
u	1) when short, something like **u** in h**u**rt, but with rounded lips 2) when long, like **u** in French s**u**r or **ü** in German f**ü**r; say **ee** and without moving your tongue, round your lips. The resulting "rounded **ee**" should be the correct sound.

Diphthongs

ai	like **igh** in s**igh**
ei, ij	like **a** in l**a**te
au, ou	Dutch short **o** followed by a weak, short **u** sound; can sound very much like **ow** in n**ow**

DUTCH

The following diphthongs have a long vowel as their first element:

aai	like **a** in c**a**rt followed by a short **ee** sound
eeuw	like **a** in l**a**te followed by a short **oo** sound
ieuw	like **ee** in fr**ee** followed by a short **oo** sound
ooi	like **o** in wr**o**te followed by a short **ee** sound
oei	like **oo** in s**oo**n followed by a short **ee** sound
ui	like **u** in f**u**r followed by a short Dutch **u** sound as described in **u**, example 2)
uw	like the sound described in **u**, example 2) followed by a weak **oo** sound

Note

1. When two consonants are next to each other, one will often influence the other even if it isn't in the same word, e.g., the **z** in *ziens* is pronounced like the **z** in **z**oo, but in the expression *tot ziens*, it's pronounced like the **s** in **s**it under the influence of the **t** before it.
2. In the **-en** ending of verbs and plural nouns, the **n** is generally dropped in everyday speech.

Some useful expressions

Hungry

I'm hungry/I'm thirsty.	**Ik heb honger/Ik heb dorst.**
Can you recommend a good restaurant?	**Kunt U een goed restaurant aanbevelen?**
Are there any good, cheap restaurants around here?	**Zijn hier ook goede, niet te dure restaurants in de buurt?**
I'd like to reserve a table for ... people.	**Ik wil graag een tafel reserveren voor ... personen.**
We'll come at ... o'clock.	**We komen om ... uur.**

Asking

Good evening. I'd like a table for ... people.	**Goedenavond. Een tafel voor ... personen, alstublieft.**
Could we have a table...?	**We willen graag een tafel...**
in the corner	**in de hoek**
by the window	**bij het raam**

outside	**buiten**
on the terrace	**op het terras**
May I please have the menu?	**Mag ik de menukaart, alstublieft?**
What's this?	**Wat is dit?**
Do you have...?	**Hebt u...?**
a set menu	**een dagschotel**
local dishes	**plaatselijke specialiteiten**
a children's menu	**een kindermenu**
Waiter/Waitress!	**Ober/Juffrouw!**
What do you recommend?	**Wat kunt U ons aanraden?**
Could I have (a/an)... please?	**Mag ik een..., alstublieft?**
ashtray	**asbak**
another chair	**stoel erbij**
fork	**vork**
glass	**glas**
knife	**mes**
napkin	**servet**
plate	**bord**
pepper mill	**pepermolen**
serviette	**servet**
spoon	**lepel**
toothpick	**tandenstoker**

Ordering

I'd like a/an/some...	**Ik wil graag ...**
aperitif	**een aperitief**
appetizer	**een voorgerecht**
beer	**een bier**
bread	**brood**
butter	**boter**
cheese	**kaas**
chips	**patates frites**
coffee	**koffie**
dessert	**een nagerecht**
fish	**vis**
french fries	**patates frites**
fruit	**fruit**

game	**wild**
ice-cream	**ijs**
lemon	**citroen**
lettuce	**stoofsla**
meat	**vlees**
mineral water	**mineraalwater**
milk	**melk**
mustard	**mosterd**
noodles	**noedels**
oil	**olie**
olive oil	**olijfolie**
pepper	**peper**
potatoes	**aardappels**
poultry	**gevogelte**
rice	**rijst**
rolls	**broodjes**
saccharin	**saccharine**
salad	**sla**
salt	**zout**
sandwich	**een boterham**
seafood	**schaal- en schelpdieren**
seasoning	**specerij**
soup	**soep**
starter	**een voorgerecht**
sugar	**suiker**
tea	**thee**
vegetables	**groenten**
vinegar	**azijn**
(iced) water	**(ijs)water**
wine	**wijn**

SMAKELIJK ETEN!
ENJOY YOUR MEAL!

baked	**in de oven gebakken**
baked in parchment	**gebraden in perkamentpapier**
boiled	**gekookt**
braised	**gesmoord**
cured	**gedroogd**

fried	**gebakken**
grilled	**geroosterd**
marinated	**gemarineerd**
poached	**gepocheerd**
roasted	**gebraden**
sautéed	**zacht gebakken**
smoked	**gerookt**
steamed	**gestoomd**
stewed	**gestoofd**
underdone (rare)	**licht gebakken**
medium	**half doorbakken**
well-done	**goed doorbakken**

GEZONDHEID!
CHEERS!

glass	**glas**
bottle	**fles**
red	**rood**
white	**wit**
rosé	**rosé**
very dry	**zeer droog**
dry	**droog**
sweet	**zoet**
light	**licht**
full-bodied	**zwaar**
sparkling	**mousserend**
neat (straight)	**puur**
on the rocks	**met ijs**

The bill

I'd like to pay.	**Mag ik afrekenen?**
We'd like to pay separately.	**We willen graag apart betalen.**
You've made a mistake in this bill, I think.	**Ik geloof dat u een fout gemaakt hebt in de rekening.**
What's this amount for?	**Waarvoor is dit bedrag?**
Is service included?	**Is de bediening inbegrepen?**
Is everything included?	**Is alles inbegrepen?**

Do you accept traveller's cheques? — **Accepteert u reischeques?**

Thank you. This is for you. — **Dank u, dit is voor u.**

Keep the change. — **Houd het wisselgeld maar.**

That was a very good meal. — **Het heeft ons prima gesmaakt.**

We enjoyed it, thank you. — **Het was lekker, dank u.**

Complaints

That's not what I ordered. — **Dat heb ik niet besteld.**
I asked for... — **Ik heb... gevraagd.**

May I change this? — **Kan ik hier iets anders voor krijgen?**

The meat is... — **Het vlees is...**

overdone — **te gaar**
underdone — **te rauw**
too rare — **te rood**
too tough — **te taai**

This is too... — **Dit is te...**

bitter/salty/sweet — **bitter/zout/zoet**

The food is cold. — **Het eten is koud.**

This isn't fresh. — **Dit is niet vers.**

What's taking you so long? — **Waarom duurt het zo lang?**

Where are our drinks? — **Waar blijven onze drankjes?**

This isn't clean. — **Dit is niet schoon.**

Would you ask the head waiter to come over? — **Wilt u de chef kelner vragen even hier te komen?**

Numbers

1	**één**	11	**elf**
2	**twee**	12	**twaalf**
3	**drie**	13	**dertien**
4	**vier**	14	**veertien**
5	**vijf**	15	**vijftien**
6	**zes**	16	**zestien**
7	**zeven**	17	**zeventien**
8	**acht**	18	**achttien**
9	**negen**	19	**negentien**
10	**tien**	20	**twintig**

Food

aalbes redcurrant
aardappel potato
~**puree** mashed potatoes
aardbei strawberry
abrikoos apricot
amandel almond
~**broodje** a sweet roll with almond-paste filling
ananas pineapple
andijvie endive (US chicory)
~**stamppot** mashed potato and endive casserole
anijs aniseed
ansjovis anchovy
appel apple
~**beignet** fritter
~**bol** dumpling
~**flap** puff-pastry containing an apple slice
~**gebak** cake
~**moes** sauce
Ardense pastei rich pork mixture cooked in a pastry crust, served cold in slices
artisjok artichoke
asperge asparagus
~**punt** tip
aubergine aubergine (US eggplant)
augurk gherkin (US pickle)
avondeten dinner, supper
azijn vinegar
baars perch
babi pangang slices of roast suck(l)ing pig, served with a sweet-and-sour sauce
bami goreng a casserole of noodles, vegetables, diced pork and shrimps
banaan banana
banketletter pastry with an almond-paste filling
basilicum basil
bediening service
belegd broodje roll with a variety of garnishes
belegen kaas pungent-flavoured cheese
biefstuk fillet of beef
~ **van de haas** small round fillet of beef
bieslook chive
bitterbal small, round breaded meatball served as an appetizer
blinde vink veal bird; thin slice of veal rolled around stuffing
bloedworst black pudding (US blood sausage)
~ **met appelen** with cooked apples

bloemkool cauliflower
boerenkool met worst kale mixed with mashed potatoes and served with smoked sausage
boerenomelet omelet with diced vegetables and bacon
bokking bloater
boon bean
borrelhapje appetizer
borststuk breast, brisket
bosbes bilberry (US blueberry)
bot 1) flounder 2) bone
boter butter
boterham slice of buttered bread
bouillon broth
braadhaantje spring chicken
braadworst frying sausage
braam blackberry
brasem bream
brood bread
~**maaltijd** bread served with cold meat, eggs, cheese, jam or other garnishes
~**pudding** kind of bread pudding with eggs, cinnamon and rum flavouring
broodje roll
~ **halfom** buttered roll with liver and salted beef
~ **kaas** buttered roll with cheese
bruine bonen met spek red kidney beans served with bacon
Brussels lof chicory (US endive)
caramelpudding caramel mould
caramelvla caramel custard
champignon mushroom
chocola(de) chocolate
citroen lemon
cordon bleu veal scallop stuffed with ham and cheese
dadel date
dagschotel day's special
dame blanche vanilla ice-cream with hot chocolate sauce
dille dill
doperwt green pea
dragon tarragon
drie-in-de-pan small, fluffy pancake filled with currants
druif grape
duif pigeon
Duitse biefstuk hamburger steak
Edam, Edammer kaas firm, mild-flavoured yellow cheese, coated with red wax
eend duck
ei egg
eierpannekoek egg pancake
erwt pea
erwtensoep met kluif pea soup with diced, smoked sausages, pork fat, pig's trotter (US feet), parsley, leeks and celery
exclusief not included
fazant pheasant
filet fillet
~ **américain** steak tartare
flensje small, thin pancake
foe yong hai omelet with leeks, onions, and shrimps served in a sweet-and-sour sauce
forel trout
framboos raspberry
Friese nagelkaas cheese made from skimmed milk, flavoured with cloves
frikadel meatball
frites, frieten chips (US french fries)
gaar well-done
gans goose
garnaal shrimp, prawn
gebak pastry, cake
gebakken fried
gebonden soep cream soup
gebraden roasted
gedroogde pruim prune

gehakt 1) minced 2) minced meat
~**bal** meatball
gekookt boiled
gekruid seasoned
gemarineerd marinated
gember ginger
~**koek** gingerbread
gemengd assorted, mixed
gepaneerd breaded
gepocheerd ei poached egg
geraspt grated
gerecht course, dish
gerookt smoked
geroosterd brood toast
gerst barley
gestoofd braised
gevogelte fowl
gevuld stuffed
gezouten salted
Goudakaas, Goudse kaas a renowned Dutch cheese, similar to *Edam*, large, flat and round; it gains in flavour with maturity
griesmeel semolina
~**pudding** semolina pudding
griet brill
groente vegetable
Haagse bluf dessert of whipped egg-whites, served with redcurrant sauce
haantje cockerel
haas hare
hachee hash of minced meat, onions and spices
half, halve half
hardgekookt ei hard-boiled egg
haring herring
hart heart
havermoutpap (oatmeal) porridge
hazelnoot hazelnut
heilbot halibut
heldere soep consommé, clear soup
hersenen brains
hete bliksem potatoes, bacon and apples, seasoned with butter, salt and sugar
Hollandse biefstuk loin section of a porterhouse or T-bone steak
Hollandse nieuwe freshly caught, filleted herring
honing honey
houtsnip 1) woodcock 2) cheese sandwich on rye bread
hutspot met klapstuk hotch-potch of mashed potatoes, carrots and onions served with boiled beef
huzarensla salad of potatoes, hard-boiled eggs, cold meat, gherkins, beetroot and mayonnaise
ijs ice, ice-cream
inclusief included
Italiaanse salade mixed salad with tomatoes, olives and tunny fish
jachtschotel a casserole of meat, onions and potatoes, often served with apple sauce
jonge kaas fresh cheese
jus gravy
kaas cheese
~**balletje** baked cheese ball
kabeljauw cod
kalfslapje, kalfsoester veal cutlet
kalfsrollade roast veal
kalfsvlees veal
kalkoen turkey
kapucijners met spek peas served with fried bacon, boiled potatoes, onions and green salad
karbonade chop, cutlet
karper carp
kastanje chestnut
kaviaar caviar
kerrie curry
kers cherry
kievitsei plover's egg
kip chicken

kippeborst breast of chicken
kippebout leg of chicken
knakworst small frankfurter sausage
knoflook garlic
koek 1) cake 2) gingerbread
koekje biscuit (US cookie)
koffietafel light lunch consisting of bread and butter with a variety of garnishes, served with coffee
kokosnoot coconut
komijnekaas cheese flavoured with cumin seeds
komkommer cucumber
konijn rabbit
koninginnesoep cream of chicken
kool cabbage
~**schotel met gehakt** casserole of meatballs and cabbage
kotelet chop, cutlet
koud cold
~ **vlees** cold meat (US cold cuts)
krab crab
krabbetje spare rib
krent currant
kroepoek large, deep-fried shrimp wafer
kroket croquette
kruiderij herb, seasoning
kruidnagel clove
kruisbes gooseberry
kwark fresh white cheese
kwartel quail
kweepeer quince
lamsbout leg of lamb
lamsvlees lamb
langoest spiny lobster
Leidse kaas cheese flavoured with cumin seeds
lekkerbekje fried, filleted haddock or plaice
lendestuk sirloin
lever liver
linze lentil
loempia spring roll (US egg roll)
maïskolf corn on the cob
makreel mackerel
mandarijntje tangerine
marsepein marzipan
meikaas a creamy cheese with high fat content
meloen melon
menu van de dag set menu
mossel mussel
mosterd mustard
nagerecht dessert
nasi goreng a casserole of rice, fried onions, meat, chicken, shrimps, vegetables and seasoning, usually topped with a fried egg
nier kidney
~**broodje** roll filled with kidneys and chopped onions
noot nut
oester oyster
olie oil
~**bol** fritter with raisins
olijf olive
omelet fines herbes herb omelet
omelet met kippelevertjes chicken liver omelet
omelet nature plain omelet
ongaar underdone (US rare)
ontbijt breakfast
~**koek** honey cake
~**spek** bacon, rasher
ossehaas fillet of beef
ossestaart oxtail
oude kaas any mature and strong cheese
paddestoel mushroom
paling eel
~ **in 't groen** braised in white sauce garnished with chopped parsley and other greens
pannekoek pancake

~ **met stroop** pancake served with treacle (US syrup)
pap porridge
paprika green or red (sweet) pepper
patates frites chips (US french fries)
pastei pie, pasty
patrijs partridge
peer pear
pekeltong salt(ed) tongue
pekelvlees slices of salted meat
peper pepper
~**koek** gingerbread
perzik peach
peterselie parsley
piccalilly pickle
pinda peanut
~**kaas** peanut butter
pisang goreng fried banana
poffertje fritter served with sugar and butter
pompelmoes grapefruit
portie portion
postelein purslane (edible plant)
prei leek
prinsessenboon French bean (US green bean)
pruim plum
rabarber rhubarb
radijs radish
rauw raw
reebout, reerug venison
reine-claude greengage
rekening bill
ribstuk rib of beef
rijst rice
~**tafel** an Indonesian preparation composed of some 30 dishes including stewed vegetables, spit-roasted meat and fowl, served with rice, various sauces, fruit, nuts and spices
rivierkreeft crayfish
rode biet beetroot
rode kool red cabbage
roerei scrambled egg
roggebrood rye bread
rolmops Bismarck herring
rolpens fried slices of spiced and pickled minced beef and tripe, topped with an apple slice
rookspek smoked bacon
rookworst smoked sausage
roomboter butter
roomijs ice-cream
rosbief roast beef
rozemarijn rosemary
runderlap beefsteak
rundvlees beef
Russische eieren Russian eggs; hard-boiled egg-halves garnished with mayonnaise, herring, shrimps, capers, anchovies and sometimes caviar; served on lettuce
salade salad
sambal kind of spicy paste consisting mainly of ground pimentos, usually served with *rijsttafel, bami* or *nasi goreng*
sardien sardine
saté, sateh skewered pieces of meat covered with a spicy peanut sauce
saucijzebroodje sausage roll
saus sauce, gravy
schaaldier shellfish
schapevlees mutton
scharretong lemon sole
schelvis haddock
schildpadsoep turtle soup
schnitzel cutlet
schol plaice
schuimomelet fluffy dessert omelet
selderij celery
sinaasappel orange

DUTCH

sjaslik skewered chunks of meat, grilled, then braised in a spicy sauce of tomatoes, onions and bacon
sla salad, lettuce
slaboon French bean (US green bean)
slagroom whipped cream
slak snail
sneeuwbal kind of cream puff, sometimes filled with currants and raisins
snijboon sliced French bean
soep soup
~ **van de dag** soup of the day
sorbet water ice (US sherbet)
speculaas spiced almond biscuit
spek bacon
sperzieboon French bean (US green bean)
spiegelei fried egg
spijskaart menu, bill of fare
spinazie spinach
sprits a kind of shortbread
spruitje brussels sprout
stamppot a stew of vegetables and mashed potatoes
steur sturgeon
stokvis stockfish (dried cod)
stroop treacle (US syrup)
suiker sugar
taart cake
tarbot turbot
tartaar steak tartare
~ **speciaal** extra-large portion, of prime quality
tijm thyme
tjap tjoy chop suey; a dish of fried meat and vegetables served with rice
toeristenmenu tourist menu
tomaat tomato
tong 1) tongue 2) sole
tonijn tunny (US tuna)
toost toast
tosti grilled cheese-and-ham sandwich
tournedos thick round fillet cut of prime beef (US rib or rib-eye steak)
truffel truffle
tuinboon broad bean
ui onion
uitsmijter two slices of bread garnished with ham or roast beef and topped with two fried eggs
vanille vanilla
varkenshaas pork tenderloin
varkenslapje pork fillet
varkensvlees pork
venkel fennel
vermicellisoep consommé with thin noodles
vers fresh
vijg fig
vis fish
vla custard
vlaai fruit tart
Vlaamse karbonade small slices of beef and onions braised in broth, with beer sometimes added
vlees meat
voorgerecht starter or first course
vrucht fruit
vruchtensalade fruit salad
wafel wafer
walnoot walnut
warm hot
waterkers watercress
waterzooi chicken poached in white wine and shredded vegetables, cream and egg-yolk
wentelteefje French toast; slice of white bread dipped in egg batter and fried, then sprinkled with cinnamon and sugar
wijnkaart wine list

wijting whiting
wild game
~ **zwijn** wild boar
wilde eend wild duck
witlof chicory (US endive)
~ **op zijn Brussels** chicory rolled in a slice of ham and oven-browned with cheese sauce
worst sausage
wortel carrot
zachtgekookt ei soft-boiled egg
zalm salmon
zeekreeft lobster
zeevis saltwater fish
zout salt
zuurkool sauerkraut
zwezerik sweetbread

Drink

advocaat egg liqueur
ananassap pineapple juice
aperitief aperitif
bessenjenever blackcurrant gin
bier beer
bisschopswijn mulled wine
bittertje bitter-tasting aperitif
boerenjongens Dutch brandy with raisins
boerenmeisjes Dutch brandy with apricots
borrel shot
brandewijn brandy
cassis blackcurrant liqueur
chocolademelk, chocomel(k) chocolate drink
citroenbrandewijn lemon brandy
citroenjenever lemon-flavoured gin
citroentje met suiker brandy flavoured with lemon peel, with sugar added
cognac brandy, cognac
donker bier porter; dark sweet-tasting beer
druivesap grape juice
frisdrank soft drink
gekoeld iced
genever see *jenever*
Geuzelambiek a strong Flemish bitter beer brewed from wheat and barley
jenever Dutch gin
jonge jenever/klare young Dutch gin
karnemelk buttermilk
kersenbrandewijn kirsch; spirit distilled from cherries
koffie coffee
~ **met melk** with milk
~ **met room** with cream
~ **met slagroom** with whipped cream
~ **verkeerd** white coffee; equal quantity of coffee and hot milk
zwarte ~ black
Kriekenlambiek a strong Brussels bitter beer flavoured with morello cherries
kwast hot or cold lemon squash
licht bier lager; light beer
likeur liqueur

DUTCH

limonade lemonade
melk milk
mineraalwater mineral water
oude jenever/klare Dutch gin aged in wood casks, yellowish in colour and more mature than *jonge jenever*
oranjebitter orange-flavoured bitter
pils general name for beer
sap juice
sinas orangeade
spuitwater soda water
sterkedrank liquor, spirit
tafelwater mineral water
thee tea
~ **met citroen** with lemon
~ **met suiker en melk** with sugar and milk
trappistenbier malt beer brewed (originally) by Trappist monks
vieux brandy bottled in Holland
vruchtesap fruit juice
warme chocola hot chocolate
wijn wine
droge ~ dry
rode ~ red
witte ~ white
zoete ~ sweet
wodka vodka

Finnish

Guide to pronunciation

Letter	Approximate pronunciation
Consonants	
k, m, n, p, t, v	as in English
d	as in rea**d**y, but sometimes very weak
g	only found after **n**; **ng** is pronounced as in si**ng**er
h	as in **h**ot, whatever its position in the word
j	like **y** in **y**ou
l	as in **l**et
r	always rolled
s	always as in **s**et

Vowels

a	like **a** in c**a**r, but shorter
e	like **a** in l**a**te

i	like **i** in p**i**n
o	like **aw** in l**aw**, but shorter
u	like **u** in p**u**ll
y	like **u** in French s**u**r or **ü** in German **ü**ber; say **ee** as in s**ee** and round your lips while still trying to pronounce **ee**
ä	like **a** in h**a**t
ö	like **ur** in f**ur**, but with the lips rounded

Note

The letters **b, c, f, q, š, sh, x, z, ž** and **å** are only found in words borrowed from foreign languages, and they're pronounced as in the language of origin.

Diphthongs

In Finnish, diphthongs occur only in the first syllable of a word, except for those ending in **-i** which can occur anywhere. They should be pronounced as a combination of the two vowel sounds represented by the spelling. The first vowel is pronounced louder in the following diphthongs: **ai, ei, oi, ui, yi, äi, öi, au, eu, ou, ey, äy, öy, iu**; the second vowel is louder in **ie, uo, yö.**

Double letters

Remember that in Finnish *every* letter is pronounced, therefore a letter written double is pronounced long. Thus, the **kk** in ku**kk**a should be pronounced like the two **k** sounds in the words thi**ck c**oat Similarly, the **aa** in k**aa**tua should be pronounced long (like **a** in English c**a**r). These distinctions are important, not least of all because ku**k**a has a different meaning from ku**kk**a and k**a**tua a different meaning from k**aa**tua.

Stress

A strong stress always falls on the first syllable of a word.

Some useful expressions

Hungry

I'm hungry/I'm thirsty.	**Minulla on nälkä/Minulla on jano.**
Can you recommend a good restaurant?	**Voitteko suositella hyvää ravintolaa?**
Are there any good, cheap restaurants around here?	**Onko täällä lähellä halpaa ja hyvää ravintolaa?**
I'd like to reserve a table for ... people.	**Haluaisin varata pöydän ... henkilölle.**
We'll come at ... o'clock.	**Tulemme kello ...**

Asking

Good evening. I'd like a table for ... people.	**Hyvää iltaa. Haluaisin pöydän ... henkilölle.**
Could we have a table...?	**Voisimmeko saada...?**
in the corner	**nurkkapöydän**
by the window	**ikkunapöydän**
outside	**pöydän ulkoa**
on the terrace	**pöydän terassilta**
May I please have the menu?	**Saisinko ruokalistan?**
What's this?	**Mitä tämä on?**
Do you have...?	**Onko teillä...?**
a set menu	**päivän ateria**
local dishes	**paikallisia erikoisuuksia**
a children's menu	**lasten ateria**
Waiter/Waitress!	**Tarjoilija/Neiti!**
What do you recommend?	**Mitä suosittelette?**
Could I have (a/an)... please?	**Voisinko saada ...?**
ashtray	**tuhkakupin**
another chair	**vielä yhden tuolin**
finger bowl	**huuhdekupin**
fork	**haarukan**
glass	**lasin**
knife	**veitsen**

napkin	**lautasliinan**
plate	**lautasen**
pepper mill	**pippurimyllyn**
serviette	**lautasliinan**
spoon	**lusikan**
toothpick	**hammastikun**

Ordering

I'd like a/an/some...	**Haluaisin...**
aperitif	**aperitiivin**
appetizer	**alkupalat**
beer	**olutta**
bread	**leipää**
butter	**voita**
cheese	**juustoa**
chips	**ranskalaisia perunoita**
coffee	**kahvia**
dessert	**jälkiruokaa**
fish	**kalaa**
french fries	**ranskalaisia perunoita**
fruit	**hedelmiä**
game	**riistaa**
ice-cream	**jäätelöä**
ketchup	**tomaattisosetta**
lemon	**sitruunaa**
lettuce	**lehtisalaattia**
meat	**lihaa**
mineral water	**kivennäisvettä**
milk	**maitoa**
mustard	**sinappia**
noodles	**nauhamakaroneja**
oil	**öljyä**
olive oil	**oliiviöljyä**
pepper	**pippuria**
potatoes	**perunoita**
poultry	**siipikarjaa**
rice	**riisiä**
rolls	**sämpylöitä**
saccharin	**sakariinia**
salad	**salaattia**

salt	**suolaa**
sandwich	**voileivän**
seafood	**kaloja ja äyriäisiä**
seasoning	**mausteita**
soup	**keittoa**
starter	**alkupalat**
sugar	**sokeria**
tea	**teetä**
vegetables	**vihanneksia**
vinegar	**etikkaa**
(iced) water	**(jää)vettä**
wine	**viiniä**

NAUTTIKAA ATERIASTANNE!
ENJOY YOUR MEAL!

baked	**uunissa paistettu**
baked in parchment	**unnissa paistettu voipaperiin kääritynä**
boiled	**keitetty**
braised	**hauduttaen kypsennetty**
cured	**suolaveteen säilötty**
fried	**paistettu**
grilled	**pariloitu**
marinated	**marinoitu**
poached	**upotettuna keitetty**
roasted	**paahdettu**
sautéed	**voissa paistettu**
smoked	**savustettu**
steamed	**höyryttäen kypsennetty**
stewed	**muhennettu**
underdone (rare)	**vähän paistettuna**
medium	**puolikypsänä**
well-done	**kypsänä**

TERVEYDEKSI!
CHEERS!

glass	**lasi**
bottle	**pullo**
red	**punaviini**
white	**valkoviini**
rosé	**roséviini**
very dry	**hyvin kuiva**
dry	**kuiva**
sweet	**makea**
light	**kevyt**
full-bodied	**täyteläisen makuinen**
sparkling	**helmeilevä**
neat (straight)	**sekoittamaton**
on the rocks	**jään kera**

The bill

I'd like to pay.	**Haluaisin maksaa.**
We'd like to pay separately.	**Maksamme kukin erikseen.**
You've made a mistake in this bill, I think.	**Luulen että tähän laskuun on tullut virhe.**
What's this amount for?	**Mitä tämä summa tarkoittaa?**
Is service included?	**Sisältyykö palvelumaksu laskuun?**
Is everything included?	**Sisältyykö siihen kaikki?**
Do you accept traveller's cheques?	**Otatteko vastaan matkašekkejä?**
Thank you. This is for you.	**Kiitos, tämä on teille.**
Keep the change.	**Pitäkää vaihtoraha.**
That was a very good meal.	**Se oli erinomainen ateria.**
We enjoyed it, thank you.	**Nautimme siitä.**

Complaints

That's not what I ordered.	**En tilannut tätä.**
I asked for...	**Pyysin...**
May I change this?	**Voinko vaihtaa tämän?**

The meat is...	**Liha on...**
overdone	**liian kypsää**
underdone	**liian vähän paistettua**
too rare	**liian raakaa**
too tough	**liian sitkeää**
This is too...	**Tämä on liian...**
bitter/salty/sweet	**kitkerää/suolaista/makeaa**
The food is cold.	**Ruoka on kylmää.**
This isn't fresh.	**Tämä ei ole tuoretta.**
What's taking you so long?	**Miksi tarjoilu on näin hidasta?**
Where are our drinks?	**Missä ovat juomamme?**
This isn't clean.	**Tämä ei ole puhdas.**
Would you ask the head waiter to come over?	**Pyytäisittekö hovimestarin tänne.**

Numbers

1	**yksi**	11	**yksitoista**
2	**kaksi**	12	**kaksitoista**
3	**kolme**	13	**kolmetoista**
4	**neljä**	14	**neljätoista**
5	**viisi**	15	**viisitoista**
6	**kuusi**	16	**kuusitoista**
7	**seitsemän**	17	**seitsemäntoista**
8	**kahdeksan**	18	**kahdeksantoista**
9	**yhdeksän**	19	**yhdeksäntoista**
10	**kymmenen**	20	**kaksikymmentä**

Food

Please note that Finnish alphabetical order is **a-z, ä, ö.**

aamiainen breakfast
ahven perch
alkupala appetizer, starter
ananas pineapple
anjovis marinated sprats
ankerias eel
ankka duck
annos portion
appelsiini orange
aprikoosi apricot
aromivoi herb butter
ateria meal
Aura blue cheese
avokado avocado (pear)
banaani banana
blini buckwheat pancake
borssikeitto borscht; beetroot soup consisting of chopped meat, cabbage and carrot, served with sour cream
broileri broiler, chicken
dieettiruoka diet food
dippikastike dip sauce
donitsi doughnut
etana snail
etikka white vinegar
~**kurkku** gherkin
~**sienet** pickled mushrooms
eturuoka warm first course
fasaani pheasant
fenkoli fennel
filee fillet
forelli trout
friteerattu deep-fried
graavi/lohi salmon cured with salt, sugar, pepper and dill
~**siika** salt- and sugar-cured whitefish
~**silakat** cured and marinated Baltic herrings
grahamleipä graham bread
gratiini gratin
gratinoitu gratinéed
greippi grapefruit
grillattu grilled
grilli/makkara grilled sausage
~**pihvi** grilled steak
halstrattu barbecued (fish)
hampurilainen hamburger
hanhenmaksa goose liver
~**pasteija** goose-liver pâté
hanhi goose
hapan/imelä sweet-and-sour
~**kaali** sauerkraut
~**kerma** sour cream
~**korppu** very thin rye crisp bread (US hardtack)
~**leipä** rye bread
hasselpähkinä hazelnut
haudutettu braised
hauki pike
hedelmä fruit
~**hilloke** stewed fruit
~**salaatti** fruit salad
herkkusieni button mushroom
herne (pl **herneet**) pea

FINNISH

~**keitto** thick pea soup with pork
hienonnettu mashed, minced
hiillostettu barbecued
hiivaleipä yeast bread
hillo jam
~**munkki** jam (US jelly) doughnut
~**sipuli** pickled pearl onion
hirven/käristys roast elk served in cream sauce
~**liha** elk meat
~**seläke** saddle of elk
hirvipaisti roast elk
hummeri lobster
hunaja honey
~**meloni** cantaloupe
hyvin paistettu well-done
hyytelö jelly
hyytelöity jellied
härän/filee fillet of beef
~**häntäkeitto** oxtail soup
~**kyljys** rib steak
~**leike** porterhouse steak
~**liha** beef
~**paisti** roast joint of beef
illallinen supper
inkivääri ginger
italiansalaatti boiled vegetables in mayonnaise
Janssonin kiusaus baked casserole of sliced potatoes, onions and marinated sprats in cream sauce
jauheliha minced meat
~**pihvi** hamburger steak
~**sämpylä** hamburger
jauhettu minced
joulu/kinkku baked ham covered with mustard and breadcrumbs
~**pöytä** buffet of Christmas specialities
jugurtti yoghurt
Juhla kind of Cheddar cheese
juomaraha tip
juottoporsas suck(l)ing pig
juurekset root vegetables
juusto cheese
~**kohokas** cheese soufflé
~**tanko** cheese straw
~**tarjotin** cheese board
jälkiruoka dessert
jälkiuunileipä rye bread baked in a slow oven
jänispaisti roast hare
jäädyke water ice (US sherbet)
jäätelö ice-cream
kaali cabbage
~**keitto** cabbage soup with mutton or pork
~**kääryleet** cabbage leaves stuffed with minced meat and rice
~**laatikko** layers of cabbage and minced meat
kahvi/aamiainen continental breakfast
~**leipä** coffee cake; generic term for cakes, sweet rolls and pastries
kakku cake
kala fish
~**keitto** fish soup
~**kukko** pie made of small whitefish and pork, baked in rye dough
~**mureke** fish mousse
~**pulla**, ~**pyörykkä** fish ball
~**ruoka** fish course
~**vuoka** fish gratin
kalkkuna turkey
kampela flounder
kana hen
kanan/koipi chicken thigh
~**maksa** chicken liver
~**muna** egg
~**poika** spring chicken
~**rinta** chicken breast

kaneli cinnamon
kantarelli chanterelle mushroom
kapris caper
karhun/liha bear meat
~**paisti** roast bear
~**vatukka** blackberry
karitsanliha lamb
karjalan/paisti stew of beef, mutton, pork, kidneys, liver and onions
~**piirakka** a thin and crisp rye-pastry shell filled with rice or mashed potatoes, served with finely chopped hard-boiled eggs mixed with butter
karpalo cranberry
karviaismarja gooseberry
kastanja chestnut
kastike sauce, gravy
kasvis (pl **kasvikset**) vegetable
~**ruoka** vegetable course
katajanmarja juniper berry
kateenkorva sweetbread
katemaksu cover charge
katkarapu shrimp
kaura/keksi oatmeal biscuit
~**puuro** oatmeal
kauris deer
kaviaari caviar
keitetty boiled, cooked
keitetyt perunat boiled potatoes
keitto soup, cream
keksi biscuit (US cookie)
keltasieni chanterelle mushroom
kerma cream
~**juusto** cream cheese
~**kakku** sponge layer cake with cream and jam filling
~**kastike** cream sauce
~**leivos** cream pastry
~**vaahto** whipped cream
~**viili** kind of sour cream
Kesti hard cheese flavoured with caraway seeds
kesäkeitto spring vegetable soup
ketsuppi catsup
kevyt/kerma coffee cream
~**viili** low-calorie yoghurt
kieli tongue
kiisseli dessert of berry or fruit juice thickened with potato flour
kinkku ham
kirjolohi salmon trout
kirsikka cherry
kohokas soufflé
kokojyväleipä whole-meal bread
kolja haddock
korppu rusk (US zwieback)
~**jauhotettu** breaded
korva/puusti cinnamon roll
~**sieni** morel mushroom
kotiruoka home cooking, plain food
kotitekoinen home-made
kovaksi keitetty muna hard-boiled egg
Kreivi semi-hard cheese, mildly pungent
kuha pike-perch
kuivattu luumu prune
kukkakaali cauliflower
kukkoa viinissä chicken stewed in red wine
kulibjaka pie stuffed with salmon, rice, hard-boiled eggs and dill, served in slices with melted butter
kumina caraway
kuoriperunat potatoes in their jacket
kuorrutettu oven-browned
kuorukka croquette
kurkku cucumber
kurpitsa gourd, pumpkin, squash
kutunjuusto goat's cheese, brown in colour
kyljys chop

FINNISH

kylkipaisti spare-rib
kylmä cold
kypsä well-done
kyyhkynen pigeon
kääre/syltty kind of brawn (US head cheese)
~**torttu** Swiss roll
kääryle thin slice of meat, stuffed and rolled
köyhät ritarit French toast; slices of bread dipped in egg batter, fried and served with jam
laatikko casserole, gratin
lahna bream
lakka Arctic cloudberry
lammas mutton
~**kaali** Irish stew; lamb and cabbage stew
~**muhennos** lamb stew
lampaan/kyljys lamb chop
~**liha** lamb
~**paisti** leg of lamb
lankkupihvi steak served on a board (US plank steak)
lanttu swede
~**laatikko** oven-browned swede purée
lapa shoulder
lasimestarinsilli pieces of herring fillets marinated in sweetened vinegar with onion, carrot, black and white peppercorns and bay leaves
laskiaispulla bun filled with almond paste and whipped cream
lasku bill, check
lasten ruokalista children's menu
lautanen plate
lehti/pihvi very thin slice of beef
~**salaatti** lettuce
leike cutlet
leikkeleet cold meat (US cold cuts)
leikkelelautanen plate of cold meat
leipä (pl **leivät**) bread
leivitetty breaded
leivos (pl **leivokset**) cake, pastry
lenkkimakkara ring-shaped sausage, eaten grilled, fried, baked or as an ingredient in stews and soups
liekitetty flamed
liemi broth
liha meat
~**keitto** beef and vegetable soup
~**liemi** meat broth, consommé
~**mureke** meat-loaf
~**piirakka** pie stuffed with rice and minced meat
~**pulla,** ~**pyörykkä** meat ball
~**ruoka** meat course
limppu sweetened rye bread
Lindströmin pihvi hamburger steak flavoured with pickled beetroot and capers
linnapaisti pot roast flavoured with brandy, molasses and marinated sprats
linturuoka fowl course
lipeäkala specially treated stockfish poached and served with potatoes and white sauce
lohi salmon
~**piirakka** pie stuffed with salmon, rice, hard-boiled eggs and dill, served in slices with melted butter
loimu/lohi salmon grilled on an open fire
~**siika** whitefish grilled very slowly on an open fire
lounas lunch
luu bone
luumu plum
luuydin bone marrow

lämmin warm
~ **ruoka** (pl **lämpimät ruoat**) main course, hot dish
länsirannikon salaatti seafood salad
maa-artisokka Jerusalem artichoke
maapähkinä peanut
made burbot
maissi maize (US corn)
maissintähkä corn on the cob
majoneesi mayonnaise
makaroni macaroni
~**laatikko** baked macaroni
makea sweet
makkara sausage
~**kastike** diced sausages stewed in a sauce
makrilli mackerel
maksa liver
~**laatikko** liver and meat-loaf flavoured with molasses, onions and raisins
~**makkara** liver sausage
~**pasteija** liver paste
mandariini mandarin (US tangerine)
mansikka strawberry
~**kakku** sponge layer cake with strawberries and whipped cream
~**leivos** strawberry pastry
~**torttu** strawberry flan
manteli almond
marenki meringue
marinoitu marinated
marja berry
marmelaati, marmeladi marmalade
mateenmäti burbot roe
mauste (pl **mausteet**) spice, condiment
~**silli** spiced, marinated herring
meetvursti kind of salami
mehukeitto dessert of berry or fruit juice slightly thickened with potato flour
meloni melon
meriantura sole
merimiespihvi sliced beef, onions and potatoes braised in beer
mesimarja Arctic raspberry
metso capercaillie, wood-grouse
metsämansikka wild strawberry
metsästäjänleike veal scallop with mushroom sauce
muhennettu stewed, mashed
muhennos stew, purée
muikku vendace (small whitefish)
~**pata** vendace casserole
muikunmäti vendace roe
multasieni truffle
muna egg
munakas omelet
munakoiso aubergine (US eggplant)
munakokkeli scrambled eggs
munariisipasteija egg and rice pasty
munavoi finely chopped hard-boiled eggs mixed with butter
munkki (jam) doughnut
munuainen (pl **munuaiset**) kidney
munuaishöystö kidney stew
mureke 1) fish or meat mousse 2) forcemeat, stuffing
murot breakfast cereals
musta viinimarja blackcurrant
mustikka blueberry
~**keitto** dessert of blueberry juice thickened with potato flour
~**piirakka** blueberry pie
muurain (pl **muuraimet**) Arctic cloudberry
mämmi dessert pudding of malted rye and rye flour flavoured

with orange rind, served cold with cream and sugar
mäti fish roe
nahkiainen lamprey
nakki (pl **nakit**) frankfurter
naudanliha beef
näkkileipä crisp bread (US hard-tack)
ohrasämpylä barley roll
ohukaiset small thin pancakes
oliivi olive
~**öljy** olive oil
omeletti omelet
omena apple
~**hilloke** stewed apples
~**paistos** baked apple
~**sose** apple sauce
oopperavoileipä toast topped with a hamburger steak and a fried egg
osteri oyster
paahdettu toasted, roasted
paahto/leipä toast
~**paisti** roast beef
~**vanukas** caramel custard
painosyltty brawn (US head cheese)
paistettu fried, roasted
~ **muna** fried egg
paistetut perunat fried potatoes
paisti roast
paistinliemi gravy
paistos generic term for fried or baked dishes
pala piece
~**paisti** beef stew
palvattu cured, smoked
palvikinkku cured ham
pannu generic term for sautéed dishes
~**kakku** kind of pancake
~**pihvi** hamburger steak served with fried onions
paprika sweet pepper
papu (pl **pavut**) bean
pariloitu grilled, barbecued
parsa asparagus
~**kaali** broccoli
pasteija 1) paste 2) pastry, pie
pata (baked) casserole
~**kukko** rye-flour pie with vendace and bacon
~**paisti** pot roast
patonki French bread
pehmeäksi keitetty muna soft-boiled egg
pekoni bacon
~**pannu** fried bacon, sausages, potatoes and eggs
peltopyy partridge
persikka peach
persilja parsley
~**voi** parsley butter
peruna potato
~**lastut** crisps (US potato chips)
~**pannukakku** potato pancake
~**muhennos** mashed potatoes
pihlajanmarja rowanberry
~**jäädyke** rowanberry water-ice
pihvi beefsteak
piimä sour milk
~**juusto** fresh curd cheese
~**piirakka** kind of cheese cake
piirakka pie
piiras (pl **piiraat**) small pie, pasty
pikkuleipä biscuit (US cookie)
pinaatti spinach
piparjuuri horse-radish
~**liha** boiled beef with horse-radish sauce
piparkakku gingerbread
pippuri pepper
~**juusto** pepper cheese
~**pihvi** pepper steak
porkkana carrot
~**raaste** grated carrots

poron/kieli reindeer tongue
~**käristys** roast reindeer served in cream sauce
~**liha** reindeer meat
~**paisti** roast reindeer
~**seläke** saddle of reindeer
porsaan/kyljys pork chop
~**paisti** roast joint of pork
~ **selkäpaisti** roast loin of pork
potka leg, shank
pulla bun
punainen viinimarja redcurrant
puna/juuri beetroot
~**kaali** red cabbage
puolikypsä medium (done)
puolukka lingonberry, kind of cranberry
~**puuro** lingonberry and semolina pudding
purjo leek
puuro porridge
pyttipannu kind of bubble and squeak; diced meat, potatoes and onions fried and served with a raw egg-yolk or a fried egg
pyy hazelhen
pähkinä nut
päivällinen dinner
päivän annos speciality of the day
pääruoka main course
päärynä pear
raaka raw
~**pihvi** steak tartare; raw, spiced minced beef
~**suolattu** cured in brine
raastettu grated
raavaanliha heifer meat
raejuusto cottage cheese
rahkapiirakka kind of cheese cake
ranskalaiset pavut French beans (US green beans)
ranskalaiset perunat chips (US French fries)
ranskanleipä white bread
raparperi rhubarb
rapu (pl **ravut**) freshwater crayfis
~**silakat** poached Baltic herrings, flavoured with tomato sauce and dill, served cold
reikäleipä ring-shaped rye bread
retiisi radish
riekko ptarmigan
rieska unleavened barley bread
riisi rice
~**puuro** rice pudding
riista game
rinta breast, brisket
rosolli herring salad with pickled beetroot, onions, hard-boiled eggs, capers and sour cream
rouhesämpylä whole-meal roll
ruijanpallas halibut
ruisleipä rye bread
ruohosipuli chive
ruoka (pl **ruoat**) food
~**laji** dish, course
~**lista** menu
rusina raisin
ruskea kastike gravy
ruskistettu sautéed
ruusukaali brussels sprout
saksanpähkinä walnut
salaatti salad
sammakonreidet frogs' legs
savu/kala smoked fish
~**kinkku** smoked ham
~**poro** smoked reindeer meat
~**silakat** smoked Baltic herrings
~**silli** smoked herring
savustettu smoked
sei, seiti black cod
seisova pöytä buffet with a large variety of hot and cold dishes, salads, cheeses and desserts
sekasalaatti mixed salad
seljanka salmon soup

selleri celery
setsuuri sweetened rye bread
sianliha pork
~**kastike** sliced pork in gravy
siansorkka (pl **siansorkat**) pigs' trotters (US pigs' feet)
sieni (pl **sienet**) mushroom
~**kastike** mushroom sauce
~**muhennos** creamed mushrooms
~**salaatti** salad of chopped mushrooms and onions with a cream sauce
siianmäti whitefish roe
siika whitefish
silakka Baltic herring
~**laatikko** baked casserole of sliced potatoes and Baltic herring
~**pihvi** breaded Baltic herring fillets stuffed with dill and parsley
~**rulla** salted and pickled Baltic herring
silavapannukakku pancake with diced bacon
silli herring
~**lautanen** plate of assorted herring
~**pöytä** buffet of a large variety of herring specialities
~**salaatti** herring salad with pickled beetroot, hard-boiled eggs, onions, apples, capers and topped with sour cream
~**tarjotin** assorted herring served on a tray
~**voileipä** open-faced sandwich with hard-boiled eggs and herring
simpukka mussel
sinappi mustard
~**silakat** Baltic herrings in mustard sauce
sipuli onion
~**pihvi** steak and fried onions
siskonmakkarakeitto vegetable soup with diced veal sausage
sitruuna lemon
smetana sour cream
sokeri sugar
~**herneet** sugar peas
~**kakku** sponge cake
sokeriton sugarless
sokeroitu sweetened
sorsa wild duck
sose mash, purée
stroganoff beef Stroganoff: thin sliced beef and mushrooms in a sour-cream sauce
suklaa chocolate
sulatejuusto processed cheese
suola salt
~**kurkku** pickled and salted gherkin
~**liha** cured beef, sliced and served cold
~**sienet** mushrooms preserved in brine
~**silli** salted herring
suolattu salted; preserved in brine
suomuurain (pl **suomuuraimet**) Arctic cloudberry
suutarinlohi sugar-salted, marinated Baltic herring
sveitsinleike cordon bleu; breaded veal scallop stuffed with ham and Swiss cheese
sämpylä roll
T-luupihvi T-bone steak
tahkojuusto kind of Swiss cheese
taimen trout
tarjoilupalkkio service charge
~ **ei sisälly hintaan** not included
~ **sisältyy hintaan** included
tartarpihvi steak tartare; raw,

spiced minced beef
taskurapu crab
tatti boletus mushroom
teeri black grouse
terveysruoka health food
tilli dill
~**liha** boiled lamb or veal in dill sauce, flavoured with lemon juice or vinegar
~**silli** poached herring seasoned with dill, white pepper and lemon juice
tomaatti tomato
tonnikala tunny (US tuna)
torttu tart, flan, cake
tumma leipä dark bread
tuore fresh
~**suolattu lohi** fresh and slightly salted salmon
turska cod
täyte stuffing, filling
~**kakku** layer cake
täytetty stuffed, filled
upotettu muna, uppomuna poached egg
uudet perunat spring potatoes
uuniperuna baked potato
uunissa paistettu baked
vadelma raspberry
valikoima assorted, mixed
valkoinen leipä white bread
valkokaali white cabbage
valkokastike white sauce
valkosipuli garlic
~**perunat** baked sliced potatoes flavoured with butter and garlic
~**voi** garlic butter
valkoturska whiting
vanilja vanilla
~**kastike** vanilla sauce
vanukas pudding, custard
varhaisaamiainen breakfast
varras (pl **vartaat**) spit, skewer
vasikan/kateenkorva calf's sweetbread
~**leike** veal cutlet
~**liha** veal
~**paisti** roast veal
vatkuli beef stew flavoured with bay leaves
velli gruel
venäläinen silli herring fillets with diced, pickled beetroot and cucumber, hard-boiled eggs and lettuce, served with sour cream
veri/ohukaiset blood pancakes
~**makkara** blood sausage
~**palttu** blood (black) pudding
vesimeloni watermelon
vihannes (pl **vihannekset**) vegetable
vihreä salaatti green salad
vihreät pavut French beans (US green beans)
viili processed sour milk
viilokki fricassée
viinietikka wine vinegar
~**kastike** oil and vinegar dressing
viini/kukko chicken stewed in red wine
~**lista** wine list
~**marja** currant
~**rypäle** grape
viipale slice
viipaloitu sliced
viiriäinen quail
vohveli wafer, waffle
voi butter
voileipä sandwich, usually open-faced
~**keksi** soda cracker
~**pöytä** large buffet of cold and warm dishes; "smörgåsbord"
voipavut butter beans (US wax beans)

FINNISH

voissa paistettu fried in butter
voisula melted butter
vorschmak minced lamb, herring fillets and fried onions cooked in broth, flavoured with catsup, mustard and marinated sprats, served with sour cream and baked potatoes
vuohenjuusto goat's milk cheese
vähän paistettu rare (US underdone)
välikyljys entrecôte, rib-eye steak
wienerleipä Danish pastry
wieninleike Wiener schnitzel; breaded veal scallop
yrttivoi herb butter
äyriäinen (pl **äyriäiset**) shellfish
öljy oil

Drink

A-olut beer with highest alcoholic content
akvaviitti spirits distilled from potatoes or grain, often flavoured with aromatic seeds and spices
aperitiivi aperitif
appelsiinilimonaati orangeade
Finlandia a Finnish vodka
gini gin
glögi mulled wine (Christmas speciality)
hedelmämehu fruit juice
Jaloviina blend of spirits and brandy
jäävesi iced water
kaakao cocoa
kahvi coffee
~ **kerman (ja sokerin) kera** with cream (and sugar)
kalja a type of very light (1% alcohol) beer, often home-made
kerma cream
keskiolut medium-strong beer
kivennäisvesi mineral water
konjakki cognac
Koskenkorva very strong *akvaviitti* made of grain
kuiva dry
~ **viini** dry wine
kuohuviini sparkling wine
Lakka Arctic cloudberry liqueur
Lapponia lingonberry (kind of cranberry) liqueur
likööri liqueur
limonaati lemonade
maito milk
~**kahvi** coffee with milk
makea sweet
mehu squash (US fruit drink)
Mesimarja Arctic bramble liqueur
mineraalivesi mineral water
musta kahvi black coffee
olut beer
piimä junket
pilsneri lager; a mild, light beer
Polar cranberry liqueur
portviini port wine

punaviini red wine
rommi rum
roséviini rosé wine
samppanja champagne
siideri cider
sima beverage produced from cane and beet sugar, lemon, yeast, hops and water (May 1 speciality)
Suomuurain Arctic cloudberry liqueur
tee tea
  ~ **maidon kera** with milk
  ~ **sitruunan kera** with lemon
tonic-vesi tonic water
tumma olut porter
tuoremehu fresh fruit or vegetable juice
tynnyriolut draught (US draft) beer
vaalea olut lager
valkoviini white wine
vermutti vermouth
vesi water
viina brandy, spirits
viini wine
virvoitusjuoma lemonade, soft drink
viski whisky
väkijuomat spirits

French

Guide to pronunciation

Letter	**Approximate pronunciation**
Consonants	
b, c, d, f, k, l, m, n, p, s, t, v, x, z	are usually pronounced more or less as in English
ç	like **s** in **s**o
ch	like **sh** in **sh**ut
g	before **e, i, y,** like **s** in lei**s**ure, otherwise as in **g**o
gn	like **ni** in o**ni**on
h	always silent
j	like **s** in lei**s**ure
ll	either like **y** in **y**es or like **l** in **l**east
qu	like **k** in **k**ill
r	pronounced in the back of the mouth
w	like **v** in **v**iew or as in **w**e

Vowels

a, à, â	something like **a** in c**a**r, but shorter
ai, ay	like **a** in l**a**te
aî, aient, ais, ait	like **e** in g**e**t
au	like **oa** in m**oa**t
é, er, et, ez	like **a** in l**a**te
è, ê	like **e** in g**e**t
e	followed by one consonant, or at the end of a one-syllable word, like **a** in **a**bout; followed by two consonants, like **e** in g**e**t
eau	see **au**
ei	like **e** in g**e**t
eu	like **ur** in f**ur**, but without any **r** sound
i	like **ee** in m**ee**t
o	like **oa** in m**oa**t or like **o** in n**o**t
ô	like **oa** in m**oa**t
oi	like **wha** in **wha**ck
ou, où	like **oo** in l**oo**t
u	pronounce **ee** as in s**ee**, but round your lips as if to pronounce **oo**
ui	like **wee** in bet**wee**n
y	like **ee** in m**ee**t

Nasal vowels

When the letter **n** or **m** follows a vowel, but is neither followed by a vowel nor by **n** or **m**, then the preceding vowel is pronounced nasally (through the nose as well as the mouth, similar to the Midwestern twang in America).

aim, ain	something like **ang** in r**ang**
am, an **em, en**	something like **arn** in b**arn**
eim, ein **im, in**	see **aim**
ien	something like **yan** in **yan**k

FRENCH

oin	something like **wang**
on	something like **orn** in **corn**-cob
un	see **aim**

Note

1) The letter **e** is generally not pronounced at the end of a word, but is used to indicate that the preceding consonants should be pronounced.
2) If there's no final **e,** then final consonants are generally not pronounced unless the next word begins with a vowel, in which case the consonant is "run-on" to the vowel at the beginning of the next word. (This is called liaison.) An example of this would be *sauce aux airelles* whereby the **x** of *aux* is pronounced as a **z** at the beginning of *airelles*.

Some useful expressions

Hungry

I'm hungry/I'm thirsty.	**J'ai faim/J'ai soif.**
Can you recommend a good restaurant?	**Pouvez-vous nous/me recommander un bon restaurant?**
Are there any good, cheap restaurants around here?	**Y a-t-il un restaurant bon marché dans les environs?**
I'd like to reserve a table for ... people.	**J'aimerais réserver une table pour ... personnes.**
We'll come at ... o'clock.	**Nous viendrons à ... heures.**

Asking

Good evening. I'd like a table for ... people.	**Bonsoir. J'aimerais une table pour ... personnes.**
Could we have a table...?	**Pouvons-nous avoir une table...?**
in the corner	**dans un angle**
by the window	**près de la fenêtre**
outside	**à l'extérieur**
on the terrace	**sur la terrasse**
May I please have the menu?	**Puis-je avoir la carte?**
What's this?	**Qu'est-ce que cela?**

Do you have...?	**Avez-vous...?**
a set menu	**un menu**
local dishes	**des spécialités locales**
a children's menu	**un menu pour enfant**
Waiter/Waitress!	**Garçon/Mademoiselle!**
What do you recommend?	**Que me recommandez-vous?**
Could I have (a/an)... please?	**Puis-je avoir..., s'il vous plaît?**
ashtray	**un cendrier**
another chair	**une chaise de plus**
finger bowl	**un rince-doigts**
fork	**une fourchette**
glass	**un verre**
knife	**un couteau**
napkin	**une serviette**
plate	**une assiette**
pepper mill	**un moulin à poivre**
serviette	**une serviette**
spoon	**une cuiller**
toothpick	**un cure-dent**

Ordering

I'd like a/an/some...	**J'aimerais...**
aperitif	**un apéritif**
appetizer	**une entrée**
beer	**une bière**
bread	**du pain**
butter	**du beurre**
cheese	**du fromage**
chips	**des pommes frites**
coffee	**un café**
dessert	**un dessert**
fish	**du poisson**
french fries	**des pommes frites**
fruit	**des fruits**
game	**du gibier**
ice-cream	**une glace**
lemon	**du citron**
lettuce	**de la laitue**

meat	**de la viande**
mineral water	**de l'eau minérale**
milk	**du lait**
mustard	**de la moutarde**
noodles	**des nouilles**
oil	**de l'huile**
olive oil	**de l'huile d'olive**
pepper	**du poivre**
potatoes	**des pommes de terre**
poultry	**de la volaille**
rice	**du riz**
rolls	**des petits pains**
saccharin	**de la saccharine**
salad	**de la salade**
salt	**du sel**
sandwich	**un sandwich**
seafood	**des fruits de mer**
seasoning	**des condiments**
soup	**de la soupe**
starter	**une entrée**
sugar	**du sucre**
tea	**du thé**
vegetables	**des légumes**
vinegar	**du vinaigre**
(iced) water	**de l'eau (glacée)**
wine	**du vin**

BON APPETIT!
ENJOY YOUR MEAL!

baked	**cuit au four**
baked in parchment	**en chemise**
boiled	**bouilli**
braised	**braisé**
cured	**salé**
fried	**frit**
grilled	**grillé**
marinated	**mariné**
poached	**poché**
roasted	**rôti**

sautéed	**sauté**
smoked	**fumé**
steamed	**cuit à la vapeur**
stewed	**à l'étouffée**
underdone (rare)	**saignant**
medium	**à point**
well-done	**bien cuit**

A VOTRE SANTÉ!
CHEERS!

glass	**un verre**
bottle	**une bouteille**
red	**rouge**
white	**blanc**
rosé	**rosé**
very dry	**très sec**
dry	**sec**
sweet	**doux**
light	**léger**
full-bodied	**moelleux**
sparkling	**mousseux**
neat (straight)	**sec**
on the rocks	**avec des glaçons**

The bill

I'd like to pay.	**L'addition, s'il vous plaît.**
We'd like to pay separately.	**Nous aimerions payer chacun notre part.**
You've made a mistake in this bill, I think.	**Je crois qu'il y a une erreur dans l'addition.**
What's this amount for?	**Que représente cette somme?**
Is service included?	**Est-ce que le service est compris?**
Is everything included?	**Est-ce que tout est compris?**
Do you accept traveller's cheques?	**Acceptez-vous les chèques de voyage?**

FRENCH

Thank you. This is for you.	**Merci. Voici pour vous.**
Keep the change.	**Gardez la monnaie.**
That was a very good meal.	**Le repas était délicieux.**
We enjoyed it, thank you.	**C'était très bon, merci.**

Complaints

That's not what I ordered. I asked for…	**Ce n'est pas ce que j'ai commandé. J'ai demandé...**
May I change this?	**Pouvez-vous me le changer?**
The meat is…	**La viande est...**
overdone	**trop cuite**
underdone	**pas assez cuite**
too rare	**trop saignante**
too tough	**trop dure**
This is too…	**C'est trop...**
bitter/salty/sweet	**amer/salé/sucré**
The food is cold.	**C'est froid.**
This isn't fresh.	**Ce n'est pas frais.**
What's taking you so long?	**Pourquoi cette attente?**
Where are our drinks?	**Quand donc viendront nos boissons?**
This isn't clean.	**Ce n'est pas propre.**
Would you ask the head waiter to come over?	**Je désire voir le maître d'hôtel.**

Numbers

1	**un, une**	11	**onze**
2	**deux**	12	**douze**
3	**trois**	13	**treize**
4	**quatre**	14	**quatorze**
5	**cinq**	15	**quinze**
6	**six**	16	**seize**
7	**sept**	17	**dix-sept**
8	**huit**	18	**dix-huit**
9	**neuf**	19	**dix-neuf**
10	**dix**	20	**vingt**

FRENCH

Food

à la, à l', au, aux in the manner of, as in, with
abats, abattis giblets, innards
abricot apricot
agneau lamb
aiglefin haddock
ail garlic
ailloli garlic mayonnaise
airelle a kind of cranberry
alouette sans tête slice of veal rolled and generally stuffed with minced meat, garlic and parsley
(à l')alsacienne usually garnished with sauerkraut, ham and sausages
amande almond
amuse-gueule appetizer
ananas pineapple
anchois anchovy
(à l')ancienne old style; usually with wine-flavoured cream sauce of mushrooms, onions or shallots
(à l')andalouse usually with green peppers, aubergines and tomatoes
andouille a kind of tripe sausage
andouillette smaller kind of tripe sausage
(à l')anglaise 1) usually boiled or steamed vegetables, especially potatoes 2) breaded and fried vegetables, meat, fish or fowl
anguille eel
~ **au vert** eel braised in a white sauce served with minced parsley and other greens
anis aniseed
artichaut (globe) artichoke
asperge asparagus
assiette plate
~ **anglaise** cold meat (US cold cuts)
~ **de charcuterie** assorted pork and other meat products
assorti assorted
aubergine aubergine (US eggplant)
ballottine (de volaille) boned fowl which is stuffed, rolled, cooked and served in gelatine
banane banana
bar bass
barbue brill
basilic basil
béarnaise sauce of egg-yolk, butter, vinegar, shallots, tarragon and white wine

bécasse woodcock
béchamel white sauce
beignet fritter generally filled with fruit, vegetables or meat
(à la) Bercy butter sauce of white wine and shallots
betterave beetroot
beurre butter
~ **blanc** white butter sauce of shallots, vinegar and white wine
~ **maître d'hôtel** butter with chopped parsley and lemon juice
~ **noir** browned butter sauce of vinegar and parsley
bifteck beef steak
(à la) bigarade brown sauce generally with oranges, sugar and vinegar
biscotte rusk (US zwieback)
biscuit biscuit (US cookie)
bisque cream soup of lobster or crayfish (US chowder)
blanc de volaille boned breast of fowl
blanchaille whitebait
blanquette de veau veal stew in white sauce
(au) bleu 1) of fish (usually trout), boiled very fresh 2) of cheese, blue-veined 3) of meat, very underdone (US rare)
bœuf beef
~ **bourguignon** chunks of beef stewed in red wine with onions, bacon and mushrooms
~ **en daube** larded chunks of beef marinated in red wine with vegetables and stewed
~ **miro(n)ton** cold boiled beef or beef stew with onion sauce
~ **mode** larded chunks of beef braised in red wine with carrots and onions
~ **salé** corned beef
bolet boletus mushroom
bombe glacée moulded ice-cream dessert
(à la) bordelaise red wine sauce with shallots, beef marrow and boletus mushrooms
bouchée à la reine vol-au-vent; puff-pastry shell filled with meat, sweetbreads or seafood and sometimes mushrooms
boudin black pudding (US blood sausage)
bouillabaisse assorted fish and shellfish stewed in white wine, garlic, saffron and olive oil
bouilli 1) boiled 2) boiled beef
bouillon bouillon, broth, stock
(à la) bourguignonne button mushrooms, pearl onions or shallots braised in rich red wine
braisé braised
brandade (de morue) prepared cod with cream, oil and garlic
brie white, mellow cheese
brioche small roll or cake
(à la) broche (on a) spit
brochet pike
(en) brochette (cooked on a) skewer
cabillaud fresh cod
café glacé coffee-flavoured ice-cream dessert
caille quail
camembert soft cheese with pungent flavour
canard (caneton) duck (duckling)
~ **à l'orange** roast duck braised with oranges and orange liqueur
cannelle cinnamon
cantal smooth, firm cheese not unlike Cheddar
câpre caper

carbonnade charcoal-grilled meat
~ **flamande** beef slices, onions and herbs braised in beer
cardon cardoon (vegetable)
carotte carrot
carottes Vichy steamed carrots
carpe carp
carré loin, rack
~ **de l'Est** usually square-shaped cheese of pungent flavour
carrelet plaice
carte des vins wine list
cassis blackcurrant
cassoulet toulousain butter-bean stew of goose or with mutton, pork and sometimes sausage
céleri celery (usually celery root)
~ **en branche** branch celery
~**-rave** celeriac, celery root
cèpe boletus mushroom
cerfeuil chervil
cerise cherry
cervelle brains
champignon mushroom
~ **de Paris** button mushroom
chanterelle chanterelle mushroom
charbonnade charcoal-grilled meat
charcuterie various kinds of cold pork products
charlotte fruit dessert (usually apples) made in a deep, round mould
chasse venison
chasseur hunter's style; sauce of mushrooms, tomatoes, wine and garlic herbs
chateaubriand thick slice of beef taken from the fillet
chaud warm
chaudrée fish and seafood stew, often with garlic, herbs, onions and white wine
chausson aux pommes apple dumpling (US turnover)
chevreuil deer
chicorée endive (US chicory)
chou cabbage
~ **de Bruxelles** brussels sprouts
~ **à la crème** cream puff
~**-fleur** cauliflower
~ **rouge** red cabbage
choucroute sauerkraut
~ **garnie** usually with ham, bacon and sausage
ciboulette chive
citron lemon
civet de lapin (lièvre) jugged rabbit (hare)
clafoutis fruit baked in pancake batter, brandy often added
clémentine pipless (US seedless) tangerine
cochon de lait suck(l)ing pig
(en) cocotte casserole
cœur heart
~ **d'artichaut** artichoke heart
(à la) Colbert dipped in egg batter and breadcrumbs, fried
colin hake
concombre cucumber
confit d'oie pieces of goose preserved in its own fat
confiture jam
consommation general word for drinks
consommé clear soup served hot or cold
~ **Célestine** with chicken and noodles
~ **aux cheveux d'ange** with thin noodles
~ **Colbert** with poached eggs, spring vegetables
~ **julienne** with shredded vegetables
~ **madrilène** cold and fla-

voured with tomatoes
~ **princesse** with diced chicken and asparagus tips
~ **aux vermicelles** with thin noodles
contre-filet sirloin
coq au vin chicken stewed in red wine with mushrooms, bacon, onions and herbs
coquelet cockerel
coquillage shellfish
coquille Saint-Jacques scallop gratinéed in its shell
corbeille de fruits basket of assorted fruit
cornichon small gherkin (US pickle)
côte chop or rib
~ **de bœuf** rib of beef
~ **de veau** veal chop
côtelette cutlet, chop
~ **d'agneau** lamb chop
~ **de porc** pork chop
coupe a metal or glass dish usually for individual desserts
~ **glacée** ice-cream dessert
courgette vegetable marrow (US zucchini)
couvert cover charge
~, **vin et service compris** price includes wine, service and cover charges
crabe crab
crème 1) a dessert with cream or a creamy dessert
~ **anglaise** custard
~ **caramel** caramel custard
~ **Chantilly** whipped cream
~ **glacée** ice-cream
crème 2) a creamy soup
crêpe large, paper-thin pancake
~ **Suzette** pancake with orange sauce, flamed with brandy and often orange liqueur
cresson (water)cress
crevette shrimp
croissant crescent-shaped flaky roll (usually served for breakfast)
croque-monsieur grilled or baked ham-and-cheese sandwich
croustade pie, pastry shell filled with fish, seafood, meat or vegetables
(en) croûte (in a) pastry crust
croûton small piece of bread, toasted or fried
cru raw
crudités raw vegetables usually served sliced, grated or diced as an hors d'oeuvre
crustacé shellfish
cuisse leg or thigh
cuisses de grenouilles frogs' legs
cuit cooked
bien ~ well-done
cumin caraway, cumin
darne thick fillet of fish, usually of salmon
datte date
daurade gilt-head
déjeuner lunch
délice often used to describe a dessert speciality of the chef
demi half
~**-sel** soft cream cheese, slightly salty
demoiselle de Cherbourg small rock lobster
(à la) dieppoise garnish of mussels and shrimp served in white-wine sauce
dinde, dindon turkey
dindonneau young turkey
dîner dinner
diplomate moulded custard dessert with crystallized fruit and lined with sponge fingers

FRENCH

steeped in liqueur
dodine de canard boned duck, rolled, stuffed, sometimes served cold in gelatine
(à la) du Barry garnish of cauliflower and cheese sauce, gratinéed
(aux) duxelles with minced mushrooms sautéed with butter, white wine and herbs
échalote shallot
écrevisse (freshwater) crayfish
~ **à la nage** simmered in white wine, aromatic vegetables and herbs
églefin haddock
émincé slices of cooked meat in gravy or thick cream sauce
endive chicory (US endive)
~ **à la bruxelloise** steamed chicory rolled in a slice of ham
entrecôte rib-eye steak
entrée dish served between the hors d'oeuvre or soup and the main course; the first course in a smaller dinner (US starter)
entremets small dish served before cheese; today it often means dessert
épaule shoulder
éperlan smelt
épice spice
épicé hot, peppered
épinard spinach
escalope de veau veal scallop, thin slice of veal
escalope viennoise wiener schnitzel; breaded veal cutlet
escargot snail
estouffade braised or steamed in tightly sealed vessel with minimum of cooking liquid
estragon tarragon
étuvé steamed, stewed with minimum of cooking liquid
faisan pheasant
farci stuffed
fenouil fennel
féra dace (fish)
fève broad bean
filet meat or fish fillet
~ **de bœuf** fillet of beef (US tenderloin)
~ **mignon** small round veal or pork fillet
~ **de sole** fillet of sole
(à la) financière rich sauce of pike dumplings, truffles, mushrooms, Madeira wine, sometimes with olives and crayfish
(aux) fines herbes with herbs
(à la) flamande Flemish style; usually a garnish of braised potatoes, carrots, cabbage, turnips, bacon and sausage (sometimes simmered in beer)
flambé dish flamed usually with brandy
flétan halibut
foie liver
~ **gras** goose or duck liver
fond d'artichaut artichocke heart (US bottom)
fondue (au fromage) melted-cheese mixture in a pot into which pieces of bread are dipped
fondue bourguignonne bite-size pieces of meat dipped into boiling oil at the table and eaten with a variety of sauces
fondue chinoise paper-thin slices of beef dipped into boiling bouillon and eaten with a variety of sauces
(à la) forestière forester's style; generally sautéed in butter with morel mushrooms, potatoes

FRENCH

and bacon
(au) four baked
frais, fraîche fresh
fraise strawberry
~ **des bois** wild
framboise raspberry
frappé chilled, iced
friand patty with meat filling
fricandeau braised, larded veal
fricassée browned pieces of meat braised with seasonings and vegetables and served in a thick sauce
frit fried
frites chips (US french fries)
friture (de poisson) fried fish
fromage cheese
~ **frais** fresh curd cheese
~ **de tête** brawn (US head-cheese)
fruit confit candied fruit
fruits de mer mussels, oysters, clams
fumé smoked
galette flat, plain cake
garbure thick cabbage soup made of salted pork, spices and *confit d'oie*
garni garnished
(avec) garniture (with) vegetables
gâteau cake, flan, tart
gaufre waffle
gaufrette small, crisp, sweet wafer
(en) gelée jellied
gélinotte hazel-hen, hazel-grouse (US prairie chicken)
gibelotte de lapin rabbit stew in wine sauce
gibier game
~ **de saison** game in season
gigot d'agneau leg of lamb
girolle chanterelle mushroom
glace ice-cream
~ **(à la) napolitaine** ice-cream layers of different flavours
glacé iced, glazed
goujon gudgeon
gras-double tripe simmered in wine and onions
(au) gratin browned with bread-crumbs or cheese
gratin dauphinois sliced potatoes gratinéed in the oven with eggs, cream and cheese
gratin de fruits de mer shellfish in heavy cream sauce and gratinéed
grillade grilled meat
grillé grilled
grive thrush
groseille à maquereau gooseberry
groseille rouge redcurrant
gruyère a hard cheese rich in flavour
haché minced, hashed
hachis mince, hash
hareng herring
haricot bean
~ **de mouton** stew of mutton with beans and potatoes
~ **vert** French bean (US green bean)
Henri IV artichoke hearts garnished with béarnaise sauce
hollandaise sauce of egg-yolks, butter and lemon juice or vinegar
homard lobster
~ **à l'américaine** (or **à l'armoricaine**) lobster flamed in brandy, simmered in white wine with garlic, tomatoes and herbs
~ **cardinal** flamed in brandy, diced, served in its shell with truffles and chopped mushrooms and gratinéed
~ **Newburg** cut into sections, cooked in brandy and fish stock

~ **Thermidor** simmered in white wine, sautéed in butter with mushrooms, herbs, spices, mustard, flamed in brandy and gratinéed with cheese
huile oil
huître oyster
~ **belon** flat, pinkish oyster
~ **de claire** similar to bluepoint oyster
~ **portugaise** small, fat oyster
jambon ham
~ **de Bayonne** raw, with a slightly salty flavour
~ **cru** raw, cured
~ **à l'os** baked ham
jardinière cooked assorted vegetables
jarret shank, shin
julienne vegetables cut into fine strips
jus gravy, juice
lamproie lamprey
langouste spiny lobster
langoustine Norway lobster, prawn, crawfish
langue tongue
lapin rabbit
lard bacon
légume vegetable
lentille lentil
levraut young hare, leveret
lièvre hare
limande dab
livarot small, round cheese from Normandy
longe de veau loin of veal
(à la) lorraine usually braised in red wine with red cabbage
loup (de mer) (sea) bass
(à la) lyonnaise generally sautéed with onions
macédoine mixed, diced vegetables or fruit
(au) madère with Madeira wine
maigre lean
maïs maize (US corn)
maître d'hôtel sautéed in butter with chopped parsley and lemon juice
maquereau mackerel
marcassin young boar
marchand de vin red wine sauce seasoned with shallots
mariné marinated
marinière sailor's style; garnish of mussels with other seafood simmered in white wine and spices
marjolaine marjoram
maroilles strong, semi-hard cheese from Picardy
marron chestnut
matelote freshwater-fish stew (especially of eel) with wine, onions, mushrooms
médaillon small, round cut of meat
menthe mint
menu in France, generally means *menu à prix fixe*, set meal at a fixed price
merguez very spicey saussage
merlan whiting
merluche dried hake
meunière floured and sautéed in butter with lemon juice and chopped parsley
miel honey
mijoté simmered
millefeuille flaky pastry with cream filling (US napoleon)
(à la) Mirabeau with anchovies, olives, tarragon
mirabelle small yellow plum
(à la) mode in the style (of); often means made according to a local recipe
moelle marrow (bone)

morille morel mushroom
Mornay *béchamel* sauce with cheese
moule mussel
moules marinière mussels simmered in white wine with shallots, thyme and parsley
mousse 1) any frothy cream dish 2) chopped or pounded meat or fish with eggs and cream
mousseline 1) frothy mixture containing cream, usually whipped 2) variation of hollandaise sauce with whipped cream
moutarde mustard
mouton mutton
munster soft cheese with a pungent flavour
mûre mulberry or blackberry
myrtille bilberry (US blueberry)
nature/au naturel plain, without dressing, sauce or stuffing
navarin mutton stew with turnips
navet turnip
(à la/en) neige snow-like; i.e. with beaten egg-whites
(à la) niçoise Riviera style; usually with garlic, anchovies, olives, onions, tomatoes
(à la) nivernaise a garnish of carrots, onions, potatoes
noisette 1) hazelnut 2) boneless round piece of meat usually taken from loin or rib
noix walnut
~ **de coco** coconut
~ **(de) muscade** nutmeg
~ **de veau** pope's eye of veal
(à la) normande usually cooked with gudgeon, shrimps, mushrooms, cream and sometimes truffles
nouilles noodles
œuf egg
~ **brouillé** scrambled
~ **à la coque** soft-boiled
~ **dur** hard-boiled
~ **farci** stuffed
~ **en gelée** lightly poached and served in gelatine
~ **au jambon** ham and eggs
~ **au/sur le plat** fried
~ **poché** poached
~ **Rossini** with truffles and Madeira wine
oie goose
oignon onion
omble-chevalier freshwater fish of the char family
omelette omelet
~ **norvégienne** ice-cream dessert covered with beaten egg-whites, quickly browned in oven and served flaming (US baked Alaska)
ortolan small game bird like a finch
os bone
~ **à moelle** marrow bone
oseille sorrel
oursin sea urchin
pain bread
palourde clam
pamplemousse grapefruit
panaché mixed; two or more kinds of something
pané breaded, rolled in breadcrumbs
(en) papillote encased in greased paper and baked
parfait ice-cream dessert
Parmentier containing potatoes
pastèque watermelon
pâté 1) a moulded pastry case which holds meat or fish 2) a thickish paste often of liver (contained in an earthenware dish)

~ **ardennais** a purée of pork and seasonings encased in a loaf of bread, served in slices

~ **de campagne** strongly flavoured with a variety of meat

~ **en croûte** in a pastry crust

~ **de foie gras** goose (or duck) liver paste

pâtes noodles, macaroni, spaghetti

paupiette (de veau) veal bird, thin slice of veal rolled around stuffing

(à la) paysanne country style; usually containing various vegetables

pêche peach

perche perch

perdreau young partridge

perdrix partridge

(à la) périgourdine preparation with truffles

persil parsley

petit small

~ **déjeuner** breakfast

~ **four** small, fancy cake (US fancy cookie)

~ **pain** roll

~ **pois** green pea

~ **salé (au chou)** salt pork (with cabbage)

~**-suisse** a mild-flavoured, double-cream cheese

pied de porc pig's trotter (US pig's foot)

pigeonneau squab

piment pimento

pintade guinea hen

piperade omelet with green peppers, garlic, tomatoes, ham

piquant sharp-tasting, spicy (e.g. of a sauce)

pissaladière onion and anchovy tart with black olives

plat plate

~ **du jour** speciality of the day

~ **principal** main dish

plateau de fromages cheese board

plie plaice

poché poached

(à la) poêle fried

(à) point medium

pointe d'asperge asparagus tip

poire pear

~ **à la Condé** served hot on a bed of vanilla-flavoured rice

~ **Belle Hélène** with vanilla ice-cream and chocolate sauce

poireau leek

pois pea

~ **chiche** chick pea

poisson fish

~ **d'eau douce** freshwater

~ **de mer** saltwater

poitrine breast, brisket

(au) poivre (with) pepper

poivron sweet pepper

pomme apple

pommes (de terre) potatoes

~ **allumettes** matchsticks

~ **chips** crisps (US potato chips)

~ **dauphine** mashed in butter and egg-yolks, mixed in seasoned flour and deep-fried

~ **duchesse** mashed with butter and egg-yolks

~ **en robe des champs** in their jackets

~ **frites** chips (US french fries)

~ **mousseline** mashed

~ **nature** boiled, steamed

~ **nouvelles** new

~ **vapeur** steamed, boiled

pont-l'évêque soft cheese, strong and pungent in flavour

porc pork

port-salut soft cheese, yellow in colour, mild in taste

potage soup
~ **bonne femme** potato, leek, mushroom, onion, rice and sometimes bacon
~ **cancalais** fish consommé (often with oysters or other seafood)
~ **Condé** mashed red beans
~ **Crécy** carrots
~ **cultivateur** mixed vegetables and bacon or pork
~ **du Barry** cream of cauliflower
~ **julienne** vegetables
~ **Longchamp** peas, sorrel and chervil
~ **Saint-Germain** split-pea, leek and onion
~ **soissonnais** haricot bean
pot-au-feu 1) stockpot of beef, potatoes and aromatic vegetables 2) stew
potée boiled pork or beef with vegetables, especially cabbage
potiron pumpkin
poularde fat pullet
~ **de Bresse** grain-fed; reputedly the finest available
~ **demi-deuil** with truffles inserted under the skin and simmered in broth
poule hen
~ **au pot** stewed with vegetables
~ **au riz** stewed in bouillon and served with rice
poulet chicken
~ **Marengo** sautéed in olive oil, cooked with white wine, tomatoes, garlic, shallots and mushrooms
pourboire tip (but *service* is the percentage added to the bill)
praire clam
pré-salé lamb pastured in the salt meadows on the Atlantic seashore
(à la) printanière with spring vegetables
prix price
~ **fixe** at a fixed price
profiterole au chocolat puff pastry filled with whipped cream or custard and covered with hot chocolate
(à la) provençale often with garlic, onions, herbs, olives, oil and tomatoes
prune plum
pruneau (blue) plum
~ **sec** prune
pudding blancmange, custard
puits d'amour pastry shell filled with liqueur-flavoured custard
purée pulped and strained fruit or vegetables
~ **de pommes de terre** mashed potatoes
quenelle light dumpling made of fish, fowl or meat
queue tail
quiche flan, open tart with meat or vegetable filling, eggs and cream
~ **lorraine** tart with cheese, bacon, eggs and cream
râble de lièvre saddle of hare
raclette hot, melted cheese scraped from a block of cheese; accompanied with boiled potatoes and gherkins
radis radish
(en) ragoût stew(ed)
raie skate, ray
raisin grape
~ **sec** raisin, sultana
ramequin small cheese tart
rascasse a Mediterranean fish, an

essential ingredient of *bouillabaisse*
ratatouille Mediterranean stew of tomatoes, peppers, onions, garlic and aubergines, served hot or cold
ravigote vinegar sauce with chopped hard-boiled eggs, capers and herbs
reblochon soft, mild cheese, pale cream colour (Savoy)
(à la) reine with mince meat or fowl
reine-claude greengage
repas meal
rhubarbe rhubarb
(à la) Richelieu garnish of tomatoes, peas, bacon and potatoes
rillettes usually minced pork (sometimes goose or duck) baked in its own fat
ris de veau sweetbread
rissole fritter, pasty
riz rice
~ **pilaf** rice boiled in a bouillon, sometimes with onions
rognon kidney
romarin rosemary
roquefort blue-veined cheese made from ewe's milk; strong, salty with piquant flavour
rosbif roast beef
rôti roast(ed)
rouelle de veau shank of veal (usually a round cut)
roulade 1) a rolled slice of meat or fish with stuffing 2) dessert with cream or jam stuffing (Swiss roll)
sabayon creamy dessert of egg-yolks, sugar and white wine flavoured with a citrus fruit, served warm
safran saffron
saignant underdone (US rare)
saint-pierre John Dory (fish)
salade salad
~ **chiffonnade** shredded lettuce and sorrel in melted butter, served with a dressing
~ **de fruits** fruit salad (US fruit cocktail)
~ **niçoise** lettuce, tomatoes, green beans, hard-boiled eggs, tunny, olives, green pepper, potatoes and anchovies
~ **russe** cooked vegetables in mayonnaise
~ **verte** green
salé salted
salmis game or fowl partially roasted, then simmered in wine and vegetable *purée*
salpicon garnish or stuffing of one or various elements held together by sauce
salsifis salsify
sandre pike perch
sanglier wild boar
sarcelle teal, small freshwater duck
sauce sauce
~ **béarnaise** vinegar, egg-yolks, butter, shallots and tarragon
~ **béchamel** white sauce
~ **au beurre blanc** butter, shallots, vinegar or lemon juice
~ **au beurre noir** browned butter
~ **bordelaise** brown sauce with boletus mushrooms, red wine, shallots and beef marrow
~ **bourguignonne** red wine sauce with herbs, onions and spices (sometimes tarragon)
~ **café de Paris** cream, mustard and herbs
~ **chasseur** brown sauce with

wine, mushrooms, onions, shallots and herbs
~ **diable** hot, spicy sauce with white wine, herbs, vinegar and cayenne pepper
~ **financière** cream, Madeira wine, herbs, spices, mushrooms, truffles and olives
~ **hollandaise** butter, egg-yolks and vinegar or lemon juice
~ **lyonnaise** onions, white wine and butter
~ **madère** brown sauce with Madeira wine base
~ **Mornay** *béchamel* sauce with cheese
~ **ravigote** vinegar sauce with chopped hardboiled eggs, capers and herbs; served cold
~ **rémoulade** mayonnaise enriched with mustard and herbs
~ **suprême** chicken-stock base, thick and bland, served with fowl
~ **tartare** mayonnaise base with gherkins, chives, capers and olives
~ **vinaigrette** oil, vinegar and herbs (sometimes mustard)

saucisse sausage
~ **de Francfort** frankfurter

saucisson a large sausage

saumon salmon

sauté lightly browned in hot butter, oil or fat, sautéed

savarin sponge cake steeped in rum and usually topped with cream

sel salt

selle saddle

selon grosseur (or **grandeur**) price according to size, e.g. of a lobster, often abbreviated **s.g.**

service (non) compris service (not) included

sorbet water ice (US sherbet)

soufflé à la reine soufflé with finely chopped poultry or meat

soufflé Rothschild vanilla-flavoured soufflé with candied fruit

soupe soup
~ **au pistou** vegetables, noodles, garlic, basil and cheese
~ **à l'oignon** onion
~ **à l'oignon gratinée** onion soup topped with toast and grated cheese; gratinéed

spécialité (du chef) (chef's) speciality

steak steak
~ **haché** hamburger
~ **au poivre** broiled with crushed peppercorns (often flamed in brandy)
~ **tartare** minced beef, eaten raw, with sauce of egg-yolks, mustard, capers, onions, oil and parsley

sucre sugar

suprême de volaille boned chicken breast with creamy sauce

sur commande to your special order

(en) sus in addition, additional charge

tarte open(-faced) flan, tart
~ **Tatin** upside-down tart of caramelized apples

tartelette small tart

tendrons de veau breast of veal

(en) terrine a preparation of meat, fish, fowl or game baked in an earthenware dish called a *terrine*, served cold

tête head

thon tunny (US tuna)

(en) timbale meat, fish, seafood,

fruit or vegetables cooked in a pastry case or mould
tomate tomato
tomme a mild soft cheese
topinambour Jerusalem artichoke
tortue turtle
tournedos round cut of prime beef
~ **Rossini** garnished with foie gras and truffles, served with Madeira wine sauce
tout compris all-inclusive (price of a meal)
tranche slice
~ **napolitaine** cassata; slice of layered ice-cream and crystallized fruit
tripes tripe
~ **à la mode de Caen** baked with calf's trotters (US calf's feet), vegetables, apple brandy or cider
truffe truffle
truite trout
vacherin a mellow cheese
~ **glacé** an ice-cream dessert with meringue
vanille vanilla
(à la) vapeur steamed
varié assorted
veau veal
velouté a creamy soup (of vegetables or poultry), thickened with butter and flour
vert-pré a garnish of cress
viande meat
~ **séchée** dried beef served as hors d'oeuvre in paper-thin slices
viandes froides various cold slices of meat and ham (US cold cuts)
vinaigre vinegar
vinaigrette salad sauce of vinegar, oil, herbs and mustard
volaille fowl
vol-au-vent puff-pastry shell filled with meat, sweetbreads or fish and sometimes mushrooms
waterzooi de poulet chicken poached in white wine and shredded vegetables, cream and egg-yolks
yaourt yoghurt

Drink

Alsace (93 communes situated on the River Rhine) produces virtually only dry white wine, notably *Gewurztraminer*, *Riesling*, *Sylvaner*, *Traminer;* the terms *grand vin* and *grand cru* are sometimes employed to indicate a wine of exceptional quality
Amer Picon an aperitif with wine and brandy base and quinine flavouring
Anjou a region of the Loire district producing fine rosé and white wine
apéritif often bittersweet, some aperitifs have a wine and brandy base with herbs and bitters (like *Amer Picon*, *Byrrh*, *Dubonnet*), others, called *pastis*,

FRENCH

have an aniseed base (like *Pernod* or *Ricard*); an aperitif may also be simply vermouth (like *Noilly Prat*) or a liqueur drink like *blanc-cassis*

appellation d'origine contrôlée (A.O.C.) officially recognized wines of which there are over 250 in France; standards of quality are rigidly checked by government inspectors

armagnac a wine-distilled brandy from the Armagnac region, west of Toulouse

Beaujolais Burgundy's most southerly and extensive vineyards which produce mainly red wine, e.g., *Brouilly, Chénas, Chiroubles, Côte de Brouilly, Fleurie, Juliénas, Morgon, Moulin-à-Vent*

Belgique Belgium; though the Romans introduced wine-making to Belgium, the kingdom today only incidentally produces wine, primarily white, sometimes rosé and sparkling wine

bénédictine forest-green liqueur; brandy base, herbs and orange peel, reputedly secret formula

Berry a region of the Loire district producing red, white and rosé wine; e.g., *Châteaumeillant, Menetou-Salon, Quincy, Reuilly, Sancerre, Sauvignon*

bière beer

~ **blonde** light

~ **(en) bouteille** bottled

~ **brune** dark

~ **pression** draught (US draft)

~ **des Trappistes** malt beer brewed by Trappist monks

blanc-cassis white wine mixed with blackcurrant liqueur

Blayais a region of Bordeaux producing mainly red and white wine

boisson drink

Bordeaux divided into several regions: Blayais, Bourgeais, Entre-Deux-Mers, Fronsac, Graves, Médoc, Pomerol, St-Emilion, Sauternais; among the officially recognized wines are 34 reds, 23 whites and two rosés divided into three categories: general (e.g., *Bordeaux* or *Bordeaux supérieur*), regional (e.g., *Entre-Deux-Mers, Graves, Médoc*) and communal (e.g., *Margaux, Pauillac, Sauternes*); Bordeaux red wine is known as claret in America and Britain

Bourgeais a region of Bordeaux producing red and white table wine

Bourgogne Burgundy, divided into five regions: Beaujolais, Chablis, Côte Chalonnaise, Côte d'Or (which comprises the Côte de Beaune and the Côte de Nuits) and Mâconnais; Burgundy counts the largest number of officially recognized wines of France's wine-growing districts; there are four categories of wine: generic or regional (e.g., *Bourgogne* red, white or rosé), subregional (e.g., *Beaujolais, Beaujolais supérieur, Beaujolais-Villages, Côte de Beaune-Villages, Mâcon, Mâcon supérieur, Mâcon-Villages*), communal (e.g., *Beaune, Chablis, Fleurie, Meursault, Nuits-St-Georges, Volnay*) and vineyard *(climat)* (e.g., *Chambertin, Clos de Vougeot, Musigny*)

brut extra dry, refers to *Champagne*

Byrrh an aperitif with wine base and quinine, fortified with brandy

cacao cocoa

café coffee

~ **complet** with bread, roll, butter and jam; the Continental breakfast

~ **crème** with cream

~ **espresso** espresso

~ **filtre** percolated or dripped through a filter

~ **frappé** iced

~ **au lait** white (with milk)

~ **liégeois** cold with ice-cream, topped with whipped cream

~ **nature, noir** simple, black

~ **sans caféine** caffeine-free

calvados an apple brandy from Normandy

cassis blackcurrant liqueur

Chablis a region of Burgundy noted for its white wine

chambrer to bring wine gently to room *(chambre)* temperature

Champagne district divided into three large regions: Côte des Blancs, Montagne de Reims and Vallée de la Marne with some 200 kilometres (120 miles) of underground caves where the wine ferments; there are ordinary red, white and rosé wines but the production is overwhelmingly centered upon the sparkling white and rosé (usually referred to in English as pink Champagne) for which the region is universally known; vineyards are of little importance in classifying wines from Champagne since, according to tradition, certain varieties of Champagne are produced by blending wine from different vineyards in proportions which are carefully-guarded secrets; sparkling Champagne is sold according to the amount of sugar added: *brut* (extra dry) contains up to 1.5 per cent sugar additive, *extra-sec* (very dry), 1.5–2.5 per cent, *sec* (dry), 2.5–5 per cent, *demi-sec* (slightly sweet), 5–8 per cent and *doux* (sweet), 8–15 per cent

Chartreuse a yellow or green liqueur of herbs and spices produced by monks of Grande Chartreuse in the French Alps

château castle; term employed traditionally in the district of Bordeaux to indicate a wine of exceptional quality; synonyms: *clos, domaine*

chocolat chocolate

cidre cider

citron pressé freshly squeezed lemon juice

citronnade lemon squash (US lemon drink)

claret see *Bordeaux*

clos vineyard; generally indicates a wine of exceptional quality

cognac cognac; the famed wine-distilled brandy from the Charente and Charente-Maritime regions

Cointreau orange liqueur

Corse Corsica; this Mediterranean island, a French department, produces fine wine, particularly from the hilly areas and Cape Corsica; red, white and rosé wine is characterized by a rich, full-bodied taste; the best wine, grown near Bastia, is the rosé *Patrimonio*

Côte de Beaune the southern half of Burgundy's celebrated Côte d'Or producing chiefly red wine; e.g., the prestigious *Aloxe-Corton* as well as *Beaune, Blagny, Chassagne-Montrachet, Meursault, Pernand-Vergelesses, Puligny-Montrachet, Santenay, Savigny-lès-Beaune, Volnay*

Côte de Nuits a region of Burgundy especially noted for its red wine, e.g., *Chambolle-Musigny, Fixin, Gevrey-Chambertin, Morey-St-Denis, Nuits-St-Georges, Vosne-Romanée*

Côte d'Or a famed region of Burgundy composed of the Côte de Beaune and de Nuits which is noted for its red and white wine

Côtes du Rhône extend from Vienne to Avignon along the banks of the River Rhone between the Burgundy and Provence wine districts; over a hundred communes offer a wide diversity in white, red and rosé wine of varying character; divided into a northern and southern region with notable wine: *Château-Grillet, Châteauneuf-du-Pape, Condrieu, Cornas, Côte-Rôtie, Crozes-Hermitage, Hermitage, Lirac, St-Joseph, St-Péray, Tavel*

crème 1) cream 2) sweetened liqueur like *crème de menthe, crème de cacao*

cru growth 1) refers to a particular vineyard and its wine 2) a system of grading wine; *premier cru, grand cru, cru classé*

curaçao originally from the name of the island of the Dutch Antilles, now applied to liqueur made from orange peel

cuvée a blend of wine from various vineyards, especially, according to tradition, in the making of Champagne

domaine estate; used on a wine label it indicates a wine of exceptional quality

eau water

~ **gazeuse** fizzy (US carbonated)

~ **minérale** mineral

Entre-Deux-Mers a vast Bordeaux region called "between two seas"—actually it's between two rivers—which produces white wine

extra-sec very dry (of Champagne)

framboise raspberry liqueur or brandy

frappé 1) iced 2) milk shake

Fronsac a Bordeaux region producing chiefly red wine

Gueuzelambic a strong Flemish bitter beer brewed from wheat and barley

grand cru, grand vin indicates a wine of exceptional quality

Grand Marnier an orange liqueur

Graves a Bordeaux region especially noted for its white wine but also its red

Jura a six-kilometre- (four-mile-) wide strip which runs 80 kilometres (50 miles) parallel to the western Swiss border and Burgundy; offers white, red, rosé, golden and sparkling wine; there are four formally recognized wines: *Arbois, Château-*

FRENCH

Chalon, Côtes du Jura and *l'Etoile*

kirsch spirit distilled from cherries

Kriekenlambic a strong Brussels bitter beer flavoured with morello cherries

lait milk

~ **écrémé** skimmed

Languedoc district, formerly a French province, to the southwest of the Rhone delta; its ordinary table wine is often referred to as *vin du Midi* but other officially recognized wines, mostly white, are produced, including *Blanquette de Limoux* (sparkling), *Clairette du Languedoc, Fitou* and the *Muscats* from Frontignan, Lunel, Mireval and St-Jean-de-Minervois

limonade 1) lemonade 2) soft drink

Loire a district of 200,000 hectares (80,000 acres) sprawled over the vicinity of France's longest river, the Loire; produces much fine red, white and rosé wine in four regions: Anjou (e.g., *Coteaux-de-l'Aubance, Coteaux-du-Layon, Coteaux-de-la-Loire, Saumur*), Berry and Nivernais *(Menetou-Salon, Pouilly-sur-Loire, Quincy, Reuilly, Sancerre)*, Nantais *(Muscadet)* and Touraine *(Bourgueil, Chinon, Montlouis, Vouvray)*

Lorraine a flourishing and renowned wine district up to the 18th century, today it is of minor importance; good red, white and rosé wine continue to be produced (e.g., *Vins de la Moselle, Côtes-de-Toul*)

Mâcon a region of Burgundy producing basically red wine

marc spirit distilled from grape residue

Médoc a Bordeaux region producing highly reputed red wine including *Listrac, Margaux, Moulis, Pauillac, St-Estèphe, St-Julien*

mirabelle a brandy made from small yellow plums, particularly produced in the Alsace-Lorraine area

Muscadet a white wine from the Nantes area (Loire)

muscat 1) a type of grape 2) name given to dessert wine; especially renowned is the muscat from Frontignan (Languedoc)

Nantais a region of the Loire chiefly renowned for its *Muscadet* white wine but offers other wine, e.g., *Coteaux d'Ancenis, Gros-Plant*

Neuchâtel a Swiss region producing primarily white wine (e.g., *Auvernier, Cormondrèche, Cortaillod, Hauterive*)

Noilly Prat a French vermouth

orange pressée freshly squeezed orange juice

pastis aniseed-flavoured aperitif

Pernod an aniseed-flavoured aperitif

pétillant slightly sparkling

Pomerol a Bordeaux region producing red wine (e.g., *Château Pétrus, Lalande-de-Pomerol, Néac*)

Provence France's most ancient wine-producing district; it traces its history back over two-and-a-half milleniums when Greek colonists planted the first vineyards on the Mediterranean coast of Gaul; red, white and rosé wine is produced, e.g., *Bandol, Bellet, Cassis, Coteaux-d'Aix-en-Provence, Coteaux-des-Baux, Coteaux-de-Pierrevert, Côtes-de-Provence, Palette*

quetsche spirit distilled from plums

rancio dessert wine, especially from Roussillon, which is aged in oak casks under the Midi sun

Ricard an aniseed-flavoured aperitif

Roussillon district which was a French province with Perpignan as its capital; its wine is similar in character to that of the Languedoc to the immediate north; good red, white and rosé table wine, e.g., *Corbières du Roussillon* and *Roussillon Dels Aspres;* this region produces three quarters of France's naturally sweet wine, usually referred to as *rancio,* which is aged in oak casks under the Midi sun; notable examples among them are *Banyuls, Côtes-d'Agly, Côtes-du-Haut-Roussillon; Grand-Roussillon, Muscat de Rivesaltes, Rivesaltes*

St-Emilion a Bordeaux region producing red wine including *Lussac, Montagne, Parsac, Puisseguin, St-Georges*

St-Raphaël a quinine-flavoured aperitif

Sauternais a Bordeaux region noted for its white wine *(Sauternes),* notably the prestigious *Château d'Yquem*

Savoie Savoy; the Alpine district producing primarily dry, light and often slightly acid white wine (e.g., *Crépy, Seyssel*) but also good red, rosé and sparkling wine which is chiefly produced around Chambéry

Sud-Ouest a district in southwestern France producing quite varying types of wine, mostly white but some red and even rosé; the district includes the former province of Aquitaine, Béarn, Basque Country and Languedoc; wines of particular note are *Bergerac, Côtes-de-Duras, Gaillac, Jurançon, Madiran, Monbazillac, Montravel*

Suisse Switzerland; two-thirds of the nation's wine production consists of white wine; some 230 different vineyards are scattered over a dozen of Switzerland's 23 cantons though only four have a special significance: Neuchâtel, Tessin, Valais and Vaud

Suze an aperitif based on gentian

thé tea

Touraine for 14 centuries a celebrated wine district of the Loire producing red, white and rosé wine (e.g., *Bourgueil, Chinon, Montlouis, St-Nicolas-de-Bourgueil, Vouvray*)

Triple Sec an orange liqueur

Valais sometimes referred to as the California of Switzerland, this Swiss region produces nearly a quarter of the nation's wine; the region in the Rhone Valley is noted for providing Switzerland's best red wine (e.g., *Dôle*) and much of its finest white wine (e.g., *Arvine,*

Ermitage, Fendant, Johannisberg, Malvoisie)

Vaud a Swiss region producing primarily white wine (e.g., *Aigle, Dézaley, Mont-sur-Rolle, Lavaux, Yvorne*)

V.D.Q.S. (vin délimité de qualité supérieure) regional wine of exceptional quality, produced according to carefully defined specifications and checked by government inspectors

Vieille Cure a wine-distilled liqueur

vin wine

~ **blanc** white

~ **chambré** wine at room temperature

~ **doux** sweet, dessert

~ **gris** pinkish

~ **mousseux** sparkling

~ **ordinaire** table

~ **du pays** local

~ **rosé** rosé (pink in reference to Champagne)

~ **rouge** red

~ **sec** dry

V.S.O.P. (very special old pale) in reference to cognac, indicates that it has been aged at least 5 years

(vin de) xérès sherry

German

Guide to pronunciation

Letter	Approximate pronunciation
Consonants	
f, h, k, l, m, n, p, t, x	normally pronounced as in English
b	1) at the end of a word or between a vowel and a consonant, like **p** in **up** 2) elsewhere as in English
c	1) before **e, i, ö** and **ä,** like **ts** in hi**ts** 2) elsewhere like **c** in **c**at
ch	like **ch** in Scottish lo**ch**
d	1) at the end of a word or between a vowel and a consonant, like **t** in ea**t** 2) elsewhere, like **d** in **d**o
g	always hard as in **g**o, but at the end of a word, more like **ck** in ta**ck**
j	like **y** in **y**es
qu	like **k** followed by **v** in **v**at

r	generally rolled in the back of the mouth
s	1) before or between vowels, like **z** in **z**oo 2) before **p** and **t** at the beginning of a syllable, like **sh** in **sh**ut 3) elsewhere, like **s** in **s**it
ß	always like **s** in **s**it
sch	like **sh** in **sh**ut
tsch	like **ch** in **ch**ip
tz	like **ts** in hi**ts**
v	like **f** in **f**or
w	like **v** in **v**ice
z	like **ts** in hi**ts**

Vowels

In German, vowels are generally long when followed by **h** or by one consonant and short when followed by two or more consonants.

a	1) short, like **u** in c**u**t 2) long, like **a** in c**a**r
ä	1) short, like **e** in l**e**t 2) long, like **ai** in h**ai**r
e	1) short, like **e** in l**e**t 2) long, like **a** in l**a**te 3) in unstressed syllables, it's generally pronounced like **a** in **a**bout
i	1) short, like **i** in h**i**t 2) long, like **ee** in m**ee**t
ie	like **ee** in b**ee**
o	1) short, like **o** in g**o**t 2) long, like **o** in n**o**te
ö	like **ur** in f**ur** (long or short)
u	like **oo** in m**oo**n (long or short)
ü	like French **u** in **u**ne; no English equivalent. Round your lips and try to say **ea** as in m**ea**n (long or short)
y	like German **ü**

Diphthongs

ai, ay, ei, ey	like **igh** in h**igh**
au	like **ow** in n**ow**
äu, eu	like **oy** in b**oy**

GERMAN

Some useful expressions

Hungry

I'm hungry/I'm thirsty.	**Ich habe Hunger/Ich habe Durst.**
Can you recommend a good restaurant?	**Können Sie mir ein gutes Restaurant empfehlen?**
Are there any good, cheap restaurants around here?	**Gibt es gute und preiswerte Restaurants in der Nähe?**
I'd like to reserve a table for ... people.	**Ich möchte einen Tisch für ... Personen reservieren lassen.**
We'll come at ... o'clock.	**Wir kommen um ... Uhr.**

Asking

Good evening. I'd like a table for ... people.	**Guten Abend. Ich hätte gern einen Tisch für ... Personen.**
Could we have a table...?	**Können wir einen Tisch... haben?**
in the corner	**in der Ecke**
by the window	**am Fenster**
outside	**im Freien**
on the terrace	**auf der Terrasse**
May I please have the menu?	**Kann ich bitte die Speisekarte haben?**
What's this?	**Was ist das?**
Do you have...?	**Haben Sie ...?**
a set menu	**ein Tagesgedeck**
local dishes	**Spezialitäten**
a children's menu	**ein Menü für Kinder**
Waiter/Waitress!	**Herr Ober/Fräulein!**
What do you recommend?	**Was empfehlen Sie mir?**
Could I have (a/an)... please?	**Könnte ich bitte... haben?**
ashtray	**einen Aschenbecher**
another chair	**noch einen Stuhl**
finger bowl	**eine Fingerschale**

fork	**eine Gabel**
glass	**ein Glas**
knife	**ein Messer**
napkin	**eine Serviette**
pepper mill	**eine Pfeffermühle**
plate	**einen Teller**
serviette	**eine Serviette**
spoon	**einen Löffel**
toothpick	**einen Zahnstocher**

Ordering

I'd like a/an/some...	**Ich hätte gern...**
aperitif	**einen Aperitif**
appetizer	**eine Vorspeise**
beer	**ein Bier**
bread	**etwas Brot**
butter	**etwas Butter**
cheese	**etwas Käse**
chips	**Pommes frites**
coffee	**einen Kaffee**
dessert	**einen Nachtisch**
fish	**ein Fischgericht**
french fries	**Pommes frites**
fruit	**etwas Obst**
game	**Wild**
ice-cream	**ein Eis**/(Switzerland: **eine Glace)**
lemon	**etwas Zitrone**
lettuce	**Kopfsalat**
meat	**Fleisch**
mineral water	**ein Mineralwasser**
milk	**Milch**
mustard	**etwas Senf**
noodles	**Nudeln**
oil	**etwas Öl**
olive oil	**etwas Olivenöl**
pepper	**etwas Pfeffer**
potatoes	**Kartoffeln**
poultry	**Geflügel**
rice	**Reis**
rolls	**einige Brötchen**

saccharin	**Süßstoff**
salad	**Salat**
salt	**etwas Salz**
sandwich	**ein Sandwich**
seafood	**Meeresfrüchte**
seasoning	**etwas Würze**
soup	**eine Suppe**
starter	**eine Vorspeise**
sugar	**etwas Zucker**
tea	**einen Tee**
vegetables	**Gemüse**
vinegar	**etwas Essig**
(iced) water	**(Eis-)Wasser**
wine	**(einen) Wein**

GUTEN APPETIT!/
MAHLZEIT!
ENJOY YOUR MEAL!

baked	**gebacken**
baked in parchment	**in Pergamentpapier gebacken**
boiled	**gekocht**
braised	**gedünstet**
cured	**gepökelt**
fried	**(in der Pfanne) gebraten**
grilled	**gegrillt**
marinated	**mariniert**
poached	**pochiert**
roasted	**(im Ofen) gebraten**
sautéed	**geschwenkt**
smoked	**geräuchert**
steamed	**gedämpft**
stewed	**geschmort**
underdone (rare)	**blutig**
medium	**mittel**
well-done	**gut durchgebraten**

ZUM WOHL!/PROST!
CHEERS!

glass	**ein Glas**
bottle	**eine Flasche**
red	**rot**
white	**weiß**
rosé	**rosé**
very dry	**sehr trocken**
dry	**trocken**
sweet	**süß**
light	**leicht**
full-bodied	**vollmundig**
sparkling	**moussierend**
neat (straight)	**pur**
on the rocks	**mit Eis**

The bill

I'd like to pay.	**Ich möchte gern zahlen.**
We'd like to pay separately.	**Wir möchten getrennt bezahlen.**
You've made a mistake in this bill, I think.	**Ich glaube, Sie haben sich verrechnet.**
What's this amount for?	**Wofür ist dieser Betrag?**
Is service included?	**Ist Bedienung inbegriffen?**
Is everything included?	**Ist alles inbegriffen?**
Do you accept traveller's cheques?	**Kann ich mit Reiseschecks bezahlen?**
Thank you. This is for you.	**Danke, das ist für Sie.**
Keep the change.	**Behalten Sie das Wechselgeld.**
That was a very good meal.	**Das Essen war sehr gut.**
We enjoyed it, thank you.	**Danke, es hat gut geschmeckt.**

Complaints

That's not what I ordered. I asked for...	**Das habe ich nicht bestellt. Ich wollte...**
May I change this?	**Können Sie mir dafür etwas anderes bringen?**

The meat is…	**Das Fleisch ist…**
overdone	**zu stark gebraten**
underdone	**zu roh**
too tough	**zu zäh**
This is too…	**Das ist zu…**
bitter/salty/sweet	**bitter/salzig/süß**
The food is cold.	**Das Essen ist kalt.**
This isn't fresh.	**Das ist nicht frisch.**
What's taking you so long?	**Weshalb dauert es so lange?**
Where are our drinks?	**Wo bleiben unsere Getränke?**
This isn't clean.	**Das ist nicht sauber.**
Would you ask the head waiter to come over?	**Würden Sie den Oberkellner zu uns bitten?**

Numbers

1	**eins, ein, eine**	11	**elf**
2	**zwei**	12	**zwölf**
3	**drei**	13	**dreizehn**
4	**vier**	14	**vierzehn**
5	**fünf**	15	**fünfzehn**
6	**sechs**	16	**sechzehn**
7	**sieben**	17	**siebzehn**
8	**acht**	18	**achtzehn**
9	**neun**	19	**neunzehn**
10	**zehn**	20	**zwanzig**

GERMAN

Food

Aal eel
Abendbrot, Abendessen evening meal, supper
Allgäuer Bergkäse hard cheese from Bavaria resembling *Emmentaler*
Allgäuer Rahmkäse a mild and creamy Bavarian cheese
Altenburger a mild, soft goat's milk cheese
Ananas pineapple
Anis aniseed
~**brot** aniseed-flavoured cake or biscuit
Apfel apple
Apfelsine orange
Appenzeller (Käse) slightly bitter, fully flavoured cheese
Appetithäppchen, Appetitschnittchen appetizer, canapé
Aprikose apricot
Artischocke artichoke
Artischockenboden artichoke bottom
Aubergine aubergine (US eggplant)
Auflauf 1) soufflé 2) a meat, fish, fowl, fruit or vegetable dish which is oven-browned
Aufschnitt cold meat (US cold cuts)
Auster oyster
Backforelle baked trout
Backhähnchen, Backhendl, Backhuhn fried chicken
Backobst dried fruit
Backpflaume prune
Backsteinkäse strong cheese from Bavaria resembling *Limburger*
Banane banana
Barsch perch
Bauernbrot rye or wholemeal bread
Bauernfrühstück breakfast usually consisting of eggs, bacon and potatoes
Bauernomelett diced bacon and onion omelet
Bauernschmaus sauerkraut garnished with bacon, smoked pork, sausages and dumplings or potatoes
Bauernsuppe a thick soup of sliced frankfurters and cabbage
Baumnuß walnut
Bayerische Leberknödel veal-liver dumplings, served with sauerkraut
Bedienung (nicht) (e)inbegriffen service (not) included

Beere berry
Beilage side dish, sometimes a garnish
belegtes Brot/Brötchen roll with any of a variety of garnishes
Berliner (Pfannkuchen) jam-filled doughnut (US jelly donut)
Berliner Luft dessert made of eggs and lemon, served with raspberry juice
Berner Platte a mound of sauerkraut or French beans liberally garnished with smoked pork chops, boiled bacon and beef, sausages, tongue, ham and boiled potatoes
Beuschel heart, kidney and liver of calf or lamb in a slightly sour sauce
Bienenstich cake with honey and almonds
Bierrettich black radish, generally cut, salted and served with beer
Biersuppe a sweet, spicy soup made on beer
Birchermus, Birchermüsli uncooked oats with raw, shredded fruit, chopped nuts in milk or yoghurt
Birne pear
Bischofsbrot fruit-nut cake
Biskuitrolle Swiss roll; jelly and butter-cream roll
Bismarckhering pickled herring, seasoned with onions
blau word to designate fish freshly poached
Blaubeere bilberry (US blueberry)
Blaukraut red cabbage
Blumenkohl cauliflower
Blutwurst black pudding (US blood sausage)
Bockwurst boiled sausage
Bohne bean
Bouillon broth, consommé
Brachse, Brasse bream
Bratapfel baked apple
Braten roast, joint
 ~soße gravy
Bratfisch fried fish
Brathähnchen, Brathendl, Brathuhn roast chicken
Bratkartoffel fried potato
Bratwurst fried sausage
Braunschweiger Kuchen rich cake with fruit and almonds
Brei porridge, mash, purée
Brezel salted, knot-shaped roll (US pretzel)
Bries, Brieschen, Briesel sweetbread
Brombeere blackberry
Brot bread
 ~suppe broth with stale bread
Brötchen roll
Brühe broth, consommé
Brunnenkresse watercress
Brüsseler Endivie chicory (US endive)
Brust breast
 ~stück brisket
Bückling bloater
Bulette meat- or fishball
Bündnerfleisch cured, dried beef served in very thin slices
Butt(e) brill
Champignon button mushroom
Chicorée chicory (US endive)
Cornichon small gherkin (US pickle)
Dampfnudel steamed sweet dumpling, served warm with vanilla sauce
Dattel date
deutsches Beefsteak hamburger, sometimes topped with a fried egg
doppeltes Lendenstück a thick fil-

let of beef (US tenderloin)
Dörrobst dried fruit
Dorsch cod
Dotterkäse cheese made from skimmed milk and egg-yolk
durchgebraten well-done
Egli perch
Ei egg
~**dotter,** ~**gelb** egg-yolk
~**schnee** beaten egg-white
~**weiß** egg-white
Eierauflauf egg soufflé
Eierkuchen pancake
Eierschwamm(erl) chanterelle mushroom
eingemacht preserved (of fruit or vegetables)
Eintopf stew, usually of meat and vegetables
Eis ice, ice-cream
~**bombe** ice-cream dessert
~**krem** ice-cream
Eisbein mit Sauerkraut pickled pig's knuckle with sauerkraut
Emmentaler (Käse) a semi-hard, robust Swiss cheese with holes
Endivie endive (US chicory)
Ente duck
Erbse pea
Erdbeere strawberry
Erdnuß peanut
errötende Jungfrau raspberries with cream
Essig vinegar
~**gurke** gherkin (US pickle)
Eßkastanie chestnut
Extraaufschlag extra charge, supplementary charge
Fadennudel thin noodle, vermicelli
falscher Hase a meat loaf of beef and pork
Fasan pheasant
Faschiertes minced meat
faschiertes Laibchen meatball
Feige fig
Felchen variety of lake trout
Fenchel fennel
fester Preis, zu festem Preis fixed price
Filet fillet
~ **Stroganoff** thin slices of beef cooked in a sauce of sour cream, mustard and onions
Fisch fish
~**klößchen** fishball
~**schüssel** casserole of fish and diced bacon
Fladen pancake
Flädle, Flädli thin strips of pancake added to soup
flambiert flambé (food set aflame with brandy)
Flammeri a pudding made of rice or semolina and served with stewed fruit or vanilla custard
Fleisch meat
~**käse** seasoned meat loaf made of beef and other minced meats
~**kloß** meat dumpling
~**roulade,** ~**vogel** slice of meat rolled around a stuffing and braised; veal bird
Flunder flounder
Forelle trout
Frankfurter (Würstchen) frankfurter (sausage)
Frikadelle a meat, fowl or fish dumpling
Frikassee fricassée, stew
frisch fresh
Frischling young wild boar
Froschschenkel frogs' legs
Frucht fruit
Frühlingssuppe soup with diced spring vegetables
Frühstück breakfast

Frühstückskäse a strong cheese with a smooth texture
Frühstücksspeck smoked bacon
Füllung stuffing, filling, forcemeat
Fürst-Pückler-Eis(bombe) chocolate, vanilla and strawberry ice-cream dessert
Gabelfrühstück brunch
Gans goose
Gänseklein goose giblets
Garnele shrimp
Garnitur garnish
Gebäck pastry
gebacken baked
gebraten roasted, fried
gedämpft steamed
Gedeck meal at a set price
gedünstet braised, steamed
Geflügel fowl
~**klein** giblets
Gefrorenes ice-cream
gefüllt stuffed
gegrillt grilled
gehackt minced or chopped
Gehacktes minced meat
gekocht cooked, boiled
Gelee 1) aspic 2) jelly 3) jam
gemischt mixed
Gemüse vegetable
gepökelt pickled
geräuchert smoked
Gericht dish
geröstet roasted
Gerste barley
gesalzen salted
geschmort stewed, braised
Geschnetzeltes meat cut into thin, small slices
Geselchtes cured and smoked pork
gesotten simmered, boiled
gespickt larded
gesülzt jellied, in aspic
Gewürz spice
~**gurke** gherkin (US pickle)
~**kuchen** spice cake
~**nelke** clove
gewürzt spiced, hot
Gipfel crescent-shaped roll
Gittertorte almond cake or tart with a raspberry topping
Gitzi kid
Glace ice-cream
Glattbutt brill
Gnagi cured pig's knuckle
Götterspeise fruit jelly dessert (US Jell-O)
Granat prawn
~**apfel** pomegranate
gratiniert oven-browned, gratinéed
Graubrot brown bread (US black bread)
Graupensuppe barley soup
Greyerzer (Käse) Gruyère, a cheese rich in flavour, smooth in texture
Griebenwurst a larded frying sausage
Grieß semolina
grilliert grilled
Gröstl grated, fried potatoes with pieces of meat
Gründling gudgeon
grüne Bohne French bean (US green bean)
Grünkohl kale
Gugelhopf, Gugelhupf a moulded cake with a hole in the centre; usually with almonds and raisins
Güggeli spring chicken
Gulasch goulash
Gurke cucumber, gherkin
Hachse knuckle, shank
Hackbraten meat loaf of beef and pork
Hackfleisch minced meat

Haferbrei oatmeal, porridge
Haferflocken rolled oats
Hähnchen spring chicken
halb half
~**gar** rare (US underdone)
Hamme ham
Hammel(fleisch) mutton
Handkäse cheese made from sour milk, with a pungent aroma
Haschee hash
Hase hare
Hasenpfeffer jugged hare
Haselnuß hazelnut
Hauptgericht main course
hausgemacht, von Haus home-made
Hausmannskost plain food
Haxe knuckle, shank
Hecht pike
Hefekranz ring-shaped cake
Heidelbeere bilberry (US blueberry)
Heilbutt halibut
heiß very warm (hot)
Hering herring
~ **Hausfrauenart** herring fillets with onions in sour cream
Heringskartoffeln a casserole of layers of herring and potatoes
Heringskönig John Dory (fish)
Herz heart
Himbeere raspberry
Himmel und Erde slices of black pudding served with mashed potatoes and apple sauce
Hirn brains
Hirsch stag (venison)
Hirse millet
hohe Rippe roast ribs of beef
Holsteiner Schnitzel breaded veal cutlet served with vegetables and topped with a fried egg
Honig honey
Hörnchen crescent-shaped roll
Huhn chicken
Hühnchen chicken
Hühnerklein chicken giblets
Hummer lobster
Husarenfleisch braised beef, veal and pork fillets, with sweet peppers, onions and sour cream
Hutzelbrot bread made of prunes and other dried fruit
Imbiß snack
Ingwer ginger
italienischer Salat finely sliced veal, salami, tomatoes, anchovies, cucumber and celery in mayonnaise
(nach) Jägerart sautéed with mushrooms and sometimes onions
Jakobsmuschel scallop
Johannisbeere redcurrant
jung young, spring
Jungfernbraten roast pork with bacon
Kabeljau cod
Kaisergranat Norway lobster, Dublin Bay prawn
Kaiserschmarren delicious, fluffy pancakes with raisins served with a compote or chocolate sauce
Kalb(fleisch) veal
Kalbsbries veal sweetbread
Kalbskopf calf's head
Kalbsmilch veal sweetbread
Kalbsnierenbraten roast veal stuffed with kidneys
Kaldaunen tripe
kalt cold
Kaltschale chilled fruit soup
Kammuschel scallop
kandierte Frucht crystallized fruit (US candied fruit)
Kaninchen rabbit
Kapaun capon

Kaper caper
Karamelkrem caramel custard
Karfiol cauliflower
Karotte carrot
Karpfen carp
Kartoffel potato
~**puffer** potato fritter
Käse cheese
~**platte** cheese board
~**stange** cheese straw, cheese stick
Kasseler Rippenspeer smoked pork chops, often served with sauerkraut
Kastanie chestnut
Katenrauchschinken country-style smoked ham
Katenwurst country-style smoked sausage
Katzenjammer cold slices of beef in mayonnaise with cucumbers or gherkins
Kaviar caviar
Keks biscuit (US cookie)
Kerbel chervil
Kesselfleisch boiled pork served with vegetables
Keule leg, haunch
Kieler Sprotte smoked sprat
Kipfel crescent-shaped roll
Kirsche cherry
Kitz kid
Kliesche dab
Klops meatball
Kloß dumpling
Klößchen small dumpling
Kluftsteak rumpsteak
Knackwurst a lightly garlic-flavoured sausage, generally boiled
Knoblauch garlic
Knochen bone
~**schinken** cured ham
Knödel dumpling
Knöpfli thick noodle
Kohl cabbage
~**rabi,** ~**rübe** turnip
~**roulade** cabbage leaves stuffed with minced meat
Kompott stewed fruit, compote
Konfitüre jam
Königinpastetchen vol-au-vent; puff-pastry shell filled with diced chicken and mushrooms
Königinsuppe creamy chicken soup with pieces of chicken breast
Königsberger Klops cooked meatball in white caper sauce
Kopfsalat green salad, lettuce
Korinthe currant
Kotelett chop, cutlet
Krabbe crab
Kraftbrühe broth, consommé
Krainer spiced pork sausage
Kranzkuchen ring-shaped cake
Krapfen 1) fritter 2) jam-filled doughnut (US jelly donut)
Krauskohl kale
Kraut cabbage
Kräutersoße herb dressing
Krautsalat coleslaw
Krautstiel white beet, Swiss chard
Krautwickel stuffed cabbage
Krebs freshwater crayfish
Krem cream, custard
~**schnitte** custard slice (US napoleon)
Kren horse-radish
~**fleisch** pork stew with vegetables and horse-radish
Kresse cress
Krustentier shellfish
Kuchen cake
Kukuruz maize (US corn)
Kümmel caraway
Kürbis pumpkin
Kuttelfleck, Kutteln tripe

Labskaus thick stew of minced, marinated meat with mashed potatoes
Lachs salmon
~**forelle** salmon trout
Lamm(fleisch) lamb
Languste spiny lobster, crawfish
Lattich lettuce
Lauch leek
Leber liver
~**käse** seasoned meat loaf made of minced liver, pork and bacon
Lebkuchen gingerbread
Leckerli honey-flavoured ginger biscuit
legiert thickened, usually with egg-yolk (refers to sauces or soups)
Leipziger Allerlei spring carrots, peas and asparagus (sometimes with mushrooms)
Lende loin
Lendenbraten roast tenderloin
Lendenstück fillet of beef (US tenderloin)
Limburger (Käse) a semi-soft, strong-smelling whole-milk cheese
Linse lentil
Linzer Torte almond cake or tart with a raspberry-jam topping
Löwenzahn young dandelion green, usually prepared as salad
Lunge light (lung of an animal)
Mahlzeit meal
Mainauer (Käse) semi-hard, full-cream round cheese with a red rind and yellow interior
Mainzer Rippchen pork chop
Mais maize (US corn)
Makrele mackerel
Makrone macaroon
Mandarine mandarin
Mandel almond
Mangold white beet, Swiss chard
Marille apricot
mariniert marinated, pickled
Mark (bone) marrow
Marmelade jam
Marone chestnut
Mastente fattened duckling
Masthühnchen broiler, spring chicken
Matjeshering slightly salted young herring
Matrosenbrot a sandwich with chopped, hard-boiled eggs, anchovies and seasoning
Maulbeere mulberry
Maultasche a kind of ravioli filled with meat, vegetables and seasoning
Meerrettich horse-radish
Mehlnockerl small dumpling
Mehlsuppe brown-flour soup
Melone melon
Menü meal at a set price
Meringe(l) meringue
Mettwurst spiced and smoked pork sausage, usually for spreading on bread
Miesmuschel mussel
Milke sweetbread
Mirabelle small yellow plum
Mittagessen midday meal, lunch
Mohn poppy
Möhre, Mohrrübe carrot
Mondseer (Käse) whole-milk yellow cheese with a moist texture
Morchel morel mushroom
Morgenessen breakfast
Morgenrötesuppe thick soup of meat, tapioca, tomatoes and chicken stock
Mostrich mustard
Mus stewed fruit, purée, mash
Muschel mussel

GERMAN

Muskat(nuß) nutmeg
Nachspeise, Nachtisch dessert, sweet
naturell plain
Nelke clove
Nidel, Nidle cream
Niere kidney
Nierenstück loin
Nockerl small dumpling
Nudel noodle
Nürnberger Bratwurst frying sausage made of veal and pork
Nuß 1) nut 2) approx. rumpsteak
Obst fruit
~**salat** fruit salad
Ochs(enfleisch) beef
Ochsenauge fried egg (US sunny side up)
Ochsenmaulsalat ox muzzle salad
Ochsenschwanz oxtail
Ohr ear
Öl oil
Omelett(e) omelet
Palatschinken pancake usually filled with jam or cheese, sometimes served with a hot chocolate and nut topping
Pampelmuse grapefruit
paniert breaded
Paprikaschote sweet pepper
Paradeis(er), Paradiesapfel tomato
Pastetchen filled puff-pastry case
Pastete pastry, pie
Patisserie pastry
Pellkartoffel potato boiled in its jacket
Perlgraupe pearl barley
Petersilie parsley
Pfahlmuschel mussel
Pfannkuchen pancake
Pfeffer pepper
~**kuchen** very spicy gingerbread
~**nuß** ginger(bread)-nut
~**schote** hot pepper
Pfifferling chanterelle mushroom
Pfirsich peach
~ **Melba** peach-halves poached in syrup, served over vanilla ice-cream, topped with raspberry sauce and whipped cream
Pflaume plum
Pichelsteiner (Fleisch) meat and vegetable stew
pikant spiced, highly seasoned
Pilz mushroom
Platte platter
Plätzchen biscuit (US cookie)
Plätzli scallop, cutlet
pochiert poached
Pökelfleisch marinated meat
Pomeranzensoße sauce of bitter oranges, wine and brandy, usually served with duck
Pommes frites chips (US french fries)
Porree leek
Poulet chicken
Praline praline; chocolate with a sweet filling
Preiselbeere cranberry
Preßkopf brawn (US headcheese)
Printe honey-flavoured biscuit (US cookie)
Pudding custard, pudding
Püree mash, purée
Puter turkey
Quargel a small, round cheese, slightly acid and salty
Quark(käse) fresh white cheese
Quitte quince
Radieschen radish
Ragout stew
Rahm cream
Rande beetroot
Räucheraal smoked eel

Räucherhering smoked herring
Räucherlachs smoked salmon
Räucherspeck smoked bacon
Rebhuhn partridge
Rechnung bill (US check)
Regensburger a highly spiced and smoked sausage
Reh deer, venison
~**pfeffer** jugged venison, fried and braised in its marinade, served with sour cream
Reibekuchen potato pancake
Reibkäse grated cheese
Reis rice
~**fleisch** veal braised with rice, tomatoes and other vegetables
Rettich black radish
Rhabarber rhubarb
Ribisel redcurrant
Rinderbrust brisket of beef
Rind(fleisch) beef
Rippe rib
Rippchen, Rippenspeer, Rippenstück, Rippli chop (usually smoked pork)
Rochen skate, ray
Rogen roe (generally cod's roe)
Roggenbrot rye bread
roh raw
Rohkost uncooked vegetables, vegetarian food
Rohschinken cured ham
Rollmops soused herring fillet rolled around chopped onions or gherkins
Rosenkohl brussels sprout
Rosine raisin
Rosmarin rosemary
Rostbraten rumpsteak
Rösti grated, fried (US hashed-brown) potatoes
Röstkartoffel roast potato
rote Beete/Rübe beetroot
rote Grütze fruit jelly served with cream
Rotkohl, Rotkraut red cabbage
Rotzunge lemon sole
Roulade beef olives; usually thin slices of beef, stuffed, rolled and braised
Rücken chine, saddle
Rüebli carrot
Rührei scrambled egg
russische Eier Russian eggs; egg-halves topped with caviar, served with remoulade sauce
Sachertorte rich chocolate layer cake with jam filling
Safran saffron
Saft juice
Sahne cream
Saibling char
Saitenwurst a variety of frankfurter or wiener sausage
Salat salad
Salbei sage
Salm salmon
Salz salt
~**fleisch** salted meat
~**gurke** pickled cucumber
~**kartoffel** boiled potato
Salzburger Nockerl dumpling made of beaten egg-yolks, egg-whites, sugar and flour, fried in butter
Sandmuschel clam
Sardelle anchovy
Sardellenring rolled anchovy
Sardine sardine, pilchard
Sattel chine, saddle
Saubohne broad bean
sauer sour
Sauerampfer sorrel
Sauerbraten pot roast marinated with herbs
Schalentier shellfish
Schalotte shallot
Schaschlik chunks of meat, slices

of kidneys and bacon, grilled then braised in a spicy sauce of tomatoes, onions and bacon
Schaumrolle puff-pastry rolls filled with whipped cream or custard
Scheibe slice
Schellfisch haddock
Schildkrötensuppe turtle soup
Schillerlocke pastry cornet with vanilla cream filling
Schinken ham
~**brot** ham sandwich, usually open(-faced)
Schlachtplatte cold meat, liver sausage and sauerkraut
Schlagobers, Schlagrahm, Schlagsahne whipped cream
Schlegel leg, haunch
Schleie tench
Schmelzkäse a soft and pungent cheese, usually for spreading on bread
Schmorbraten pot roast
Schmorfleisch meat stew
Schnecke 1) cinnamon roll 2) snail
Schnepfe snipe
Schnittbohne sliced French bean
Schnitte slice, cut
Schnittlauch chive
Schnitzel cutlet
Schokolade chocolate
Scholle plaice
Schulter shoulder
Schwamm(erl) mushroom
schwarze Johannisbeere/Ribisel blackcurrant
Schwarzwälder Kirschtorte a chocolate layer cake filled with cream and cherries, flavoured with *Kirsch*
Schwarzwälder Schinken a variety of smoked ham from the Black Forest
Schwarzwurzel salsify
Schwein(efleisch) pork
Seezunge sole
Selchfleisch smoked pork
Sellerie celery
Semmel roll
~**brösel** breadcrumbs
~**knödel** dumpling made of diced white bread
Senf mustard
Siedfleisch boiled meat
Soße sauce, gravy
Spanferkel suck(l)ing pig
spanische Soße a brown sauce with herbs
Spargel asparagus
Spätzle, Spätzli thick noodle
Speck bacon
~**knödel** dumpling made with bacon, eggs and white bread
Speise food
~**eis** ice-cream
~**karte** menu, bill of fare
Spekulatius spiced biscuit (US cookie)
Spezialität speciality
~ **des Hauses** chef's speciality
~ **des Tages** day's speciality
Spiegelei fried egg (US sunny side up)
(am) Spieß (on the) spit
Spinat spinach
Sprossenkohl brussels sprout
Sprotte sprat
Stachelbeere gooseberry
Steckrübe turnip
Steinbuscher (Käse) semi-hard creamy cheese; strong and slightly bitter
Steinbutt turbot
Steingarnele prawn
Steinpilz boletus mushroom
Stelze knuckle of pork

Stierenauge fried egg (US sunny side up)
Stock mashed potatoes
~**fisch** stockfish, dried cod
Stollen loaf cake with raisins, almonds, nuts and candied lemon peel
Stoßsuppe caraway soup
Stotzen leg, haunch
Strammer Max slice of bread or sandwich with spiced minced pork (sometimes sausage or ham) served with fried eggs and onions
Streichkäse any soft cheese spread, with different flavours
Streuselkuchen coffee cake with a topping made of butter, sugar, flour and cinnamon
Strudel paper-thin layers of pastry filled with apple slices, nuts, raisins and jam or honey
Stück piece, slice
Sülze 1) jellied, in aspic 2) brawn (US headcheese)
Suppe soup
süß sweet
~**sauer** sweet-and-sour (of sauces)
Süßigkeit sweet (US candy)
Süßspeise dessert, pudding
Tagesgericht day's special
Tagessuppe day's soup
Tascherl pastry turnover with meat, cheese or jam filling
Tatar raw, spiced minced beef
Tatarenbrot open(-faced) sandwich with *Tatar*
Taube pigeon (US squab)
Teigwaren macaroni, noodles, spaghetti
Teller plate, dish
~**gericht** one-course meal
Thunfisch tunny (US tuna)
Thymian thyme
Tilsiter (Käse) semi-hard cheese, mildly pungent
Tomate tomato
Topfen fresh white cheese
~**strudel** flaky pastry filled with creamed, vanilla-flavoured white cheese, rolled and baked
Topfkuchen moulded cake with raisins
Törtchen small tart or cake
Torte layer cake, usually rich
Traube grape
Trüffel truffle
Truthahn turkey
Tunke sauce, gravy
Türkenkorn maize (US corn)
Vanille vanilla
verlorenes Ei poached egg
Voressen meat stew
Vorspeise starter, first course
Wacholderbeere juniper berry
Wachtel quail
Waffel waffle
Walnuß walnut
Wassermelone watermelon
Weinbeere, Weintraube grape
Weinkarte wine list
Weinkraut white cabbage, often braised with apples and simmered in wine
weiße Bohne haricot bean (US navy bean)
Weißbrot white bread
Weißkäse fresh white cheese
Weißkohl, Weißkraut white cabbage
Weißwurst sausage made of veal and bacon, flavoured with parsley, onion and lemon peel
Weizen wheat
Welschkorn maize (US corn)
Westfälischer Schinken a well-known variety of cured and

smoked ham
Wiener Schnitzel breaded veal cutlet
Wiener Würstchen, Wienerli wiener, frankfurter (sausage)
Wild(bret) game, venison
Wildente wild duck
Wildschwein wild boar
Wilstermarschkäse semi-hard cheese, similar to *Tilsiter*
Windbeutel cream puff
Wirsing(kohl) savoy cabbage
Wittling whiting
Wurst sausage
Würstchen small sausage
würzig spiced
Zander pike-perch
Zervelat(wurst) a seasoned and smoked sausage made of pork, beef and bacon
Zichorie chicory (US endive)
Ziege goat
Zimt cinnamon
Zitrone lemon
Zucker sugar
Zunge tongue
Zutat (added) ingredient
Zwetsch(g)e plum
Zwiebel onion
~**fleisch** beef sautéed with onions
~**wurst** liver and onion sausage
Zwischenrippenstück approx. rib-eye steak, entrecôte

Drink

Abfüllung bottled, from wine brought directly from the grower
Abzug wine bottled on the estate or at the vineyard where the grapes were grown, e.g., *Schloßabzug, Kellerabzug*
Ahr the region, named after its tributary of the Rhine, has the continent's northernmost vineyards; the red wine—pale, delicious with a fine aroma—is the best in Germany, which produces little red wine; try it around the towns of Ahrweiler, Neuenahr and Walporzheim
Apfelmost apple cider
Apfelsaft apple juice
Apfelwein apple cider with a high alcoholic content
Aprikosenlikör apricot liqueur
Auslese wine produced from choice grapes
Baden this wine-producing region is situated in the southwestern part of Germany with Switzerland to the south and Alsace, France, to the west; vineyards are especially found on the outskirts of the Black Forest facing the valley of the Rhine; some examples of the wine are *Kaiserstuhl*, produced at the foot of a one-time volcano to the west of Freiburg, *Markgräfler, Mauerwein* and *Seewein* from the Lake of Constance
Beerenauslese wine produced

from choice, very mature grapes resulting in a dessert wine
Bier beer
dunkles ~ dark
helles ~ light, lager
Bock(bier) a beer with a high malt content
Branntwein brandy, spirits
Brauner coffee with milk
kleiner ~ small cup of coffee with milk
Danziger Goldwasser a caraway seed-flavoured liqueur flecked with tiny golden leaves
Doppelkorn spirit distilled from grain
Dornkaat a grain-distilled spirit, slightly flavoured with juniper berries
Eierlikör egg liqueur
Eiskaffee iced coffee
Enzian spirit distilled from gentian root
Exportbier a beer with a higher hops content than lager beer
Flasche bottle
Flaschenbier bottled beer
Franken Franconia; the best vineyards of this wine-producing region around the River Main are situated in the vicinity of Iphofen, Escherndorf, Randersacker, Rödelsee and Würzburg; Franconian white wine is dry, strong and full-bodied; Würzburg produces one of the area's best wines under the name *Steinwein*
Fruchtsaft fruit juice
Gewächs used together with the year on the label of quality wines
gezuckert sugar added, sweetened
Glühwein mulled wine
Himbeergeist spirit distilled from raspberries
Kabinett a term indicating that a wine is of high quality
Kaffee coffee
~ **Hag** caffeine-free
~ **mit Sahne (und Zucker)** with cream (and sugar)
~ **mit Schlag(obers)** served with whipped cream
schwarzer ~ black
Kakao cocoa
Kapuziner coffee with whipped cream and grated chocolate
Kirsch(wasser) spirit distilled from cherries
Klosterlikör herb liqueur
Kognak cognac
Korn(branntwein) spirit distilled from grain
Kümmel(branntwein) caraway-flavoured spirit
Likör liqueur, cordial
Limonade 1) soft drink 2) lemon drink
Lindenblütentee lime-blossom tea
Malzbier malt beer, with a low alcoholic content
Märzenbier beer with a high alcoholic content, brewed in March
Maß(krug) a large beer mug holding 1 litre (about 1 quart)
Milch milk
~**kaffee** half coffee and half hot milk
~**mix** milk shake
Mineralwasser mineral water
Mosel(–Saar–Ruwer) the official name of the Moselle region; the best Moselle wine is produced in only a part of the region, the mid-Moselle Valley which runs from Trittenheim to Traben-Trarbach; the best vineyards

are those of Bernkastel, Brauneberg, Graach, Piesport, Wehlen and Zeltingen

Most must, young wine

Nahe a wine-producing region, named after its tributary of the River Rhine, in the vicinity of Bad Kreuznach; its white wine is full-bodied and may be compared to the best wine of Rhenish Hesse; the most celebrated vineyard is Schloß Böckelheim, owned by the state; other excellent wine is produced in the vicinity of Bad Kreuznach, Bretzenheim, Münster, Niederhausen, Norheim, Roxheim, Winzerheim

Naturwein unblended, unsweetened wine

Österreich Austria; very little of its wine is exported; the red—mainly from Burgenland—is not especially notable and is usually drunk only locally; probably the best-known Austrian wine is *Gumpoldskirchner*, produced to the south of Vienna, a good white wine which generations of Viennese have enjoyed; along the banks of the River Danube to the west of Vienna, good white wine is produced in the Wachau area (e.g., *Dürnsteiner, Loibner, Kremser);* in the immediate vicinity of the Austrian capital, table wine is produced (e.g., *Nußberger, Grinzinger, Badener)* of which the best is sometimes exported

Perlwein white, semi-sparkling wine

Pfalz Palatinate; in good years this region is often first among West Germany's wine-producing regions in terms of production, predominantly of white wine; in medieval times, the Palatinate gained a reputation for being "the wine cellar of the Holy Roman Empire"; today's Palatinate is bounded on the north by Rhenish Hesse, to the east by the River Rhine, to the south and west by Alsace, and Saarland; some examples *Dürkheimer, Forster, Deidesheimer, Ruppertsberger* for white, *Dürkheimer* also for red

Pils(e)ner beer with a particularly strong aroma of hops

Pfefferminztee peppermint tea

Pflümli(wasser) spirit distilled from plums

Portwein port (wine)

Rhein Rhine wine is produced in five regions in the Rhine valley offering the country's best white wines

Rheingau region situated at the foot of the Taunus Mountains facing the River Rhine; its best wines are dessert wines which can be compared to fine Sauternes; a good red wine is produced in Aßmannshausen

Rheinhessen Rhenish Hesse, of which Mainz is the capital; no less than 155 villages are dedicated to wine production; some produce wines of exceptional quality (Alsheim, Bingen, Bodenheim, Dienheim, Guntersblum, Ingelheim, Nackenheim, Nierstein, Oppenheim and Worms); wine of lesser quality is sold under the name of *Liebfrau(en)milch*

Schillerwein rosé wine
Schloß castle, denotes a wine estate
Schnaps brandy, spirits
Schokolade chocolate
Schweiz Switzerland; the most notable wines (both red and white) are produced in French- and Italian-speaking cantons; German-speaking cantons produce mostly light red wines
Sekt sparkling wine similar to Champagne
Sirup syrup
Sodawasser soda water
Spätlese wine produced from grapes picked late in the season, often resulting in full-bodied wine
Spezialbier more strongly brewed beer than *Vollbier*
Sprudel(wasser) soda water
Starkbier strong beer with a high malt content
Steinhäger juniper-flavoured spirit
Tee tea
  ~ **mit Milch** with milk
  ~ **mit Zitrone** with lemon
trocken dry
Trockenbeerenauslese wine produced from specially selected overripe grapes; usually results in a rich, full-bodied dessert wine
ungezuckert unsweetened
verbessert in reference to wine, "improved" or sweetened
Viertel ¼ litre (about ½ pint) of wine
Vollbier the typical German beer with an alcoholic content of 3–4%
Wachstum used on a wine label with the name of the grower, guarantees natural wine
Wasser water
Wein wine
  Rot~ red
  Schaum~ sparkling
  Süß~ dessert
  Weiß~ white
Weinbrand brandy distilled from wine
Weißbier light beer brewed from wheat
Wermut vermouth
Württemberg wine from this region, rarely exported, must be drunk very young; the term *Schillerwein* is employed in the region to denote rosé wine; best wine is produced at Cannstatt, Feuerbach, Untertürckheim; *Stettener Brotwasser* is a noted wine
Zitronensaft lemon squash (US lemon soda)
Zwetschgenwasser spirit distilled from plums

GERMAN

Greek

Guide to pronunciation

Each Greek word in the following menu reader is followed by a simplified transliteration in our own alphabet to help you to recognize and pronounce the word. However, if you're even more interested in speaking the language, you'll want to obtain a copy of GREEK FOR TRAVELLERS from your favourite bookshop. This Berlitz phrase book uses imitated pronunciation which is read as if it were English.

Letter	Approximate pronunciation	Symbol
Vowels		
α	like the vowel in c**a**r, but pronounced further forward in the mouth	a
ε	like **e** in sell	e
η, ι, υ	like **ee** in meet	i
ο, ω	like **o** in got	o

Consonants

β	like **v** in **v**ine	v
γ	1) before **α**, **ο**, **ω**, **ου** and consonants, a voiced version of the **ch** sound in Scottish lo**ch**	gh
	2) before **ε, αι, η, ι, υ, ει, οι,** like **y** in **y**et	y
δ	like **th** in **th**is	dh
ζ	like **z** in **z**oo	z
θ	like **th** in **th**ing	th
κ	like **k** in **k**it	k
λ	like **l** in **l**emon	l
μ	like **m** in **m**an	m
ν	like **n** in **n**ew	n
ξ	like **x** in si**x**	x
π	like **p** in **p**ot	p
ρ	like **r** in **r**ed	r
σ, ς	1) before **β, γ, δ, ζ, μ, ν, ρ,** like **z** in **z**oo	z
	2) elsewhere, like **s** in **s**ee	s
τ	like **t** in **t**ea	t
φ	like **f** in **f**ive	f
χ	like **ch** in Scottish lo**ch**	kh
ψ	like **ps** in dro**ps**y	ps

Groups of letters

αι	like **e** in g**e**t	e
ει, οι	like **ee** in s**ee**	i
ου	like **oo** in r**oo**t	u
αυ	1) before voiceless consonants (θ, κ, ξ, π, σ, τ, φ, χ, ψ), like **uff** in p**uff**ed	af
	2) elsewhere, similar to **ave** in h**ave**	av
ευ	1) before voiceless consonants, like **ef** in l**ef**t	ef
	2) elsewhere, like **ev** in l**ev**el	ev
γγ	like **ng** in li**ng**er	ng
γκ	1) at the beginning of a word, like **g** in **g**o	g
	2) in the middle of a word, like **ng** in li**ng**er	ng

GREEK

γξ	like **nks** in li**nks**	nx
γχ	like **ng** followed by the **ch** of Scottish lo**ch**	nkh
μπ	1) at the beginning of a word, like **b** in **b**eer 2) in the middle of a word, like **mb** in lu**mb**er	b mb
ντ	1) at the beginning of a word, like **d** in **d**ear 2) in the middle of a word, like **nd** in u**nd**er	d nd
τζ	like **ds** in see**ds**	dz

Accent marks

These are written in various ways, e.g., **ὰ, ά,** or **ᾶ,** but all of them indicate the stressed syllable. The signs for the "breathing" of initial vowels (ἁ, ἀ) can be ignored. A diaeresis (two dots) written over a letter means that the letter is pronounced separately from the previous one.

The alphabet

Here are the characters which comprise the Greek alphabet. The column at left shows the printed capital and small letters, while written letters are shown in the center column. At right you'll find the names of these letters in our simplified transliteration.

Α α		alfa
Β β		vita
Γ γ		ghama
Δ δ		dhelta
Ε ε		epsilon
Ζ ζ		zita
Η η		ita
Θ θ		thita
Ι ι		iota
Κ κ		kapa
Λ λ		lamdha
Μ μ		mi
Ν ν		ni
Ξ ξ		xi
Ο ο		omikron
Π π		pi
Ρ ρ		ro
Σ σ ς		sighma
Τ τ		taf
Υ υ		ipsilon
Φ φ		fi
Χ χ		khi
Ψ ψ		psi
Ω ω		omegha

Some useful expressions

Hungry

I'm hungry/I'm thirsty.	**Πεινῶ/Διψῶ.**	pino/dhipso
Can you recommend a good restaurant?	**Μπορεῖτε νά μοῦ ὑποδείξετε ἕνα καλό ἑστιατόριο;**	borite na mu ipodhixete ena kalo estiatorio
Are there any good, cheap restaurants around here?	**Ὑπάρχουν καλά, φθηνά ἑστιατόρια ἐδῶ κοντά;**	iparkhun kala fthina estiatoria edho konda
I'd like to reserve a table for ... people.	**Θά ἤθελα νά κρατήσω ἕνα τραπέζι γιά ...**	tha ithela na kratiso eną trapezi yia...
We'll come at...	**Θά ἔλθουμε στίς ...**	tha elthume stis

Asking

Good evening, I'd like a table for ... people.	**Καλησπέρα. Θά ἤθελα ἕνα τραπέζι γιά**	kalispera. tha ithela ena trapezi yia...
Could we have a table...?	**Θά μπορούσαμε νά ἔχουμε ἕνα τραπέζι ...;**	thȧ borusame na ekhume ena trapezi
in the corner	**στή γωνία**	sti ghonia
by the window	**στό παράθυρο**	sto parathiro
outside	**ἔξω**	exo
on the terrace	**στή ταράτσα**	sti taratsa
May I please have the menu?	**Μοῦ δίνετε τό κατάλογο, παρακαλῶ;**	mu dhinete to katalogho parakalo
What's this?	**Τί εἶναι αὐτό;**	ti ine afto
Do you have...?	**Ἔχετε ...;**	ekhete
a set menu	**τάμπλ-ντότ**	tabl-dot
local dishes	**σπεσιαλιτέ τῆς περιοχῆς**	spesialite tis periokhis
a children's menu	**μενού γιά παιδιά**	menu yia pedhia
Waiter/Waitress!	**Γκαρσόν!**	garson
What do you recommend?	**Τί μοῦ προτείνετε;**	ti mu protinete
Could I have (a/an)... please?	**Θά μπορούσα νά ἔχω... παρακαλῶ;**	tha borisae na ekho...parakalo
ashtray	**ἕνα σταχτοδοχεῖο**	ena staktodhokhio
another chair	**μία καρέκλα ἀκόμη**	mia karekla akomi
fork	**ἕνα πηρούνι**	ena piruni
glass	**ἕνα ποτήρι**	ena potiri

GREEK

knife	**ἕνα μαχαίρι**	ena makheri
napkin	**μία πετσέτα**	mia petseta
plate	**ἕνα πιάτο**	ena piato
pepper mill	**μία πιπεριέρα**	mia piperiera
serviette	**μία πετσέτα**	mia petseta
spoon	**ἕνα κουτάλι**	ena kutali
toothpick	**μία ὀδοντογλυφίδα**	mia odhondoghlifidha

Ordering

I'd like a/an/some...	**Θά ἤθελα ...**	tha ithela
aperitif	**ἕνα ἀπεριτίφ**	ena aperitif
appetizer	**ἕνα ὀρεκτικό**	ena orektiko
beer	**μία μπύρα**	mia bira
bread	**ψωμί**	psomi
butter	**βούτυρο**	vutiro
cheese	**τυρί**	tiri
chips	**πατάτες τηγανιτές**	patates tighanites
coffee	**ἕνα καφέ**	ena kafe
dessert	**ἕνα γλυκό**	ena ghliko
fish	**ψάρι**	psari
french fries	**πατάτες τηγανιτές**	patates tighanites
fruit	**φροῦτα**	fruta
game	**κυνήγι**	kiniyi
ice-cream	**ἕνα παγωτό**	ena paghoto
ketchup	**λίγη κέτσαπ**	liyi ketsap
lemon	**ἕνα λεμόνι**	ena lemoni
lettuce	**μαρούλι**	maruli
meat	**κρέας**	kreas
mineral water	**μεταλλικό νερό**	metaliko nero
milk	**γάλα**	ghala
mustard	**μουστάρδα**	mustardha
noodles	**ζυμαρικά**	zimarika
oil	**λάδι**	ladhi
olive oil	**λάδι ἐλιᾶς**	ladhi elias
pepper	**πιπέρι**	piperi
potatoes	**πατάτες**	patates
poultry	**πουλερικά**	pulerika
rice	**ρύζι**	rizi
rolls	**ψωμάκια**	psomakia
saccharin	**ζαχαρίνη**	zakharini
salad	**σαλάτα**	salata
salt	**ἁλάτι**	alati
sandwich	**ἕνα σάντουϊτς**	ena sanduïts
seafood	**θαλασσινά**	thalasina
seasoning	**καρύκευμα**	karikevma
soup	**μία σούπα**	mia supa

GREEK

starter	**ἕνα ὀρεκτικό**	ena orektiko
sugar	**λίγη ζάχαρη**	liyi zakhari
tea	**ἕνα τσάϊ**	ena tsaï
vegetables	**λαχανικά**	lakhanika
vinegar	**ξύδι**	xidhi
(iced) water	**(παγωμένο) νερό**	(paghomeno) nero
wine	**κρασί**	krasi

ΚΑΛΗ ΣΑΣ ΟΡΕΞΗ

(kali sas orexi)

ENJOY YOUR MEAL!

baked	**στό φοῦρνο**	sto furno
baked in parchment	**ψητό στό χαρτί**	psito sto kharti
boiled	**βραστό**	vrasto
braised	**μέ σάλτσα**	me saltsa
cured	**παστό**	pasto
fried	**τηγανιτό**	tighanito
grilled	**στή σχάρα**	sti skhara
marinated	**μαρινάτο**	marinato
poached	**βραστό**	vrasto
roasted	**ψητό**	psito
sautéed	**σωτέ**	sote
smoked	**καπνιστό**	kapnisto
steamed	**στόν ἀτμό**	ston atmo
stewed	**γιαχνί**	yiakhni
underdone (rare)	**λίγο ψημένο**	ligho psimeno
medium	**μέτριο**	metrio
well-done	**καλοψημένο**	kalopsimeno
glass	**ἕνα ποτήρι**	ena potiri
bottle	**ἕνα μπουκάλι**	ena bukali

ΣΤΗΝ ΥΓΕΙΑ ΣΑΣ

(stin iyia sas)

CHEERS!

red	**κόκκινο**	kokino
white	**ἄσπρο**	aspro
rosé	**ροζέ**	roze
very dry	**πολύ ξηρό**	poli xiro
dry	**ξηρό**	xiro
sweet	**γλυκό**	ghliko
light	**ἐλαφρό**	elafro

full-bodied	**πολύ γευστικό**	poli yefstiko
sparkling	**ἀεριοῦχο**	aeriukho
neat (straight)	**σκέτο**	sketo
on the rocks	**μέ παγάκια**	me paghakia

The bill

I'd like to pay.	**Θά ἤθελα νά πληρώσω.**	tha ithela na pliroso
We'd like to pay separately.	**Θέλουμε χωριστό λογαριασμό.**	thelume khoristo loghariazmo
You've made a mistake in this bill, I think.	**Νομίζω ὅτι κάνατε ἕνα λάθος στό λογαριασμό.**	nomizo oti kanate ena lathos sto loghariazmo
What's this amount for?	**Γιά τί εἶναι αὐτό τό ποσό;**	yia ti ine afto to poso
Is service included?	**Τό ποσοστό ὑπηρεσίας περιλαμβάνεται;**	to pososto ipiresias perilamvanete
Is everything included?	**Περιλαμβάνονται τά πάντα;**	perilamvanonde ta panda
Do you accept traveller's cheques?	**Δέχεστε τράβελερς τσέκ;**	dhekheste travelers tsek
Thank you. This is for you.	**Εὐχαριστῶ, αὐτό εἶναι γιά σᾶς.**	efkharisto afto ine yia sas
Keep the change.	**Κρατῆστε τά ψιλά.**	kratiste ta psila
That was a very good meal.	**Τό γεῦμα ἦταν πολύ ὡραῖο.**	to yevma itan poli oreo
We enjoyed it, thank you.	**Τό ἀπολαύσαμε, εὐχαριστοῦμε.**	to apolafsame efkharistume

Complaints

That's not what I ordered. I asked for...	**Δέν παρήγγειλα αὐτό. Ζήτησα ...**	dhen paringila afto. zitisa
May I change this?	**Μπορῶ νά ἀλλάξω αὐτό;**	boro na alakso afto
The meat is...	**Τό κρέας εἶναι ...**	to kreas ine
overdone	**πολύ ψημένο**	poli psimeno
underdone	**ἄψητο**	apsito
too rare	**ὠμό**	omo
too tough	**πολύ σκληρό**	poli skliro
This is too...	**Αὐτό εἶναι πολύ ...**	afto ine poli
bitter/salty/sweet	**πικρό/ἁλμυρό/ γλυκό**	pikro/almiro/ghliko

The food is cold.	**Τό φαγητό εἶναι κρῦο.**	to fayito ine krio
This isn't fresh.	**Αὐτό δέν εἶναι φρέσκο.**	afto dhen ine fresko
What's taking you so long?	**Γιατί ἀργεῖτε τόσο πολύ;**	yiati aryite toso poli
Where are our drinks?	**Ποῦ εἶναι τά ποτά μας;**	pu ine ta pota mas
This isn't clean.	**Αὐτό δέν εἶναι καθαρό.**	afto dhen ine katharo
Would you ask the head waiter to come over?	**Μπορεῖτε νά ζητήσετε στόν ἀρχισερβιτόρο νά ἔλθη ἐδῶ;**	borite na zitisete ston arkhiservitoro na elthi edho

Numbers

1	**ἕνας, μία, ἕνα**	enas, mia, ena
2	**δύο**	dhio
3	**τρία**	tria
4	**τέσσερα**	tesera
5	**πέντε**	pende
6	**ἕξη**	exi
7	**ἑπτά**	epta
8	**ὀκτώ**	okto
9	**ἐννέα**	enea
10	**δέκα**	dheka
11	**ἕντεκα**	endeka
12	**δώδεκα**	dhodheka
13	**δεκατρία**	dhekatria
14	**δεκατέσσερα**	dhekatesera
15	**δεκαπέντε**	dhekapende
16	**δεκαέξη**	dhekaexi
17	**δεκαεπτά**	dhekaepta
18	**δεκαοκτώ**	dhekaokto
19	**δεκαεννέα**	dhekaenea
20	**εἴκοσι**	ikosi

Food

ἀγγούρι (anguri) cucumber
ἀγκινάρες (anginares) artichoke
~ **ἀ λά πολίτα** (a la polita) with potatoes, carrots and chopped dill in oil and lemon dressing
~ **γεμιστές** (yemistes) stuffed with rice
~ **(μέ)κουκιά** ([me]kukia) with broad beans
~ **τηγανιτές** (tighanites) fried
ἁλάτι (alati) salt
ἁλατισμένο (alatizmeno) salted
ἀλεύρι (alevri) flour
ἁλμυρό (almiro) highly salted
ἀμύγδαλο (amighdhalo) almond
ἀμυγδαλωτό (amighdhaloto) marzipan
ἀνάλατο (analato) unsalted
ἄνηθος (anithos) dill
ἀρακᾶς (arakas) peas
ἀραβοσιτέλαιο (aravositeleo) Indian-corn oil (US corn oil)
ἀραχιδέλαιο (arakhidheleo) peanut oil
ἀρνί (arni) lamb
~ **ἀτζέμ πιλάφι** (adzem pilafi) lamb and rice stewed in tomato sauce
~ **βραστό** (vrasto) boiled lamb
~ **(τοῦ) γάλακτος** ([tu] ghalaktos) baby lamb
~ **ἐξοχικό** (exokhiko) spiced lamb and cheese baked in parchment
~ **καπαμᾶς Μωραΐτικος** (kapamas moraïtikos) lamb braised in wine with tomatoes (Peloponnesos)
~ **(τῆς) κατσαρόλας** ([tis] katsarolas) lamb casserole with lemon dressing
~ **μπούτι** (buti) leg of lamb
~ **μπούτι στό χαρτί** (buti sto kharti) leg of lamb baked in parchment
~ **σέλινο αὐγολέμονο** (selino avgholemono) lamb braised with celery, served with egg and lemon dressing
~ **σκορδοστούμπι ζακυνθινό** (skordhostumbi zakinthino) spiced lamb in tomato and wine gravy (Zakinthos)
~ **σούβλας** (suvlas) spit-roasted
~ **τάς-κεμπάπ** (tas-kebap) with rice and tomato sauce
~ **φρικασέ** (frikase) braised with celery root, spring onions and carrots; served with white sauce
~ **ψητό** (psito) roasted
ἀστακός (astakos) lobster
~ **μαγιονέζα** (mayioneza) lobster with mayonnaise
ἀτζέμ πιλάφι (adzem pilafi) rice boiled in tomato sauce
(στόν) ἀτμό ([ston] atmo) steamed

αὐγό (avgho) egg
~ **βραστό** (vrasto) boiled egg
~ **μάτι** (mati) fried egg
~ **μελάτο** (melato) soft-boiled egg
~ **σφικτό** (sfikto) hard-boiled
~ **τηγανιτό** (tighanito) fried egg
αὐγολέμονο (avgholemono) egg and lemon dressing
ἀχινός (akhinos) sea urchin
ἀχλάδι (akhladhi) pear
βασιλικός (vasilikos) basil
βασιλόπιττα (vasilopita) cake flavoured with orange or mastic; traditionally served on New Year's Eve; a coin baked in the cake is to bring luck to the finder
βατόμουρα (vatomura) blackberries
βερύκοκα (verikoka) apricots
βουτήματα (vutimata) biscuits (US cookies)
βούτυρο (vutiro) butter
βραστό (vrasto) boiled
βυσσινάδα (visinadha) wild-cherry juice
γάλα (ghala) milk
γαλακτομπούρεκο (ghalaktobureko) flaky pastry filled with custard, steeped in syrup
γαλέος (ghaleos) lamprey eel
~ **σκορδαλιά** (skordhalia) with thick garlic sauce
~ **τηγανιτός** (tighanitos) fried
γαλοπούλα (ghalopula) turkey
~ **γεμιστή** (yemisti) stuffed with chestnuts, minced meat and pine nuts; a Christmas speciality
~ **ψητή** (psiti) roast turkey
γαρίδες (gharidhes) shrimp
~ **πιλάφι** (pilafi) shrimp with rice in tomato sauce
~ **σαλάτα** (salata) shrimp cocktail in oil, lemon and parsley sauce
~ **τηγανιτές** (tighanites) fried
γεμιστό (yemisto) stuffed
γεῦμα (yevma) meal, lunch
γιαούρτι (yiaürti) yogurt
γιαουρτόπιττα (yiaürtopita) yogurt cake
γιουβαρλάκια αὐγολέμονο (yiuvarlakia avgholemono) rice- and meat-balls in egg and lemon sauce
γιουβέτσι (yiuvetsi) meat with noodles or macaroni, usually baked in a Dutch oven
γλυκά (ghlika) sweets (US candy)
~ **τοῦ ταψιοῦ** (tu tapsiu) refers to any sweet or pastry baked on a *tapsi* (baking sheet)
γλυκό (ghliko) sweet (adj.)
γλῶσσα (ghlosa) 1) tongue 2) sole
~ **πανέ** (pane) breaded sole
~ **φιλέτο** (fileto) fillet of sole
γουρουνόπουλο τοῦ γάλακτος (ghurunopulo tu ghalaktos) sucking pig
~ **σούβλας** (suvlas) roasted on the spit
γραβιέρα (ghraviera) swiss cheese, best varieties made in Corfu and Crete
γρανίτα (ghranita) water-ice (US sherbet)
δαμάσκηνα (dhamaskina) plums
δάφνη (dhafni) bay leaf
δεῖπνο (dhipno) dinner
δεντρολίβανο (dhendrolivano) rosemary
δίπλες (dhiples) puff pastry with walnuts, steeped in honey syrup
δυόσμος (dhiozmos) mint
ἐλαιόλαδο (eleoladho) olive oil
ἐλιές (elies) olives
~ **Καλαμῶν** (kalamon) big brown olives from Kalamata

GREEK

πιδόρπιο (epidhorpio) dessert
αμπόν (zambon) ham
~ **καπνιστό** (kapnisto) smoked ham
άχαρη (zakhari) sugar
ελέ φρούτων (zele fruton) fruit jelly, eaten as a dessert
εστό (zesto) hot, warm
υμαρικά (zimarika) noodles, spaghetti, etc.
ωμός (zomos) broth
~ **κότας** (kotas) chicken broth
~ **κρέατος** (kreatos) meat broth
αλασσινά (thalasina) seafood
αβούρι (kavuri) crab
ακαβιά (kakavia) fish stew
αλαμάρια (kalamaria) squid
~ **τηγανιτά** (tighanita) fried
αλαμπόκι (kalamboki) Indian corn (US corn)
αλοψημένο (kalopsimeno) well done
ανέλλα (kanela) cinnamon
απαμᾶς (kapamas) the way of braising meat in tomato and wine sauce (Peloponessos)
άπαρη (kapari) capers
αραβίδα (karavidha) crawfish
στά) κάρβουνα ([sta]karvuna) the coals, barbecued
αρπούζι (karpuzi) watermelon
αρύδα (karidha) coconut
αρύδια (karidhia) walnuts
αρυδόπιττα (karidhopita) walnut cake
~ **'Αθηναϊκή** (athinaïki) walnut cake steeped in cinnamon syrup (Athens)
αρύκευμα (karikevma) spice
αρῶτα (karota) carrots
ασέρι (kaseri) light yellow cheese, rich in cream with a soft texture
αταΐφι (kataïfi) a sweet made of sugared thin noodles, almonds, walnuts and syrup
κατάλογος (kataloghos) menu
κατσαρόλα (katsarola) casserole
τῆς ~ ς (tis) in a casserole
κεράσια (kerasia) cherries
κεφτέδες (keftedhes) meatballs
~ **μέ σάλτσα ντομάτα**(me saltsa domata) in tomato sauce
~ **στή σχάρα**(sti skhara) grilled
~ **τηγανιτοί** (tighaniti) fried
~ **φούρνου μέ αὐγά** (furnu me avgha) baked with eggs
κεφαλογραβιέρα(kefaloghraviera) mild yellow cheese, hard texture
κέφαλος (kefalos) mullet
κεφαλοτύρι (kefalotiri) yellow, very strong and salty cheese with tiny holes
κιμᾶς (kimas) minced meat
κόκορας (kokoras) stewing hen
~ **κοκκινιστός** (kokinistos) braised in tomato sauce
~ **μέ κρασί** (me krasi) braised in wine and tomato sauce
κόκκαλο (kokalo) bone
κοκκινιστό (kokinisto) meat or vegetables braised in tomato sauce
κοκορέτσι (kokoretsi) kidneys, tripe and liver grilled on a skewer
κολοκύθα (kolokitha) pumpkin
κολοκύθια (kolokithia) baby marrow (US zucchini)
~ **βραστά σαλάτα** (vrasta salata) as a salad with oil and vinegar dressing, flavoured with oregano
~ **γεμιστά**(yemista) stuffed with rice and/or meat
~ **μουσακᾶς** (musakas) layers of baby marrows (US zucchini) and minced meat topped with a white sauce and oven-browned
~ **μπριάμ** (briam) layers of baby

marrows (US zucchini), potatoes and tomatoes; baked
~ **παπουτσάκια** (paputsakia) baby marrows (US zucchini) stuffed with rice and/or minced meat, topped with sauce; baked

κολοκυθοκεφτέδες (kolokithokeftedhes) baby marrow (US zucchini) croquettes

κομπόστα (kombosta) stewed or tinned (US canned) fruit
~ **ἀχλάδι** (akhladhi) pears
~ **βερύκοκο** (verikoko) apricots
~ **κυδώνι** (kidhoni) quince
~ **μῆλο** (milo) apples
~ **ροδάκινο** (rodhakino) peaches

κοπενχάγη (kopenkhayi) tea bread (US sweet roll) with almond filling, steeped in syrup

κοτολέττα (kotoleta) cutlet, chop
~ **ἀρνίσια** (arnisia) lamb chop
~ **βωδινή** (vodhini) veal cutlet
~ **μοσχαρίσια** (moskharisia) rib or rib-eye steak
~ **πανέ** (pane) breaded cutlet, usually veal
~ **χοιρινή** (khirini) pork chop

κοτόπουλο (kotopulo) chicken
~ **βραστό** (vrasto) boiled
~ **(τῆς) κατσαρόλας** ([tis]katsarolas) in a casserole; served with a butter and lemon sauce
~ **κοκκινιστό** (kokinisto) braised with tomatoes
~ **μέ μπάμιες** (me bamies) braised in tomato sauce with okra
~ **μπούτι** (buti) chicken leg
~ **στή σούβλα** (sti suvla) spit-roasted
~ **στή σχάρα** (sti skhara) grilled
~ **στῆθος** (stithos) breast of chicken
~ **τηγανιτό** (tighanito) fried
~ **ψητό** (psito) roasted

κοτόσουπα (kotosupa) chicken broth

κουζίνα (kuzina) 1) kitchen 2) way of cooking in general

κουνουπίδι (kunupidhi) cauliflower
~ **σαλάτα** (salata) cauliflower salad with oil and lemon sauce

κουκιά (kukia) broad beans
~ **μέ ἀγκινάρες** (me anginares) with artichoke

κουλούρα (kulura) round bread, usually found in villages

κουλουράκια (kulurakia) round biscuits (US cookies)

κουλούρι (kuluri) doughnut-shaped rolls with sesame seeds

κουνέλι (kuneli) rabbit
~ **κρασάτο** (krasato) braised in wine
~ **στιφάδο** (stifadho) braised with spring onions, bay leaf, cloves, red wine and tomato sauce

κουραμπιές (kurambies) almond biscuits (US cookies)

κρέας (kreäs) meat
~ **ἀρνίσιο** (arnisio) lamb
~ **βραστό** (vrasto) boiled meat
~ **βωδινό** (vodhino) veal
~ **μοσχαρίσιο** (moskharisio) beef
~ **χοιρινό** (khirino) pork
~ **ψητό** (psito) roasted meat

κρεατόπιττα (kreätopitta) minced-meat pie
~ **Γιαννιώτικη** (yianiotiki) with eggs, grated cheese, onions and parsley (Yannina)
~ **Κεφαλληνίας** (kefalinias) very spicy meat pie with *feta* cheese, rice, potatoes, onions

GREEK

garlic (Cephalonia)
κρέμα (krema) cream
~ **καραμελέ** (karamele) caramel mousse (US caramel pudding)
κρεμμύδι (kremidhi) onions
~ **φρέσκο** (fresko) spring onions
κρεμμυδόσουπα (kremidhosoupa) onion soup
κροκέττες (kroketes) meat, vegetable or fish fritters, croquettes
~ **ἀπό ψάρι** (apo psari) fish fritters
~ **μέ κρέας** (me kreäs) deep-fried meat fritters
~ **μέ μελιτζάνες** (me melidzanes) fried aubergine (eggplant) croquettes
~ **μέ ρύζι** (me rizi) rice fritters
κρύο (krio) cold
~ **κρέας** (kreäs) cold cuts
κυδώνι (kidhoni) quince
~ **πελτές** (peltes) quince jelly
κυδώνια (kidhonia) clams
κύμινο (kimino) cumin
κυνήγι (kiniyi) fowl
λαγός (laghos) hare
~ **στιφάδο** (stifadho) braised with pearl onions in tomato sauce
~ **στό φοῦρνο** (sto furno) roasted
λαδερό (ladhero) cooked in oil
~ **φαγητό** (fayito) cooked vegetable dish, usually stuffed with rice and cooked or served with olive oil
λάδι (ladhi) oil
λαδολέμονο (ladholemono) olive oil and lemon dressing
λαδόξυδο (ladhoxidho) olive oil and vinegar dressing
λακέρδα (lakerdha) salted tunny (US tuna)
λαρδί (lardhi) bacon
λαχανικά (lakhanika) vegetables
λάχανο (lakhano) cabbage
~ **ντολμᾶδες** (dolmadhes) cabbage leaves stuffed with rice and minced meat, braised in white sauce
~ **σαλάτα** (salata) cole slaw
λεμόνι (lemoni) lemon
λῖπος (lipos) fat
λουκάνικο (lukaniko) sausage
~ **χωριάτικο** (khoriatiko) hot pork sausage
λουκουμάδες (lukumadhes) light, deep-fried, crisp puffs; served warm in honey syrup
λουκούμι (lukumi) Turkish delight
λυθρίνι (lithrini) grey mullet
~ **στή σχάρα** (sti skhara) grilled
~ **τηγανιτό** (tighanito) fried
μαγειρίτσα (mayiritsa) soup made of minced lamb entrails, dill, egg and lemon sauce; served traditionally at Easter
μαγιονέζα (mayioneza) mayonnaise
μαϊντανός (maïdanos) parsley
μακαρόνια (makaronia) macaroni
~ **μέ κιμᾶ** (me kima) with meat sauce
~ **μέ σάλτσα ντομάτα** (me saltsa domata) in tomato sauce
~ **παστίτσιο** (pastitsio) layers of macaroni and minced meat with white sauce; baked
~ **παστίτσιο μέ φύλλο** (pastitsio me filo) macaroni and minced meat rolled and baked in a crust
μαλακό (malako) soft
μανέστρα (manestra) noodles
~ **σούπα** (supa) noodle and tomato soup

μανιτάρια (manitaria) mushrooms
μανούρι (manuri) a kind of fresh whey cheese, often mixed with honey as a dessert
μανταρίνι (mandarini) tangerine
μάντολες (mandoles) sugared almonds (Cephalonia)
μαντολάτο (mandolato) nougat (Zakinthos)
μαργαρίνη (margharini) margarine
μαρίδες (maridhes) whitebait
μαρινᾶτο (marinato) marinated
μαρμελάδα (marmeladha) jam
μαρούλι (maruli) lettuce
~ **σαλάτα** (salata) lettuce salad
μεζές (mezes) titbit
μεζεδάκια (mezedhakia) titbits served as appetizers
μέλι (meli) honey
μελιτζάνες (melidzanes) aubergine (eggplant)
~ **γεμιστές μέ ρύζι** (yemistes me rizi) stuffed with rice and onions
~ **ἰμάμ** (imam) stuffed with chopped tomato, onion and parsley and covered with grated cheese and breadcrumbs; baked
~ **κροκέττες** (kroketes) fritters
~ **μέ κρέας** (me kreäs) stewed with meat
~ **μουσακᾶς** (musakas) layers of aubergine (eggplant) and minced meat topped with white sauce, baked
~ **παπουτσάκια** (paputsakia) stuffed with rice and/or meat topped with white sauce; baked
~ **πουρές** (pures) mashed
~ **τηγανιτές** (tighanites) fried
~ **τουρσί** (tursi) pickled
μελιτξανοκεφτέδες (melidzanokeftedhes) fried aubergine (eggplant) and meatballs
μελιτζανοσαλάτα (melidzano-salata) aubergine (eggplant baked and mashed, flavourec with olive oil, minced onion garlic and parsley; servec chilled as an appetizer or salac
μελοκάρυδο (melokaridho) smal cake made of honey and walnuts
μελομακάρονα (melomakarona pastry steeped in honey syrup
μερίδα (meridha) portion
μέτριο (metrio) medium (of meat
μῆλο (milo) apple
μηλόπιττα (milopitta) apple tart
μισό (miso) half
μοσχάρι (moskhari) beef
~ **βραστό** (vrasto) boiled beef
~ **καπαμᾶς** (kapamas) braise with tomatoes and wine
~ **κοκκινιστό** (kokinisto braised with tomatoes
~ **σέλινο αὐγολέμονο** (selinc avgholemono) braised witł celery in egg and lemon sauc
~ **σουβλάκι** (suvlaki) spit-roasted chunks of beef
~ **φρικασέ** (frikase) braised witł celery root, spring onions, carrots and white sauce
~ **ψητό στό φοῦρνο** (psito st furno) roast beef
μοσχοκάρυδο (moskhokaridho nutmeg
μουσακᾶς (musakas) layers of vegetables and minced meat toppec with white sauce; baked
~ **κολοκύθια** (kolokithia) witł baby marrows (US zucchini)
~ **μελιτζάνες** (melidzanes) witł aubergine (eggplant)
~ **πατάτες** (patates) with potatoes
μουσταλευριά (mustalevria) grap

GREEK

jam with almonds and cinnamon
μουστάρδα (mustardha) mustard
μουστοκούλουρα (mustokulura) grape biscuits (US cookies)
μπακαλιάρος (bakaliaros) cod
~ **ἁλμυρός** (almiros) dried cod
~ **γιαχνί** (yiakhni) dried cod in tomato sauce
~ **σκορδαλιά** (skordhalia) cod with garlic sauce
~ **φιλέττα πανέ** (fileta pane) breaded cod fillets
μπακλαβᾶς (baklavas) flaky pastry filled with nuts and steeped in syrup
μπάμιες (bamies) okra
~ **λαδερές** (ladheres) stewed in oil
~ **μέ κοτόπουλο** (me kotopulo) with chicken
~ **στό φοῦρνο** (sto furno) baked with tomatoes and onions
μπανάνα (banana) banana
μπαρμπούνια (barbunia) red mullet
~ **στή σχάρα** (sti skhara) grilled
~ **τηγανιτό** (tighanito) fried
μπαχαρικά (bakharika) spices
μπεκάτσες (bekatses) woodcock
~ **σαλμί** (salmi) in spicy tomato and wine sauce
μπεσαμέλ (besamel) white sauce
μπιζέλια (bizelia) green peas
μπισκότα (biskota) biscuits (US cookies)
μπιφτέκια (biftekia) meat rissoles (US patties)
~ **στή σχάρα** (sti skhara) grilled
~ **στό φοῦρνο** (sto furno) baked
~ **τηγανιτά** (tighanita) fried
μπουρεκάκια (burekakia) stuffed pasties, rissoles
~ **μέ κιμᾶ** (me kima) minced meat
~ **μέ σπανάκι** (me spanaki) spinach
~ **μέ τυρί** (me tiri) cheese
μπούτι (buti) leg
μπριάμι (briami) baked casserole of baby marrow (US zucchini), potatoes and tomatoes
μπριζόλα (brizola) cutlet, chop
~ **ἀρνίσια** (arnisia) lamb chop
μυαλά (miala) brains
~ **πανέ** (pane) breaded and fried
~ **τηγανιτά** (tighanita) fried
μύδια (midhia) mussels
~ **μέ πιλάφι** (me pilafi) cooked with rice and tomatoes
~ **τηγανιτά** (tighanita) fried
μυζήθρα (mizithra) soft, salted cheese made from ewe's milk
νεφρά (nefra) kidneys
νεφραμιά (neframia) sirloin steak
ντολμᾶδες (dolmadhes) cabbage or grape leaves stuffed with rice or minced meat
~ **αὐγολέμονο** (avgholemono) served with egg and lemon dressing
~ **γιαλαντζῆ** (yialandzi) stuffed with rice; steeped in oil
~ **μέ λάχανο** (me lakhano) served with white sauce
~ **μέ φύλλα μαρουλιοῦ** (me fila maruliu) stuffed lettuce leaves
ντομάτες (domates) tomatoes
~ **γεμιστές** (yemistes) baked stuffed tomatoes
~ **μέ κιμᾶ** (me kima) tomatoes stuffed with meat and/or rice
~ **μέ ρύζι** (me rizi) baked tomatoes stuffed with rice and onions
ντοματοσαλάτα (domatosalata) tomato salad
ντοματόσουπα (domatosoupa) tomato soup

ντονέρ (doner) leg of lamb or mutton broiled on a vertical spit; as the meat cooks, thin slices are cut off and served on a flat, round bread
ξυδᾶτο (xidhato) cooked in a vinegar solution
ξύδι (xidhi) vinegar
ὀμελέττα (omeleta) omelet
~ **μέ ζαμπόν** (me zambon) ham
~ **μέ λουκάνικα** (me lukanika) sausage
~ **μέ ντομάτα** (me domata) tomato
~ **μέ πατάτες** (me patates) potato
~ **μέ συκωτάκια πουλιῶν** (me sikotakia pulion) chicken-liver
~ **μέ τυρί** (me tiri) cheese
ὀρεκτικά (orektika) appetizers
ὀρτύκια (ortikia) quail
~ **μέ ντομάτα** (me domata) with tomato sauce
οὐρά βωδινή (ura vodhini) oxtail
παγωμένο (paghomeno) iced
παγωτό (paghoto) ice-cream
~ **ἀνάμικτο** (anamikto) mixed
~ **βανίλλια** (vanilia) vanilla
~ **κασσάτα** (kasata) Neapolitan ice cream (US spumoni)
~ **σοκολάτα** (sokolata) chocolate
~ **φράουλα** (fraula) strawberry
παϊδάκια ἀρνίσια (païdhakia arnisia) lamb chops
πανέ (pane) breaded
πάπια (papia) duck
πάστα (pasta) pastry, plain cake
~ **ἀμυγδάλου** (amighdhalu) almond
~ **σοκολατίνα** (sokolatina) chocolate
~ **φλώρα** (flora) jam
~ **φρούτου** (frutu) fruit
παστέλι (pasteli) honey and sesame bar
παστιτσάδα (pastitsadha) veal or beef braised with garlic, onions, bay leaves and noodles (Corfu)
παστίτσιο (pastitsio) layers of noodles and minced meat topped with white sauce and baked
παστό (pasto) cured
πατάτες (patates) potatoes
~ **βραστές** (vrastes) boiled
~ **γεμιστές** (yemistes) stuffed with rice and/or minced meat
~ **πουρέ** (pure) mashed
~ **στό φοῦρνο** (sto furno) baked
~ **τηγανιτές** (tighanites) fried
~ **τσίπς** (tsips) crisps (US potato chips)
~ **ψητές** (psites) roasted
πατατοκεφτέδες (patatokeftedhes) fried potato croquettes
πατζάρι (padzari) beetroot
~ **α σκορδαλιά** (a skordhalia) with garlic dressing
πατσᾶς (patsas) tripe
παχύ (pakhi) thick
πεπόνι (peponi) melon
πέρδικα (perdhika) partridge
περιστέρι (peristeri) pigeon
πέρκα (perka) perch
πέστροφα (pestrofa) trout
πηχτή (pikhti) aspic
πιατέλα (piatela) platter
πιάτο (piato) plate, dish
πικρό (pikro) bitter
πιλάφι (pilafi) rice casserole
~ **ἀτζέμ** (adzem) with tomatoes
~ **μέ γαρίδες** (me gharidhes) with shrimp
~ **μέ κιμᾶ** (me kima) with minced meat and tomatoes
~ **μέ μύδια** (me midhia) with mussels
~ **τάς-κεμπάπ** (tas-kebap) with

tomatoes and meat

πιπέρι (piperi) black pepper

πιπεριά (piperia) sweet pepper

~ **πράσινη** (prasini) green pepper

πιπεριές γεμιστές (piperies yemistes) green peppers stuffed with rice

πιτσούνια (pitsunia) young pigeon, squab

~ **γεμιστά** (yemista) stuffed

~ **σαλμί** (salmi) braised with tomatoes and wine in a spicy broth

πίττα (pitta) a flat, round bread

πληγούρι (plighuri) cracked-wheat noodles

~ **γιουβέτσι** (yiuvetsi) roasted leg of lamb or mutton served with tomatoes and cracked-wheat noodles

ποδαράκια ἀρνίσια αὐγολέμονο (podharakia arnisia avgholemono) leg of lamb with egg and lemon dressing

ποικιλία ὀρεκτικῶν (pikilia orektikon) assorted appetizers

πορτοκάλι (portokali) orange

πουλερικά (pulerika) fowl

πουρές (pures) mashed or puréed vegetables or fruit

~ **μελιτζάνες** (melidzanes) aubergines (eggplant)

~ **πατάτες** (patates) mashed potatoes

~ **σπανάκι** (spanaki) spinach

πράσσα (prassa) leeks

~ **μέ ρύζι** (me rizi) with rice

πρόγευμα (proyevma) breakfast

προϊόντα (proïonda) products

~ **κατεψυγμένα** (katepsighmena) frozen food

~ **φρέσκα** (freska) fresh produce

ραδίκια (radhikia) dandelion greens

ραπανάκια (rapanakia) radishes

ρεβανί (revani) kind of sponge cake steeped in syrup

ρεβίθια (revithia) chick-peas

ρέγγα (renga) herring

~ **καπνιστή** (kapnisti) smoked herring

ρίγανη (righani) oregano

ροδάκινο (rodhakino) peach

ρόδι (rodhi) pomegranate

ρολλό μέ αὐγά (rollo me avgha) meatloaf stuffed with eggs

ρύζι (rizi) rice

ρυζόγαλο (rizoghalo) rice pudding

σαγανάκι (saghanaki) cheese croquette with lemon and butter dressing

σαλάμι (salami) salami

σαλάτα (salata) salad

~ **ἀγγούρι** (anguri) cucumber

~ **γαρίδες** (gharidhes) shrimp

~ **λάχανο** (lakhano) cole slaw with lemon and olive oil dressing

~ **μελιτζάνες** (melidzanes) aubergine (eggplant)

~ **ντομάτα** (domata) tomato

~ **πατζάρια** (padzaria) beetroot

~ **σατζίκι** (sadziki) salad made of yogurt, cucumber, garlic, olive oil and mint

~ **σκορδαλιά** (skordhalia) crushed garlic combined with mashed potatoes and olive oil

ταραμο ~ (taramo~) cod or mullet roe combined with bread, olive oil, lemon juice seasoning

~ **φρούτων** (fruton) fruit cocktail

~ **χόρτα** (khorta) greens, such as endive (US chicory) or dandelion, boiled and served cold with an olive oil and lemon

dressing
~ **χωριάτικη** (khoriatiki) salad of tomatoes, cucumber, onion, peppers, olives, *feta* cheese, parsley and oregano
σάλτσα (saltsa) sauce
~ **ἄσπρη** (aspri) white sauce
~ **αὐγολέμονο** (avgholemono) egg and lemon dressing
~ **λαδολέμονο** (ladholemono) oil and lemon dressing
~ **λαδόξυδο** (ladhoxidho) vinegar and oil dressing
~ **μαγιονέζα** (mayioneza) mayonnaise
~ **ντομάτα** (domata) tomato sauce with parsley and onions
~ **πράσινη** (prasini) parsleyed mayonnaise
~ **ψητοῦ** (psitu) gravy
σαντιγύ (sandiyi) whipped cream
σαρδέλλες (sardheles) sardines
σβίγγοι (svingi) fritters
σέλινο (selino) celery
~ **κρέας αὐγολέμονο** (kreäs avgholemono) meat with celery in egg and lemon dressing
σιμιγδάλι (simighdhali) farina
σιρόπι (siropi) syrup
σκαλτσουνάκια σιφνέϊκα (skaltsunakia sifneïka) a turnover stuffed with fruit, chopped almonds or nuts and cinnamon (Sifnos)
σκέτο (sketo) plain
σκληρό (skliro) hard
σκορδαλιά (skordhalia) a salad of minced garlic, potatoes or bread with onions
σκόρδο (skordho) garlic
σοκολάτα (sokolata) chocolate
σοκολατάκια (sokolatakia) assorted chocolates
σολομός (solomos) salmon
(στή) σούβλα ([sti]suvla) on a spit
σουβλάκι (suvlaki) meat on a spit
~ **μέ πίττα** (me pitta) snack consisting of pieces of meat grilled on a spit with tomatoes, onions and parsley wrapped in round, flat bread (*pitta*)
~ **χωριάτικο** (khoriatiko) meat on a spit served at counters with a slice of bread
σούπα (supa) soup
~ **αὐγολέμονο** (avgholemono) poultry or meat broth with rice, egg, lemon juice
~ **βραστό** (vrasto) broth meat
~ **κακαβιᾶ** (kakavia) fish stew
κοτό ~ (koto~) chicken broth
~ **μαγειρίτσα** (mayiritsa) Easter soup made of minced lamb entrails, dill, egg and lemon juice
~ **ντομάτα** (domata) tomato
~ **πατσᾶς** (patsas) tripe
~ **ρεβύθια** (revithia) chick-pea
~ **τραχανᾶς** (trakhanas) made with yoghurt or sour cream with cracked-wheat dumplings
~ **φακή** (faki) lentil
~ **φασόλια** (fasolia) butter bean (US navy-bean)
χορτό ~ (khorto~) vegetable
~ **χυλοπίττες** (khilopites) tomato with square noodles
ψαρό ~ (psaro~) fish
σουπιές (supies) cuttlefish
~ **μέ σπανάκι** (me spanaki) braised with spinach
σουτζουκάκια σμυρνέϊκα (sudzukakia smirneïka) cumin-flavoured meat-balls braised with tomato sauce
σοφρίτο (sofrito) meat stewed in a wine-vinegar with garlic (Corfu)
σπανάκι (spanaki) spinach

σπανακόπιττα (spanakopita) spinach pasty
σπανακόρυζο (spanakorizo) spinach cooked with rice
σπαράγγια (sparangia) asparagus
σπιτικό (spitiko) homemade
σπλήνα (splina) spleen
~ **γεμιστή** (yemisti) stuffed with rice, onions, pine nuts and tomatoes; baked
σταφίδα (stafidha) raisins
~ **σουλτανιά** (sultania) sultanas, raisins
σταφύλι (stafili) grapes
~ **ἄσπρο** (aspro) green grapes
~ **κόκκινο** (kokino) red grapes
~ **μαῦρο** (mavro) black grapes
~ **σουλτανιά** (sultania) seedless grapes
στῆθος (stithos) breast
στιφάδο (stifadho) a method of braising meat with spring onions, tomatoes and wine
~ **κουνέλι** (kuneli) with rabbit
στό φοῦρνο (sto furno) baked
στρείδια (stridhia) oysters
~ **τηγανιτά** (tighanita) fried
σῦκα (sika) figs
συκώτι (sikoti) liver
~ **στή σχάρα** (sti skhara) grilled
~ **τηγανιτά** (tighanita) fried
~ **τάς-κεμπάπ** (tas-kebap) sliced liver in tomato sauce, usually served with rice
συναγρίδα (sinaghridha) sea bream
σφυρίδα (sfiridha) whiting
σφολιάτα ζύμη (sfoliata zimi) crust, short-pastry dough
(στή) σχάρα ([sti] skhara) grilled
ταραμᾶς (taramas) cod or mullet roe
ταραμοκεφτέδες (taramokeftedhes) balls of cod or mullet roe
ταραμοσαλάτα (taramosalata) cod- or mullet-roe salad with bread, olive oil and lemon juice
ταψί (tapsi) baking sheet
~ **γλυκά τοῦ ταψιοῦ** (ghlika tu tapsiu) refers to any sweet or pastry baked on a *tapsi*
τουρσί (tursi) pickles (US pickled vegetables)
τηγανίτα (tighanita) fritter
τηγανιτό (tighanito) fried
τῆς ὥρας (tis oras) made to order
τιμή (timi) price
~ **καθωρισμένη** (kathorizmeni) set price
τόννος (tonos) tunny (US tuna)
τριμμένο (trimeno) chopped or grated
τρόφιμα (trofima) food
τρυφερό (trifero) tender
τσάϊ (tsaï) tea
τσιπούρα (tsipura) gifthead (fish)
τσουρέκι (tsureki) bun
τυρί (tiri) cheese
τυρόπιττα (tiropita) cheese tart
τυροπιττάκια (tiropitakia) small cheese tarts
φάβα (fava) yellow lentils
φακή (faki) lentils
φασιανός (fasianos) pheasant
φασόλια (fasolia) beans
~ **γιαχνί** (yiakhni) butter beans (US navy beans) in tomato sauce
~ **ξερά** (xera) dried butter beans (US navy beans)
~ **πράσινα** (prasina) green beans
~ **σαλάτα μπιάζ** (salata biaz) butter beans (US navy beans) with tomatoes, onions and parsley
φέτα (feta) 1) slice; 2) the best

known Greek cheese, made of goat's or ewe's milk, white and crumbly
φιδές (fidhes) thin noodles
~ **σούπα** (supa) noodle soup
φιλέτο (fileto) fillet
φιλοδώρημα (filodhorima) tip
φουντούκια (fundukia) hazelnuts
φράουλες (fraüles) strawberries
φράπα (frapa) grapefruit
φρατζόλα (fradzola) white bread; like English or American white bread
φρέσκο (fresko) fresh
φρικασέ (frikase) cooked with onions and carrots in a creamy sauce
φροῦτα (fruta) fruit
~ **ἐποχῆς** (epokhis) fruit of the season
φρουτοσαλάτα (frutosalata) fruit cocktail
φτερούγα (fterugha) wing
φυστίκια (fistikia) nuts
~ **Αἰγίνης** (eyinis) pistachios
~ **ἀράπικα** (arapika) peanuts
χαλβᾶς (khalvas) a sugary loaf made from farina and almonds
~ **τῆς Ρήνας** (tis rinas) flavoured with cinnamon
χέλι (kheli) eel
~ **τηγανιτό** (tighanito) fried
χήνα (khina) goose
~ **γεμιστή** (yemisti) stuffed
χοιρινή μπριζόλα (khirini brizola) pork chop
χοιρινό (khirino) pork
~ **μέ σέλινα** (me selina) with celery in egg and lemon
χόρτα (khorta) herbs
~ **σαλάτα** (salata) greens, such as endive (US chicory) or dandelion, boiled and served cold with an olive oil and lemon dressing
χορτόπιττα (khortopita) herb tart
χορτόσουπα (khortosupa) vegetable soup
χουρμάδες (khurmadhes) dates
χταπόδι (khtapodhi) octopus
~ **βραστό** (vrasto) boiled
~ **κρασσᾶτο** (krasato) stewed in wine
~ **μέ πιλάφι** (me pilafi) stewed with rice and tomatoes
~ **στιφάδο** (stifadho) braised with onions and tomatoes
χυλοπίττες (khilopittes) square noodles
ψάρι (psari) fish
~ **βραστό** (vrasto) poached
~ **μαγιονέζα 'Αθηναϊκή** (mayioneza athinaïki) fish salad
~ **μαρινάτο** (marinato) marinated
~ **πανέ** (pane) breaded, fried
~ **πλακί** (plaki) baked sliced with tomatoes, parsley and bread crumbs
~ **στή σχάρα** (sti skhara) grilled
~ **φούρνου** (furnu) baked
~ **φούρνου σπετσιώτικο** (furnu spetsiotiko) braised with tomatoes, olive oil, parsley and spices (Spetse)
ψαρόσουπα (psarosupa) fish soup
ψητό (psito) roasted
~ **τῆς κατσαρόλας** (tis katsarolas) pot roasted, baked in a Dutch oven
ψωμί (psomi) bread
~ **ἡμίλευκο** (imilefko) white bread, using unblanched flour
~ **μαῦρο** (mavro) wholemeal bread (US wholewheat bread)
~ **μέ σουσάμι** (me susami) sesame bread
~ **χωριάτικο** (khoriatiko) rye

bread, called village bread because in the villages it's still homemade
ὠμό (omo) raw, cured

Drink

ἀεριοῦχο (aeriukho) sparkling
Ἄλφα(alfa) one of the best-known brands of Greek beer
ἀναψυκτικό (anapsiktiko) soft drink
Ἀττική (attiki) Attica, the vicinity of Athens; nearly all the country's resinated wine is produced here; most of it white but there is some rosé
Βερντέα (verndea) dry white wine (Zakinthos)
βυσσινάδα (vissinadha) morello-cherry juice
γάλα (ghala) milk
~ **ἀποβουτυρωμένο** (apovutiromeno) skim milk
γκαζόζα (gazoza) soda water
γλυκό (ghliko) sweet
ζεστό (zesto) warm
Ζίτσα (zitsa) sparkling white wine (Epirus)
Ἤπειρος (ipiros) Epirus, the northwestern part of Greece bordering on the Ionian Sea, produces much white table wine
θερμοκρασία δωματίου (thermokrasia domatiu) room temperature
Ἰόνιοι Νῆσοι (ionii nisi) Ionian Islands; vineyards are found on most of the islands in the Ionian Sea; the white table wine of Cephalonia (its *Rombola*) and of Zakinthos (its *Verdea*) are considered quite good; Corfu and Levkas (*Santa Mavra*) have red table wine
κακάο (kakao) cocoa
καράφα (karafa) carafe
καφές (kafes) coffee
~ **(μέ) γάλα** ([me]ghala) white
~ **ἐξπρέσσο** (expreso) espresso
τούρκικος ~ (turkikos) "Turkish coffee"; boiled
~ **φραπέ** (frape) iced
~ **χωρίς καφεΐνη** (khoris kafeïni) caffeine-free
κίτρο (kitro) lemon liqueur (Naxos)
κοκτέϊλ (kokteïl) cocktail
κονιάκ (koniak) brandy
κουμ-κουάτ (kum-kuat) kumquat liqueur (Corfu)
κρασί (krasi) wine
~ **ἀεριοῦχο** (aeriukho) sparkling
~ **ἀρετσίνωτο** (aretsinoto) non-resinated
~ **ἄσπρο** (aspro) white
~ **γλυκό** (ghliko) dessert wine
~ **κόκκινο** (kokkino) red
~ **μοσχᾶτο** (moskhato) muscat wine
~ **ξηρό** (xiro) dry
~ **ρετσίνα** (retsina) resinated wine; about half of the Greek wines contain sandarac, a pine resin; the best resinated wine is produced in the Attica region

GREEK

~ **ροζε** (rose) rosé wine
Κρήτη (kriti) Crete, an important island to the south of Athens, produces predominantly red table wine
κρύο (krio) cold
λεμονάδα (lemonadha) lemon drink
~ **μέ ἀνθρακικό** (me anthrakiko) lemon soda
λικέρ (liker) liqueur
λίτρο (litro) litre
Μακεδονία (makedhonia) Macedonia, the region to the north of Greece, produces mostly red table wine
μαστίχα (mastikha) mastic liqueur (Chios)
μαυροδάφνη (mavrodhafni) red dessert wine (Peloponnesus)
Μεταξᾶ (metaxa) the best-known brand of Greek brandy
μηλίτης (militis) apple cider
μισό (miso) half
μπουκάλι (bukali) bottle
μπύρα (bira) beer
νερό (nero) water
μεταλλικό ~ (metaliko) mineral water
Νῆσοι Αἰγαίου (nisi egheu) Aegean Islands; nearly all the islands scattered throughout the Aegean produce table wine, some of it of very good quality; Samos is noted for its white muscat wine; either red or white table wine is found on islands like Andros, Kos, Milos or Naxos while Karpathos, Chios and Rhodes produce white table wine; red wine is produced on the islands of Ikaria and Lemnos
οἰνοπνευματῶδες (inopnevmatodhes) alcoholic drink
οὖζο (uzo) aniseed-flavoured liqueur; best brands: *San Rival, Masters, Achaia Clauss, 22, Tyrnavos*
παγάκια (paghakia) ice cubes
(μέ) πάγο ([me] pagho) on the rocks
πάγος (paghos) ice
παγωμένο (paghomeno) iced, chilled
Πελοπόννησος (peloponisos) Peloponnesus, the penisula forming the southern part of the Greek mainland; the nation's most important wine-growing region; over a third of Greece's vineyards are located here; the Peloponnesus is noted for its red dessert wine like *Malvasia; Mavrodaphni,* a sweet red wine, is considered the region's most notable wine
πικρό (pikro) bitter
πορτοκαλάδα (portokaladha) orangeade
~ **(μέ) ἀνθρακικό** ([me] anthrakiko) orange soda
ποτήρι (potiri) glass
ποτό (poto) drink
ρακί (raki) aniseed-flavoured liqueur
ρετσίνα (retsina) resinated wine; about half of the Greek wines contain sandarac, a pine resin; the best resinated wine is produced in the Attica region
Ρομπόλα (rombola) dry white wine produced on the island of Cephalonia
ροῦμι (rumi) rum
σαμπάνια (sambania) a sparkling, champagne-like wine; best brands: *Cuvée Réservée, Achaia*

Clauss] *Côte d'Or*
Σάντα Μαύρα (santa mavra) red dry wine produced in the island of Levkas
σκέτο (sketo) neat (US straight)
σοκολάτα (sokolata) chocolate
σουμάδα (sumadha) soft drink made with almonds
Στερεά Ἑλλάς (stereä elas) Sterea Ellas, the region to the north-west of Athens, has red table wine
τσάϊ (tsaï) tea
~ **(μέ) γάλα** ([me] ghala) with milk
~ **(μέ) λεμόνι** ([me] lemoni) with lemon
Φίξ (fiks) best-known brand of Greek beer
Θεσσαλία (thesalia) Thessaly, located between Sterea Ellas and Macedonia; has mainly red table wine
Θράκη (thraki) Thrace, on the northeastern corner of Greece, produces principally red table wine
φλυτζάνι (flidzani) cup
χυμός (himos) juice
~ **μανταρινιοῦ** (mandariniu) tangerine
~ **μήλου** (milu) apple juice
~ **πορτοκαλιοῦ** (portokaliu) orange
~ **ντομάτας** (domatas) tomato
~ **φρούτου** (frutu) fruit

Hungarian

Guide to pronunciation

Letter	Approximate pronunciation
Consonants	
b, d, f, h, m, n, v, x, z	as in English
c	like **ts** in ne**ts**
cs	like **ch** in **ch**ap
g	always as in **g**o, never as in **g**in
gy	like **di** in me**di**um, said fairly quickly
j	like **y** in **y**es
k	always as in si**ck**, never as in **k**ill
l	always as in **l**eap, never as in ba**ll**
ly	like **y** in **y**es
ny	quite like **ni** in o**ni**on
p	always as in si**p**, never as in **p**ill
r	pronounced with the tip of the tongue, like Scottish **r**
s	like **sh** in **sh**oot
sz	like **s** in **s**o
t	always as in si**t**, never as in **t**ill

ty	like **ty** in a fast pronunciation of pu**t y**our
zs	like **s** in plea**s**ure

Vowels

a	quite like **o** in n**o**t (British pronunciation)
á	like the exclamation "ah!"
e	quite like **e** in y**e**s, but with the mouth a little more open, i.e. a sound betweeen **e** in y**e**s and **a** in h**a**t
é	like **ay** in s**ay**, but a pure vowel, not a diphthong, i.e. neither the tongue nor the lips move during the pronunciation of it
i	like **ee** in f**ee**t (short)
í	like **ee** in s**ee** (long)
o	quite like **aw** in s**aw** (British pronunciation), but shorter
ó	like **aw** in s**aw**, but with the tongue higher in the mouth
ö	like **ur** in f**ur**, but short, without any **r**-sound, and with rounded lips
ő	like **ur** in f**ur**, but without any **r**-sound, and with the lips tightly rounded
u	as in the British pronunciation of p**u**ll
ú	like **oo** in f**oo**d
ü	round your lips and try to say **ee**; the resulting sound should be as in French **u**ne or German f**ü**nf
ű	the same sound as **ü**, but long and with the lips more tightly rounded

N.B.

1) There are no "silent' letters in Hungarian, so all letters must be pronounced. This means that double consonants are pronounced long, e.g. **tt** in ke**tt**ő sounds rather like **t-t** in a fast pronunciation of par**t-t**ime. (But a double consonant appearing at the end of a word is pronounced short.) It also means that vowels standing next to each other are pronounced separately and do not combine to produce diphthongs.
2) When two or more consonants stand next to each other, the last one can influence the pronunciation of the others. If it is "voiceless", it will make a preceding "voiced' consonant into a "voiceless" one, and vice versa., e.g. *végtelen* is pronounced as if it were written *véktelen*. The "voiceless" consonants are **c, f, k, p, s, sz, t, ty**, and the corresponding "voiced' ones are **dz, v, g, b, zs, d, gy**.
3) Every word, when pronounced alone, has a strong stress on the first syllable. When words are combined in sentences, the stress on the less important words weaken.
4) The "double" forms of **cs, gy, ly, ny, sz, ty, zs**, are **ccs, ggy, lly, nny, ssz, tty, zzs**.

HUNGARIAN

5) In Hungarian, the letter **j** can combine with a preceding vowel to produce diphthongs, e.g. *új, fej, sajt*. In all these cases, the **y** should be pronounced only fleetingly, as in boy.

Some useful expressions

Hungry?

I'm hungry/I'm thirsty.	**Éhes vagyok./Szomjas vagyok.**
Can you recommend a good restaurant?	**Tudna ajánlani egy jó éttermet?**
Are there any inexpensive restaurants around here?	**Vannak a környéken olcsó éttermek?**
I'd like to reserve a table for 4.	**4 személy részére szeretnék asztalt foglalni.**
We'll come at 8.	**8 órakor jövünk.**
Could we have a table ...?	**Van szabad asztaluk ...?**
in the corner	**a sarokban**
by the window	**az ablaknál**
outside	**kint**
on the terrace	**a teraszon**
in a non-smoking area	**a nemdohányzó részben**
Where are the toilets?	**Hol van a WC?**

Asking and ordering

Waiter/Waitress!	**Pincér/Kisasszony**
I'd like something to eat/drink.	**Szeretnék valamit enni/inni.**
May I have the menu, please?	**Kérek egy étlapot.**
Do you have a set menu/local dishes?	**Van menüjük/helyi specialitásuk?**
What do you recommend?	**Mit ajánlana?**
Do you have anything ready quickly?	**Van valami, ami gyorsan elkészül?**
I'm in a hurry.	**Sietek.**
I'd like ...	**Kérnék ...**
Could we have a/ an ..., please?	**Kaphatnánk egy ...?**
ashtray	**hamutartót**

cup	**csészét**
fork	**villát**
glass	**poharat**
knife	**kést**
napkin (serviette)	**szalvétát**
plate	**tányért**
spoon	**kanalat**
May I have some ...?	**Kaphatnék ...?**
bread	**kenyeret**
butter	**vajat**
lemon	**citromot**
oil	**olajat**
pepper	**borsot**
salt	**sót**
seasoning	**fűszereket**
sugar	**cukrot**
vinegar	**ecetet**
baked	**sült**
barbecued	**roston sült**
boiled	**főtt**
braised	**dínsztelt**
fried	**sült**
grilled	**roston sült**
marinated	**pácolt**
poached	**buggyantott**
roast	**sült**
sautéed	**hirtelen sült**
smoked	**füstölt**
steamed	**párolt**
stewed	**főtt**
underdone (rare)	**félig átsütve**
medium	**közepesen átsütve**
well-done	**jól átsütve**
a bottle	**üveg**
half a bottle	**fél üveg**
a carafe	**kancsó**

a small carafe	**kis kancsó**
a glass	**pohár**
I'd like a bottle of … wine.	**Egy üveg … bort kérek.**
red	**vörös**
white	**fehér**
rosé	**rosé**
sweet	**édes**
dry	**száraz**
sparkling	**pezsgő**
chilled	**hűtött**
at room temperature	**szobahőmérsékletű**

Complaints

There's a plate/glass missing.	**Hiányzik egy tányér/pohár.**
I don't have a knife/ fork/spoon.	**Nincs késem/villám/kanalam.**
That's not what I ordered.	**Nem ezt rendeltem.**
I asked for ...	**... kértem.**
There must be some mistake.	**Itt valami félreértés van.**
May I change this?	**Hozna valami mást ehelyett?**
I asked for a small portion (for the child).	**Kis adagot kértem (a gyereknek).**
The meat is ...	**A hús ...**
overdone	**túl van sütve**
underdone	**nincs rendesen átsütve**
too rare	**nincs eléggé átsütve**
too tough	**túl rágós**
This is too ...	**Túl ...**
bitter/salty/sweet	**keserű/sós/édes**
I don't like this.	**Ez nem ízlik.**
The food is cold.	**Hideg az étel.**
This isn't fresh.	**Ez nem friss.**
What's taking you so long?	**Mi tartott ilyen sokáig?**
Have you forgotten our drinks?	**Az italunkat elfelejtette?**

This isn't clean.	**Ez nem tiszta.**
Would you ask the head waiter to come over?	**Kérem hívja ide a főpincért.**

The bill (check)

I'd like to pay.	**Fizetni szeretnék.**
We'd like to pay separately.	**Külön-külön szeretnénk fizetni.**
I think there's a mistake in this bill.	**Azt hiszem, hogy hibás a számla.**
What's this amount for?	**Ez az összeg mire vonatkozik?**
Is service included?	**Ebben a felszolgálás is benne van?**
Is the cover charge included?	**Ebben minden extra is benne van?**
Is everything included?	**Ebben minden benne van?**
Do you accept traveller's cheques?	**Utazási csekket elfogadnak?**
Can I pay with this credit card?	**Ezzel a hitelkártyávalfizethetek?**
Keep the change.	**Az apró a magáé.**
That was delicious.	**Nagyon finom volt.**
We enjoyed it, thank you.	**Nagyon ízlett, köszönjük.**

Numbers

0	**nulla**	11	**tizenegy**
1	**egy**	12	**tizenkettő**
2	**kettő**	13	**tizenhárom**
3	**három**	14	**tizennégy**
4	**négy**	15	**tizenöt**
5	**öt**	16	**tizenhat**
6	**hat**	17	**tizenhét**
7	**hét**	18	**tizennyolc**
8	**nyolc**	19	**tizenkilenc**
9	**kilenc**	20	**húsz**
10	**tíz**		

Food

Please note that **cs, é, gy, í, ly, ny, ó, ö, ő, sz, ty, ú, ü, ű** and **zs** are treated as separate letters in Hungarian alphabetical order.

alföldi saláta salad Alföldi style: slices of sausage in vinaigrette sauce
alföldi marharostélyos steak Alföldi style: with a rich sauce and stewed vegetables
alig sütve very rare
alma apple
almaleves apple soup
almamártás apple sauce
almás palacsinta apple pancake
agyvelő brains
ananász pineapple
apró uborka gherkins
aranygaluska sweet dumpling filled with jam
articsóka (szív) artichokes (hearts)
aszalt szilva prunes
avokádó avocado
áfonya blueberries
angolna matróz módra eels marinière
ánizsmag aniseed
árpa barley
babérlevél bay leaf
babok beans
 ~**lima** lima beans
 ~**spanyol** kidney beans
 ~**vaj** butter beans
 ~**zöld** green beans
bajai halászlé fish and potato soup
bakonyi gombamártás mushroom sauce
bakonyi betyárleves "outlaw soup" – soup Bakony style; a mix of chicken, beef chunks, thin noodles, mushrooms and vegetables, richly spiced
banán banana
bazsalikom basil
bámia okra
bárányhús lamb
bécsi heringsaláta herring salad Vienna style
bécsi szelet Wiener Schnitzel; breaded veal escalope
békacomb gombával és rákkal frog's legs with freshwater crab and mushrooms
békacomb paprikásan frog's legs in a paprika sauce
birkahús mutton
birsalma quince
borjúhús veal
borjúmirigy sweetbreads
borjúpörkölt a stew composed of a veal chunks, onions, tomatoes, pepper rings, seasoned with paprika and garlic
bors pepper
borsó peas
brokkoli broccoli
buggyantott poached

bukta bun
burger burger
burgonya saláta potato salad
burgonya/krumpli potatoes
~ **főtt** boiled potatoes
~**hasáb** chips (French fries)
~**püré** mashed potatoes
~**sült** baked potatoes
burgonyakrémleves cream of potato soup
búza wheat
cékla beetroot
cigányrostélyos steak gypsy style: with a brown sauce and braised vegetables
citrom lemon
comb leg
~**bárány** leg of lamb
cukkini courgette (eggplant)
cukor sugar
cukorrépa beets
csabai szarvascomb venison stuffed with spicy csabai sausage served in a paprika sauce
császármorszsa "Emperor's delight"; Viennese fluffy, scrambled pancake
császárszalonna bacon
cseresznye cherries
cseresznyepaprika chilli
csiga snail
csikós tokány strips or chunks of beef braised in a mixture of bacon strips or bits, onion rings and sour cream and tomato concentrate
csípős hot
csiperke gomba champignon mushrooms
csipetke tiny dumplings
csipkebogyó hip
csirke chicken
~**comb** leg
~**mell** breast
~**roston sült csirke** barbecued chicken
~**szárny** wing
csirkeaprólék chicken giblets
csokoládé chocolate
csokoládéfánk chocolate doughnut
csont bone
csontleves bone consommé
csontvelő marrow bones
csuka tejfölben sütve pike fried and served with sour cream
csuka pike
csúsztatott palacsinta multi-layer pancake
csülök pig's trotters
dara semolina
darab piece
daragaluska semolina dumplings
darált minced
datolya dates
debreceni fatányéros a Debrecen speciality, prepared only for parties of three or more, usually containing pork chops and choice fillets as well as some veal; garnished with lettuce
diéta diet
dinnye melon
dínsztelt braised
dió walnuts
disznófej pig's head
disznóhús pork
disznózsír lard
disznózsíron sült larded roast
dobostorta caramel-topped chocolate cream cake
ebéd lunch
ecet vinegar
ecetes torma horseradish sauce
egres gooseberries

HUNGARIAN

egy tábla csokoládé chocolate bar
egytálétel one-course meal
előételek appetisers, starters
Ementáli (sajt) a semi-hard, robust Swiss cheese with holes
endívia saláta endive (chicory)
eper strawberries
erdei szalonka woodcock
erdélyi rakottkáposzta a Transylvanian dish consisting of layers of cabbage interspersed with rice and minced, spiced pork, covered with sour cream and baked in the oven
erdélyi tokány a dish originating in Transylvania: virtually the same as csikós tokány, but without the sour cream
erőleves consommé
~ **húsgombóccal** consommé with meat balls
erős hot
édes sweet
édeskömény caraway
édességek desserts
éhes hungry
élesztő yeast
étel food
étkezés meal
étlap menu
fagylalt ice cream
fahéj cinnamon
fasírozott meatball
fácán pheasant
fácán gesztenyével, gombával töltve pheasant with mushroom and chestnut filling
fácánleves pheasant soup
fehérhagyma mártás onion sauce
fehérrépa turnip
fejeskáposzta-főzelék boiled cabbage
fejes saláta lettuce
fekete áfonya blueberries
fekete cseresznye heart cherry
fekete ribizli black currants
felfújt soufflé
felvágott cold plate of carved meat
fél half
félig átsütve underdone (rare)
fiatal kacsa duckling
fiatal liba grouse
fogas giant pike-perch, a local fish of the pike-perch family
~ **fehérbor mártásban** in a white-wine sauce
~ **rákpörkölttel** with crayfish pörkölt
~**szeletek Gundel módra** Gundel style (after the famous Hungarian restaurateur); breaded fillet of pike
fogoly partridge
fokhagyma garlic
fokhagymás majonézes fejes saláta lettuce salad with garlic flavoured mayonnaise
fokhagymás mártás garlic sauce
forró hot
földimogyoró peanuts
főfogás main course
főtt boiled, stewed
főtt tojás boiled egg
~**kemény** hard boiled
~**lágy** soft boiled
főzelékek vegetables
francia saláta Russian salad
friss fresh
frissen sültek made to order
füge figs
fürj quail

~ **májjal töltve** stuffed with liver
füstölt smoked
fűszer spice
fűszerkeverék mixed herbs
galamb pigeon
galuska dumplings, noodles
gesztenye chestnuts
~**püré tejszínhabbal** chestnut purée with whipped cream
gesztenyés libamájas pulyka turkey with goose liver and chestnut stuffing
gomba mushrooms
~**fejek májkrémmel töltve** mushrooms stuffed with liver paté
gombaleves mushroom soup
görögdinnye watermelon
grapefruit grapefruit
grillezett grilled
gríz semolina
gulyásleves the traditional Hungarian speciality, goulash soup: a rich soup with beef, onion, potatoes, mild paprika, caraway seeds, garlic, vegetables and tiny dumplings (csipetke)
Gundel palacsinta pancake with nut-cream and raisin filling, flambéd
gyömbér ginger
gyöngytyúk guinea fowl
Gyulai kolbász spicy, slightly hot smoked sausage
gyümölcs fruit
gyümölcskenyér Bishop's bread; fruit and nut cake
hagyma onion
hal fish
halászlé fisherman's soup
halételek fish and seafood
hal fatányéros assorted fish, some breaded or fried, served on a wooden plate, accompanied by tartar sauce
hallal töltött paradicsom tomato stuffed with fish
halsaláta szegedi módra fish salad Szeged style: fish pieces, diced peppers, tomatoes and chives turned in oil and accompanied by lettuce and hard-boiled eggs
harcsa catfish
~**szelet fűszermártásban** fillet of catfish in a spicy sauce doused with white wine
hasábburgonya chips (U.S. french fries)
hátrész saddle
hátszín sirloin
házias home-made
hideg cold
hideg fogas tartármártással giant pike-perch with tartar sauce (mayonnaise with gherkins, chives, capers and olives)
hidegtál cold meals
hideg sülthús cold cuts
hirtelen sült sautéed
hortobágyi húsos palacsinta stuffed pancakes Hortobágyi style: filled with veal or pork meat and sour cream
hortobágyi rostélyos steak Hortobágyi style: braised in a mix of stock and bacon and accompanied by a large semolina dumpling
hozzávalók ingredient
húsételek meat
Ischler a traditional Hungarian cookie coated with chocolate glaze and filled with jam
jérce koktél chicken cocktail

Jó étvágyat! Have a nice meal!
joghurt yoghurt
Jókai bableves bean soup Jókai style: a mix of smoked pig's knuckles, butter beans and carrots, seasoned with pepper, garlic, paprika and parsley
jól átsütve well-done
jonatán alma Jonathan apple
kacsa duck
kagyló shellfish
kakukkfű thyme
kalács fluffy white milk-bread, available also as rolls called "puffancs"
kalocsai halászlé fish soup in red wine
kapor dill
~**mártás** dill sauce
káposztás rétes cabbage strudel
káposztás ürü mutton with cabbage
kappan capon
kapribogyó caper
kapros túrógombóc dill flavoured cottage cheese dumplings
kapros túrós rétes curd strudel with dill
kapros zöldborsófőzelék green peas with dill
kapucineres felfújt mocha soufflé
karaj chop/cutlet
karalábé kohlrabi; a green-leaf vegetable
karfiol cauliflower
kaszinó tojás eggs with mayonnaise
kaviár caviar
káposzta cabbage
kecsege sterlet
~ **tejszínes paprikás mártásban** in a cream and paprika sauce
kecske goat
kecskeméti barackpuding apricot pudding with vanilla cream
keksz biscuits, cookies
kelbimbó Brussels sprouts
kelkáposzta Savoy cabbage
~**s fácán** pheasant with Savoy cabbage
~**s fogoly** partridge with Savoy cabbage
kelt tészta puff pastry
kenyér bread
~**barna** brown bread
~**fehér** white bread
keserű bitter
keszeg bream
képviselőfánk cream puff
készétel ready-made meal
kocsonyázott halászlé jellied fisherman's soup
kókusz coconut
kolbász sausage
komló hops
kompót stewed fruit, compote
kovászos uborka dill gherkins
könnyű light
könnyű ételek snacks
köret garnish
körözött juhtúró ewe-cheese spread
körte pear
közepesen átsütve medium
kukorica sweet corn
kukoricapehely cornflake
kunsági pandúrleves chicken or pigeon soup Kunság style: seasoned with paprika, grated nutmeg, ginger and garlic
különlegesség speciality
lábszár shank
lebbencs broken pasta
lecsó a mixture of pepper slices,

tomatoes and rice
lecsós borjúmáj rántva breaded veal liver, garnished with a mix of pepper slices, tomatoes, rice, spiced with paprika and garlic
lecsós rostélyos sirloin steak in *lecsó*
lekvár jam
  ~os bukta sweet bun filled with jam
  ~os derelye jam pockets
  ~os táska pastry filled with jam
lencse lentils
  ~püré szárnyasmájjal puréed lentils with poultry liver
leves soup
liba goose
libamáj goose liver
  ~jal töltött pisztráng trout stuffed with goose liver
  ~ pástétom goose liver paté mixed with butter and béchamel (white)sauce, spices and brandy, served in a flakey pastry shell
  ~püré goose liver purée
  ~ rizottó goose liver risotto
  ~ zsírjában goose liver in goose fat
lime lime
liszt flour
magok nuts
magyaros burgonyaleves Hungarian potato soup: diced potatoes and onions with paprika
magyaros csirkeaprólék leves Hungarian chicken giblets soup with mushrooms, diced potatoes, pepper rings and tomatoes
magyaros ízelítő a choice of salami, sausages, goose liver, eggs, green pepper
majonézes kukorica sweet corn with mayonnaise
majoránna marjoram
malac suckling pig
malackocsonya jellied pork
malacpecsenye roast pig
mandarin tangerine
mandula almonds
  ~ felfújt almond soufflé
mandulás rétes almond strudel
marhahús beef
marhanyelv ox-tongue
marhasült roast beef
mazsola raisins
mazsolás borleves wine soup with raisins
máglyarakás apple and jam pudding
máj liver
  ~gombóc liver dumplings
mák poppy-seed
  ~os kalács poppy-seed cake
  ~os rétes poppy-seed strudel
málna raspberries
mártások sauces
meggy morello
  ~mártás morello sauce
menta mint
menü menu for a set price
méz honey
mézes csók honey kisses (cookie made with honey)
mogyoró hazelnuts
mogyoróhagyma shallot
mustár mustard
napi ajánlat day speciality
narancs orange
nokedli noodles
nyelv tongue
nyelvhal sole
nyúl rabbit
  ~szeletek pirított

szárnyasmájjal rabbit with roasted chicken liver
olaj oil
oldalas rib
omlett omelette
~ **debreceni módra** omelette Debrecen style: filled with lecsó (a mix of sliced green peppers, tomatoes, rice and spices) and dry sausage slices
oregáno oregano
óriás kifli large, flaky crescent-shaped roll
orosz hússaláta Russian salad with meat
ökörfarok oxtail
őszibarack peach
őz venison
pacal tripe
~**pörkölt** tripe *pörkölt*
padlizsán aubergine (eggplant)
palacsinta pancake
palócleves a mix of mutton, French beans, potatoes and sour cream, seasoned with paprika, garlic and caraway seeds
paprika paprika; (sweet) peppers
~**piros** red peppers
~**zöld** green peppers
~**csemege** delicate paprika
~**csípősségmentes** mild paprika
~**édes-nemes** fine-sweet paprika
~**félédes** semi-sweet paprika
~**különleges** special paprika
paprika szeletek körözöttel töltve green peppers sliced in four, filled with a mix of ewe's cheese, butter, mustard, paprika, caraway seeds and beer
paprikás csirke galuskával chicken paprika with gnocchi
paprikás mártás paprika sauce
paprikás ponty carp served in a paprika sauce
paradicsom tomatoes
~**leves** tomato soup
pattogatott kukorica popcorn
pácolt marinated
párolt steamed
párolt húsok stews
párolt hús pot roast
petrezselyem parsley
petrezselymes újburgonya fried new potatoes with parsley
péksütemény bakery product
pirítós kenyér toast
pisztácia pistachio
pisztráng trout
~ **tejszín mártásban** baked in cream
ponty carp
póréhagyma leeks
Pozsonyi kifli Pozsony crescent
pörkölt variety of stews (ingredients: lard, onion, paprika, meat, salt, green pepper, tomato)
pulyka turkey
~**comb tejfeles gombamártással** turkey cutlet in a mushroom sauce
püré mash, purée
rablóhús nyárson alternating pieces of pork, onions, mushrooms, bacon and veal roasted and served on a skewer
rakott palacsinta multi-layer pancakes with various fillings
Rác ponty carp with potatoes and sour cream dressing
rágós tough
rák crab

~**pörkölt** broiled crab
rántott gombafejek tartármártással fried mushrooms with tartar sauce
rántott hús breaded veal cutlet
rántott sajt fried cheese
rántott zöldbab fried string beans
rebarbara rhubarb
reggeli breakfast
retek radishes
réce teal; a type of small duck
répa carrots
rétes strudel
ringló greengage
rizibizi rice mixed with green peas
rizs rice
rizses libaaprólék goose giblets with rice
roston sült barbecued; grilled
rozmaring rosemary
róseibni chips (French fries)
sajt cheese
sajtos pogácsa scone with cheese
saláta lettuce; salad
savanyúkáposzta sauerkraut
~ **főzelék** stewed sauerkraut
savanyú malac sour pork
savanyú tojásleves sour egg soup
sáfrány saffron
sárgabarack apricots
sertésborda pork-chop
sertéshús pork
sertéskaraj cutlet of pork
sertéssült roast pork
sertészsír lard
sima héjú őszibarack nectarine
snidling chives
só salt
somlói galuska sweet dumplings made with vanilla, nuts and chocolate, in an orange and rum sauce
sonka ham; gammon
~**füstölt** smoked ham
~**tojással** ham and egg
spanyol paprika pimiento
spárga asparagus (tips)
~**krémleves** cream of asparagus soup
spenót spinach
starking alma starking apple
süllő pike perch
~ **rákpörkölttel** pike-perch with crayfish pörkölt
sült baked; roast; fried
~ **kolbász** fried sausage
~ **derelye** fried jam pockets
Sümegi torta delicious chocolate and hazelnut cake
sütemény cakes
szaharin artificial sweetener
szalámi salami (the two most famous types are Pick and Herz, but there is a wide range of different salamis, for example prepared with sweet paprika)
szalonna smoked bacon
szardínia sardine
számla bill
szárított gyümölcs dried fruit
szárnyas poultry
szarvas deer
szeder mulberries/blackberries
szegedi halászlé fisherman's soup - a mix of various kinds of fish (usually carp, pike and wels), tomato and pepper rings, with hot paprika seasoning
szegfűszeg clove
szelet slice
szelethús escalope
szendvics open sandwich

~**sajtos** with cheese
~**sonkás** with ham
szerecsendió nutmeg
szilva plums
~**s gombóc** plum dumpling
~**s rétes** plum strudel
szív heart
szomjas thirsty
szőlő grapes
tarhonya egg barley
tárkony tarragon
~**os bárány** lamb with tarragon
~**os mártás** tarragon sauce
tejbedara semolina pudding
tejberizs milk-rice
tejföl sour cream
~**ös bableves** bean soup with sour cream
~**ös-gombás sertésborda** pork chop with mushrooms and sour cream
tejszín cream
~**hab** whipped cream
tejtermék dairy-product
tepertős pogácsa crispy scone, seasoned with salt and pepper, topped with crackling
tészták pastries
tojás eggs
~**buggyantott** poached
~**főtt** boiled
~**kemény** hard boiled
~**lágy** soft boiled
~**rántotta** scrambled
~**tükör** fried
~ **ételek** egg dishes
tonhal tuna
torma horseradish
tormás sonkatekercs slices of ham filled with horseraddish
torta cake
tök pumpkin; squash; vegetable marrow
~**főzelék** braised squash
tőkehal cod
töltelék stuffing
töltött stuffed
~ **alma** apple stuffed with vanilla, raisins and cream
~ **káposzta** stuffed cabbage
~ **malac újfalusi módra** stuffed suckling-pig *újfalu* style: with a mix of spiced minced meat, liver, egg and bread
~ **paprika** stuffed green pepper in tomato sauce
~ **tojás kaviárral** eggs stuffed with caviar
~ **uborka** stuffed dill gherkins
túró cottage cheese
~**gombóc** cottage cheese dumplings
~**s rétes** cottage cheese strudel
~**s csusza** cottage cheese noodles
~**s táska/ökörszem** pastry filled with cottage cheese and raisins
~**torta** cheese cake
tüdő lung
tükörtojás sonkával bacon and eggs
tyúkhúsleves chicken-broth
uborka cucumber; gherkins
~**savanyú** pickles
Ujházi tyúkleves a rich chicken soup with vegetables
vacsora dinner; supper
vad game
vadasmártás brown sauce
vaddisznó wild boar
~ **borókamártással** wild boar served in a juniper sauce
vadételek game

vadnyúl hare
~**párolt** jugged hare
vaj butter
vajas galuska butter dumplings
vajassütemény butter pastry
vajastészta short pastry
vanília vanilla
Vargabéles Cobbler's delight
vargánya chanterelle (mushroom)
vegetáriánus vegetarian
vegyes gyümölcsleves hidegen chilled fruit soup
vegyeszöldség mixed vegetables
vese kidney
vesepecsenye tenderloin
véreshurka black pudding
villásreggeli brunch
virsli sausage; frankfurter
vízitorma watercress
zab oat
zabpehely oat-flake
zeller celery
zónaadag small portion
zöldbab French beans; green beans
~**főzelék** stewed green beans
zöldpaprika saláta green pepper salad
zöldség vegetable
zsálya sage
zselé jelly
zsemlegombóc white-bread dumplings
zsemlemorzsa bread crumbs
zsenge young
zsír fat
zsírpapírban sült baked in grease-proof paper
zsömle roll

Drink

alkoholmentes italok non-alcoholic drinks
almabor apple cider
almalé apple juice
aperitif aperitif
ásványvíz mineral water
~**szénsavas** fizzy (carbonated)
~**szénsavmentes** still
asztali bor table wine
Badacsony wine-growing region on the north-western shore of Lake Balaton, most noted for its *kéknyelű* (blue stalk), a medium-dry white, and *szürkebarát* (Grey Monk), an exquisite, slightly bitter wine with a sweet aftertaste
Bak sör dark beer, produced in Hungary
Balatonfüred-Csopak region around lake Balaton producing light, golden-coloured, fruity riesling white wines
baracklé apricot juice
barackpálinka apricot brandy
borok wine
~**vörös** red
~**fehér** white
~**édes** sweet
~**könnyű** light
~**száraz** dry
borpince wine cellar
citromlé lemon juice
cola coke
csapolt sör draught beer
cseresznyepálinka cherry

brandy
Debrői hárslevelű distinguished dessert wine from the slopes of the Mátra mountains; fragrant, sweet and with a hint of Muscat
diólikőr nut liqueur
Dréher sör lager, produced in Hungary
Egészségére! Cheers!
Egri bikavér Bull's blood (dramatic, dark, heavy and powerful wine, made from a blend of mainly Kadarka grapes)
fehér white
féldeci half a decilitre, approximately 1/10 pint
feljavított in reference to wine: "improved" or sweetened
fél üveg half a bottle
filter tea tea bags
fröccs mixture of soda water and wine
gin gin
grapefruitlé grapefruit juice
gyógytea herb tea
gyümölcslé fruit juice
  ~grapefruit grapefruit
  ~narancs orange
habzó bor sparkling wine
házmesterfröccs mixture of 3 mesures of wine and 2 of soda water
Homoki siller the main rosé wine produced in Hungary
hosszúlépés mixture of 1 measure of wine and 2 of soda water
hűtött chilled
itallap wine list
italok beverages, drinks
jég ice
jéggel on the rocks
kakaó (hot) chocolate
kancsó a carafe
kávé coffee
  ~espresso, presso espresso
  ~fekete black
  ~jeges iced
  ~koffeinmentes decaffeinated
  ~mokka mocha
  ~tejes with milk
  ~tejszínes with cream
kisfröccs mixture of 1 measure of wine and 1 of soda water
kis kancsó a small carafe
konyak cognac
korsó sör half a liter of beer
Kőbányai sör lager, produced in Hungary
körtepálinka pear brandy
likőr liqueur
limonádé lemonade
málnaszörp raspberry drink
Mecsek region near Pécs in southern Hungary specially famed for the fragrant bouquet of their *cirfandli* wines
Móri ezerjó a sweetish, full-bodied wine from the region just west of Budapest; goes well with heavy fish or meat dishes
must must, young wine
nagyfröccs mixture of 2 measure of wine and 1 of soda water
narancslé orange juice
narancsszörp orangeade
palackozott bottled
paradicsomital tomato juice
pezsgő champagne
pohár glass
Puszta cocktail a mixture of apricot brandy, liqueur and Tokay wine, chilled and served with a slice of lemon

rosé rosé
rum rum
Somló the smallest of Hungary's wine-producing regions; its best wines are from *furmint* and *tramini* grapes
Sopron region touching the border with Austria, where the popular *Soproni kékfrankos* is produced; a strong, acid wine which complements rich games stews perfectly
sör beer
~**barna** dark beer
~**világos** lager
söröző beer-house
száraz dry
szeszes ital alcoholic drinks
szilvapálinka plum brandy
szóda soda water
szőlőlé grape juice
tea tea
~**citrommal** with lemon
~**jeges** iced
~**tejjel** with milk
tej milk
~**hideg** cold
~**meleg** hot
tisztán neat (straight)
tojáslikőr egg liqueur
Tokaji aszú full-bodied, very sweet wine, best drunk on their own or with fruit desserts (3 *puttony* is the least concentrated, 6 *puttony* is the most concentrated)
Tokaji Szamorodni medium sweet or medium dry wine, made from bunches of grapes that are not suitable for *aszú*
tonik tonic water
törkölypálinka marcbrandy
turmix milkshake
Unicum a bitter liqueur made from a secret herbal recipe
üdítőital soft drink
üveg bottle
~**es sör** bottled beer
vegyes gyümölcspálinka mixed fruit brandy
vermut vermouth
víz water
~**forró** hot
~**hideg** cold
vodka vodka
vörös red
whisky whisky

Italian

Guide to pronunciation

Letter	Approximate pronunciation
Consonants	
b, d, f, k, l, m, n, p, qu, t, v	are pronounced as in English
c	1) before **e** and **i**, like **ch** in **ch**ip 2) elsewhere, like **c** in **c**at
ch	like **c** in **c**at
g	1) before **e** and **i**, like **j** in **j**et 2) elsewhere, like **g** in **g**o
gh	like **g** in **g**o
gl	like **lli** in mi**lli**on
gn	like **ni** in o**ni**on
h	always silent
r	trilled like a Scottish **r**
s	1) generally like **s** in **s**it 2) sometimes like **z** in **z**oo

sc	1) before **e, i,** like **sh** in **sh**ut 2) elsewhere, like **sk** in **sk**in
z or **zz**	1) generally like **ts** in hi**ts** 2) sometimes like **ds** in roa**ds**

Vowels

a	1) short, like **a** in c**a**r, but shorter 2) long, like **a** in c**a**r
e	1) can always be pronounced like **ay** in g**ay** 2) in correct speech, it's sometimes pronounced like **e** in g**e**t or, when long, more like **ai** in h**ai**r
i	like the **ee** in m**ee**t
o	1) can always be pronounced like **oa** in g**oa**t 2) in correct speech, it's sometimes pronounced like **o** in g**o**t or, when long, more like **aw** in l**aw**
u	like the **oo** in f**oo**t

Two or more vowels

In groups of vowels, **a, e** and **o** are strong, and **i** and **u** are weak. When two strong vowels are next to each other, they're pronounced as two separate syllables, e.g., *beato*. When a strong and weak vowel are next to each other, the weak one is pronounced more quickly and with less stress (less loudly) than the strong one, e.g., *piede;* such sounds are diphthongs and constitute only one syllable. If the weak vowel is stressed, then it's pronounced as a separate syllable, e.g., *due*. Two weak vowels together are pronounced as a diphthong, and it's generally the second one that's more strongly stressed, e.g., *guida*.

Stressing of words

Generally, the vowel of the next to the last syllable is stressed. When a final vowel is stressed, it has an accent written over it (´ or `). Normally an accent is used only when the stress falls on a final vowel and not when it falls on syllables before the next to the last one.

Some useful expressions

Hungry

I'm hungry/I'm thirsty.	**Ho fame/Ho sete.**
Can you recommend a good restaurant?	**Può consigliarmi un buon ristorante?**
Are there any good, cheap restaurants around here?	**Vi sono dei buoni ristoranti economici qui vicino?**
I'd like to reserve a table for ... people.	**Vorrei riservare un tavolo per ... persone.**
We'll come at ... o'clock.	**Verremo alle ...**

Asking

Good evening. I'd like a table for ... people.	**Buona sera. Vorrei un tavolo per ... persone.**
Could we have a table...?	**Potremmo avere un tavolo...?**
in the corner	**d'angolo**
by the window	**vicino alla finestra**
outside	**all'aperto**
on the terrace	**sulla terrazza**
May I please have the menu?	**Per favore, mi può dare il menù?**
What's this?	**Cos'è questo?**
Do you have...?	**Avete...?**
a set menu	**un menù a prezzo fisso**
local dishes	**piatti locali**
a children's menu	**un menù per bambini**
Waiter/Waitress!	**Cameriere/Cameriera!**
What do you recommend?	**Cosa consiglia?**
Could I have (a/an)... please?	**Posso avere... per favore?**
ashtray	**un portacenere**
another chair	**un'altra sedia**
finger bowl	**una vaschetta lavadita**
fork	**una forchetta**
glass	**un bicchiere**
knife	**un coltello**

napkin	**un tovagliolo**
plate	**un piatto**
pepper mill	**un macinapepe**
serviette	**un tovagliolo**
spoon	**un cucchiaio**
toothpick	**uno stuzzicadenti**

Ordering

I'd like a/an/some...	**Vorrei...**
aperitif	**un aperitivo**
appetizer	**un antipasto**
beer	**una birra**
bread	**del pane**
butter	**del burro**
cheese	**del formaggio**
chips	**delle patatine fritte**
coffee	**un caffè**
dessert	**un dolce**
fish	**del pesce**
french fries	**delle patatine fritte**
fruit	**della frutta**
game	**della cacciagione**
ice-cream	**un gelato**
lemon	**un limone**
lettuce	**della lattuga**
meat	**della carne**
mineral water	**dell'acqua minerale**
milk	**del latte**
mustard	**della mostarda**
noodles	**della pasta asciutta**
oil	**dell'olio**
olive oil	**dell'olio d'oliva**
pepper	**del pepe**
potatoes	**delle patate**
poultry	**del pollo**
rice	**del riso**
rolls	**dei panini**
saccharin	**della saccarina**
salad	**dell'insalata**
salt	**del sale**

sandwich	**un sandwich**
seafood	**dei frutti di mare**
seasoning	**dei condimenti**
soup	**una minestra**
starter	**un antipasto**
sugar	**dello zucchero**
tea	**un tè**
vegetables	**delle verdure**
vinegar	**dell'aceto**
(iced) water	**dell'acqua (ghiacciata)**
wine	**del vino**

BUON APPETITO!
ENJOY YOUR MEAL!

baked	**al forno**
baked in parchment	**al cartoccio**
boiled	**lesso**
braised	**brasato**
cured	**salato**
fried	**fritto**
grilled	**ai ferri**
marinated	**marinato**
poached	**affogato**
roasted	**arrostito**
sautéed	**fritto in padella**
smoked	**affumicato**
steamed	**cotto a vapore**
stewed	**in umido**
underdone (rare)	**al sangue**
medium	**a puntino**
well-done	**ben cotto**

CIN-CIN!
CHEERS!

glass	**un bicchiere**
bottle	**una bottiglia**

red	**rosso**
white	**bianco**
rosé	**rosatello**
very dry	**molto secco**
dry	**secco**
sweet	**dolce**
light	**leggero**
full-bodied	**pieno**
sparkling	**spumante**
neat (straight)	**liscio**
on the rocks	**con ghiaccio**

The bill

I'd like to pay.	**Vorrei pagare.**
We'd like to pay separately.	**Vorremmo pagare separatamente.**
You've made a mistake in this bill, I think.	**Penso che abbiate fatto un errore nel conto.**
What's this amount for?	**Per che cos'è questo importo?**
Is service included?	**È compreso il servizio?**
Is everything included?	**È tutto compreso?**
Do you accept traveller's cheques?	**Accettate i traveller's checques?**
Thank you. This is for you.	**Grazie, questo è per lei.**
Keep the change.	**Tenga la moneta.**
That was a very good meal.	**È stato un pasto molto buono.**
We enjoyed it, thank you.	**Ci è piaciuto, grazie.**

Complaints

That's not what I ordered.	**Non è ciò che avevo ordinato.**
I asked for...	**Avevo chiesto...**
May I change this?	**Posso cambiare questo?**
The meat is...	**La carne è...**
overdone	**troppo cotta**
underdone	**poco cotta**
too rare	**troppo al sangue**
too tough	**troppo dura**

ITALIAN

This is too...	**Questo è troppo...**
bitter/salty/sweet	**amaro/salato/dolce**
The food is cold.	**Il cibo è freddo.**
This isn't fresh.	**Questo non è fresco.**
What's taking you so long?	**Perchè avete impiegato tanto tempo?**
Where are our drinks?	**Dove sono le nostre bevande?**
This isn't clean.	**Questo non è pulito.**
Would you ask the head waiter to come over?	**Vuole chiedere al capo cameriere di venire qui?**

Numbers

1	**uno, una**	11	**undici**
2	**due**	12	**dodici**
3	**tre**	13	**tredici**
4	**quattro**	14	**quattordici**
5	**cinque**	15	**quindici**
6	**sei**	16	**sedici**
7	**sette**	17	**diciassette**
8	**otto**	18	**diciotto**
9	**nove**	19	**diciannove**
10	**dieci**	20	**venti**

ITALIAN

Food

abbacchio grilled lam
~ alla cacciatora pieces of lamb, often braised with garlic, rosemary, white wine, anchovy paste and hot peppers
(all') abruzzese Abruzzi style; with red peppers and sometimes ham
acciughe anchovies
~ al limone fresh anchovies served with a sauce of lemon, oil, breadcrumbs and oregano
(all')aceto (in) vinegar
acetosella sorrel
acquacotta soup of bread and vegetables, sometimes with eggs and cheese
affettati sliced cold meat, ham and salami (US cold cuts)
affumicato smoked
agliata garlic sauce; garlic mashed with breadcrumbs
aglio garlic
agnello lamb
agnolotti kind of ravioli with savoury filling of vegetables, chopped meats, sometimes with garlic and herbs
(all')agro dressing of lemon juice and oil
agrodolce sweet-sour dressing of caramelized sugar, vinegar and flour to which capers, raisins or lemon may be added
al, all', alla in the style of: with
ala wing
albicocca apricot
alice anchovy
allodola lark
alloro bay leaf
ananas pineapple
anguilla eel
~ alla veneziana braised with tunny (tuna) and lemon sauce
anguria watermelon
anice aniseed
animelle (di vitello) (veal) sweetbreads
anitra duck
~ selvatica wild duck
annegati slices of meat in white wine or Marsala wine
antipasto hors-d'oeuvre
~ di mare seafood
~ a scelta to one's own choosing
arachide peanuts
aragosta spiny lobster
arancia orange
aringa herring

arista loin of pork
arrosto roast(ed)
arsella kind of mussel
asiago cheese made of skimmed milk, semi hard to hard, sweet when young
asparago asparagus
assortito assorted
astice lobster
attorta flaky pastry filled with fruit and almonds
avellana hazelnut
babbaluci snails in olive-oil sauce with tomatoes and onions
baccalà stockfish, dried cod
~ **alla fiorentina** floured and fried in oil
~ **alla vicentina** poached in milk with onion, garlic, parsley, anchovies and cinnamon
(con) bagna cauda simmering sauce of butter, olive oil, garlic and chopped anchovies, into which raw vegetables and bread are dipped
barbabietola beetroot
basilico basil
beccaccia woodcock
Bel Paese smooth cheese with delicate taste
ben cotto well-done
(alla) besciamella (with) white sauce
bigoli in salsa noodles with an anchovy or sardine sauce
biscotto rusk, biscuit (US zwieback, cookie)
bistecca steak, usually beef, but may be another kind of meat
~ **di manzo** beef steak
~ **(alla) pizzaiola** with tomatoes, basil and sometimes garlic
~ **di vitello** veal scallop
bocconcini diced meat with herbs
bollito 1) boiled 2) meat or fish stew
(alla) bolognese in a sauce of tomatoes and meat or ham and cheese
(alla) brace on charcoal
braciola di maiale pork chop
bracioletta small slice of meat
~ **a scottadito** charcoal-grilled lamb chops
braciolone alla napoletana breaded rumpsteak with garlic, parsley, ham and currants; rolled, sautéed and stewed
branzino bass
brasato braised
broccoletti strascinati brocoli sautéed with pork fat and garlic
brodetto fish soup with onions and tomato pulp
brodo bouillon, broth, soup
~ **vegetale** vegetable broth
bruschetta a thick slice of countrystyle bread, grilled, rubbed with garlic and sprinkled with olive oil
budino blancmange, custard
bue beef
burrida fish casserole strongly flavoured with spices and herbs
burro butter
~ **maggiordomo** with lemon juice and parsley
busecca thick tripe and vegetable soup
cacciagione game
(alla) cacciatora often with mushrooms, herbs, shallots, wine, tomatoes, strips of ham and tongue
cacciucco spicy fish soup, usually with onions, green pepper, garlic and red wine topped with garlic flavoured croutons

caciocavallo firm, slightly sweet cheese from cow's or sheep's milk
calamaretto young squid
calamaro squid
caldo hot
calzone pizza dough envelope with ham, cheese, herbs and baked
(alla) campagnola with vegetables, especially onions and tomatoes
canederli dumplings made from ham, sausage and breadcrumbs
cannella cinnamon
cannelloni tubular dough stuffed with meat, cheese or vegetables, covered with a white sauce and baked
~ **alla Barbaroux** with chopped ham, veal, cheese and covered with white sauce
~ **alla laziale** with meat and onion filling and baked in tomato sauce
~ **alla napoletana** with cheese and ham filling in tomato and herb sauce
cannolo rolled pastry filled with sweet, white cheese, sometimes nougat and crystallized fruit
capitone large eel
capocollo smoked salt pork
caponata aubergine, green pepper, tomato, vegetable marrow, garlic, oil and herbs; usually served cold
cappelletti small ravioli filled with meat, herbs, cheese and eggs
cappero caper
cappon magro pyramid of cooked vegetables and fish salad
cappone capon
capretto kid
~ **ripieno al forno** stuffed with herbs and roasted
caprino a soft goat's cheese
~ **romano** hard goat's milk cheese
capriolo roebuck
caramellato caramelized
(alla) carbonara *pasta* with smoked ham, cheese, eggs and olive oil
carbonata 1) grilled pork chop 2) beef stew in red wine
carciofo artichoke
~ **alla romana** stuffed, sautéed in oil, garlic and white wine
carciofino small artichoke
cardo cardoon
carne meat
~ **a carrargiu** spit-roasted
carota carrot
carpa, carpione carp
(della) casa chef's speciality
(alla) casalinga home-made
cassata ice-cream with a crystallized fruit filling
~ **(alla) siciliana** sponge cake garnished with sweet cream cheese, chocolate and crystallized fruit
(in) casseruola (in a) casserole
castagnaccio chestnut cake with pine kernels, raisins, nuts, cooked in oil
castagne chestnuts
caviale caviar
cavolfiore cauliflower
cavolino di Bruxelles brussels sprout
cavolo cabbage
cazzoeula a casserole of pork, celery, onions, cabbage and spices
cece chick-pea
cena dinner, supper
cerfoglio chervil
cervella brains

cervo stag
cetriolino gherkin (US pickle)
cetriolo cucumber
chiodo di garofano cloves
ciambella ringshaped bun
cicoria endive (US chicory)
ciliegia cherry
cima cold, stuffed veal
~ **alla genovese** stuffed with eggs, sausage and mushrooms
cinghiale (wild) boar
cioccolata chocolate
cipolla onion
cipollina pearl onion
ciuppin thick fish soup
cocomero watermelon
coda di bue oxtail
colazione lunch
composta stewed fruit
coniglio rabbit
~ **all'agro** stewed in red wine, with the addition of lemon juice
contorno garnish
copata small wafer of honey and nuts
coppa kind of raw ham, usually smoked
corda lamb tripes roasted or braised in tomato sauce with peas
cornetti 1) string beans 2) crescent rolls
cosce di rana frogs' legs
coscia leg, thigh
cosciotto leg
costata beef steak or chop, entrecôte
~ **alla fiorentina** grilled over an olive-wood fire, served with lemon juice and parsley
~ **alla pizzaiola** braised in sauce with tomatoes, marjoram, parsley and *mozzarella* cheese
~ **al prosciutto** with ham, cheese and truffles; breaded and fried
costoletta cutlet, chop (veal or pork)
~ **alla bolognese** breaded veal cutlet topped with a slice of ham, cheese and tomato sauce
~ **alla milanese** veal cutlet, breaded, then fried
~ **alla parmigiana** breaded and baked with parmesan cheese
~ **alla valdostana** with ham and *fontina* cheese
~ **alla viennese** breaded veal scallop, wiener schnitzel
cotechino spiced pork sausage, served hot in slices
cotto cooked
~ **a puntino** medium (done)
cozza mussel
cozze alla marinara mussels cooked in white wine with parsley and garlic
crauti sauerkraut
crema cream, custard
cremino 1) soft cheese 2) type of ice-cream bar
crescione watercress
crespolino spinach-filled pancake baked in cheese sauce
crocchetta potato or rice croquette
crostaceo shellfish
crostata pie, flan
crostini small pieces of toast, croutons
~ **in brodo** broth with croutons
~ **alla provatura** diced bread and *provatura* cheese toasted on a spit
crostino alla napoletana small toast with anchovies and melted cheese
crudo raw
culatello type of raw ham, cured

in white wine
cuore heart
 ~ **di sedano** celery heart
cuscusu di Trapani fish soup with semolina flakes
dattero date
datteri di mare mussels, small clams
dentice dentex (Mediterranean fish, similar to sea bream)
(alla) diavola usually grilled with a lavish amount of pepper, chili pepper or pimento
diverso varied
dolce 1) sweet 2) sweet, dessert
dolci pastries, cakes
(alla) Doria with cucumbers
dragoncello tarragon
fagiano pheasant
fagiolino French bean (US green bean)
fagiolo haricot bean
faraona guinea hen
farcito stuffed
farsumagru rolled beef or veal stuffed with bacon, ham, eggs, cheese, parsley and onions; braised with tomatoes
fatto in casa home-made
fava broad bean
favata casserole of beans, bacon, sausage and seasoning
fegatelli di maiale alla Fiorentina pork liver grilled on a skewer with bay leaves
fegato liver
 ~ **alla veneziana** slices of calf's liver fried with onions
(ai) ferri on the grill, grilled
fesa round cut taken from leg of veal
 ~ **in gelatina** roast veal in aspic jelly
fettina small slice
fettuccine flat narrow noodles
 ~ **verdi** green noodles
fico fig
filetto fillet
finocchio fennel
 ~ **in salsa bianca** in white sauce
(alla) fiorentina with herbs, oil and often spinach
focaccia 1) flat bread, sprinkled with olive oil, sometimes with fried chopped onions or cheese 2) sweet ring-shaped cake
 ~ **di vitello** veal patty
fondo di carciofo artichoke heart (US bottom)
fonduta melted cheese with egg-yolk, milk and truffles
fontina a soft, creamy cheese from Piedmont, chiefly used in cooking
formaggio cheese
(al) forno baked
forte hot, spicy
fra diavolo with a spicy tomato sauce
fragola strawberry
 ~ **di bosco** wild
frattaglie giblets
fregula soup with semolina and saffron dumplings
fresco cool, fresh, uncooked
frittata omelet
 ~ **semplice** plain
frittatina di patate potato omelet
frittella fritter, pancake, often filled with ham and cheese or with an apple
fritto deep-fried
 ~ **alla milanese** breaded
 ~ **misto** deep-fried bits of seafood, vegetables or meat
 ~ **alla napoletana** fried fish, vegetables and cheese

~ **alla romana** sweetbread, artichokes and cauliflower
~ **di verdura** fried vegetables
frutta fruit
~ **candita** crystallized (US candied)
~ **cotta** stewed
frutti di mare shellfish
fungo mushroom
galantina tartufata truffles in aspic jelly
gallina hen
gallinaccio 1) chanterelle mushroom 2) woodcock
gallinella water-hen
gallo cedrone grouse
gamberetto shrimp
gambero crayfish, crawfish
garofolato beef stew with cloves
(in) gelatina (in) aspic jelly
gelato ice-cream; iced dessert
(alla) genovese with basil and other herbs, pine kernels, garlic and oil
ghiacciato iced, chilled
ginepro juniper (berry)
girello round steak from the leg
gnocchi dumplings
gorgonzola most famous of the Italian blue-veined cheese, rich with a tangy flavour
grana hard cheese; also known as *parmigiano(-reggiano)*
granchio crab
grasso rich with fat or oil
(alla) graticola grilled
gratinata sprinkled with breadcrumbs and grated cheese and oven-browned
grattugiato grated
(alla) griglia from the grill
grissino breadstick
gruviera mild cheese with holes, Italian version of Swiss *gruyère*
guazzetto meat stew with garlic, rosemary, tomatoes and pimentos
incasciata layers of dough, meat sauce, hard-boiled eggs and grated cheese
indivia chicory (US endive)
insalata salad
~ **all'americana** mayonnaise and shrimps
~ **russa** diced boiled vegetables in mayonnaise
~ **verde** green
~ **di verdura cotta** boiled vegetables
involtino stuffed meat or ham roll
lampone raspberry
lampreda lamprey
lardo bacon
lasagne thin layers of generally green noodle dough alternating with tomato, sausage meat, ham, white sauce and grated cheese; baked in the oven
latte alla portoghese baked custard with liquid caramel
lattuga lettuce
lauro bay leaf
(alla) laziale with onions
legume vegetable
lenticchia lentil
lepre hare
~ **al lardo con funghi** with bacon and mushrooms
~ **in salmì** jugged
leprotto leveret
lesso 1) boiled 2) meat or fish stew
limone lemon
lingua tongue
linguine flat noodles
lista dei vini wine list
lodigiano kind of parmesan cheese
lombata loin
luganega pork sausage

lumaca snail
lupo di mare sea perch
maccheroni macaroni
macedonia di frutta fruit salad
maggiorana marjoram
magro 1) lean 2) dish without meat
maiale pork
~ **al latte** cooked in milk
~ **ubriaco** cooked in red wine
maionese mayonnaise
mandarino mandarin
mandorla almond
manzo beef
~ **arrosto ripieno** stuffed roast
~ **lesso** boiled
~ **salato** corned beef
(alla) marinara sauce of tomatoes, olives, garlic, clams and mussels
marinato marinated
maritozzo soft roll
marmellata jam
~ **d'arance** marmalade
marrone chestnut
mascarpone soft, butter-coloured cheese, often served as a sweet dish
medaglione round fillet of beef or veal
mela apple
~ **cotogna** quince
melanzana aubergine (US eggplant)
melanzane alla parmigiana aubergines baked with tomatoes, parmesan cheese and spices
melanzane ripiene stuffed with various ingredients and gratinéed
melone melon
~ **con prosciutto** with cured ham
menta mint
meringa meringue
merlano whiting
merluzzo cod
messicani veal scallops rolled around a meat, cheese or herb stuffing
midollo marrow (bone)
miele honey
(alla) milanese 1) Milanese style of cooking 2) breaded (of meat)
millefoglie custard slice (US napoleon)
minestra soup
~ **in brodo** bouillon with noodles or rice and chicken liver
~ **di funghi** cream of mushroom
minestrone thick vegetable soup
~ **alla genovese** with spinach, basil, macaroni
~ **verde** with French beans and herbs
mirtillo bilberry (US blueberry)
misto mixed
mitilo mussel
(alla) montanara with different root vegetables
montone mutton
mora blackberry, mulberry
mortadella bologna (sausage)
mostarda mustard
~ **di frutta** spiced crystallized fruits (US candied fruits) in a sweet-sour syrup
mozzarella soft, unripened cheese with a bland, slightly sweet flavour, made from buffalo's milk in southern Italy, elsewhere with cow's milk
(alla) napoletana with cheese, tomatoes, herbs and sometimes anchovies
nasello whiting
naturale plain, without sauce or

filling
navone yellow turnip
nocciola hazelnut
noce nut
~ **di cocco** coconut
~ **moscata** nutmeg
nostrano local, home-grown
oca goose
olio oil
~ **d'arachide** peanut oil
~ **di semi** seed oil
olive agrodolci olives in vinegar and sugar
olive ripiene stuffed olives (e.g. with meat, cheese, pimento)
ombrina umbrine (fish)
orata John Dory (fish)
origano oregano
osso bone
~ **buco** veal shanks cooked in various ways depending on the region
ostrica oyster
ovalina small *mozzarella* cheese from buffalo's milk
ovolo egg mushroom
(alla) paesana with bacon, potatoes, carrots, vegetable marrow and other root vegetables
pagliarino medium-soft cheese from Piedmont
palomba wood-pigeon, ring-dove
pan di Genova almond cake
pan di Spagna sponge cake
pan tostato toasted Italian bread
pancetta bacon
pandolce heavy cake with dried fruit and pine kernels
pane bread
~ **casareccio** home-made
~ **scuro** dark
~ **di segale** rye
panettone tall light cake with a few raisins and crystallized fruit
panforte di Siena flat round slab made mostly of spiced crystallized fruit
pangrattato breadcrumbs
panicielli d'uva passula grapes wrapped in citron leaves and baked
panino roll
~ **imbottito** sandwich
panna cream
~ **montata** whipped
panzarotti fried or baked large dough envelopes often with a filling of pork, eggs, cheese, anchovies and tomatoes
pappardelle long, broad noodles
~ **con la lepre** garnished with spiced hare
parmigiano(-reggiano) parmesan, a hard cheese generally grated for use in hot dishes
passatelli pasta made from a mixture of egg, parmesan cheese, breadcrumbs, often with a pinch of nutmeg
passato purée, creamed
~ **di verdura** mashed vegetable soup, generally with croutons
pasta the traditional Italian first course; essentially a dough consisting of flour, water, oil (or butter) and eggs; produced in a variety of shapes and sizes (e.g. spaghetti, macaroni, broad noodles, ravioli, shell- and star-shaped *pasta*); may be eaten on its own, in a bouillon, seasoned with butter or olive oil, stuffed or accompanied by a savoury sauce, sprinkled with grated cheese
~ **asciutta** any pasta not eaten in a bouillon; served with any of various dressings

pasticcino tart, cake, small pastry
pasticcio 1) pie 2) type of *pasta* like *lasagne*
pastina small *pasta* in various shapes used principally as a bouillon or soup ingredient
pasto meal
patate potatoes
~ **fritte** deep fried
~ **lesse** boiled
~ **novelle** new
~ **in padella** fried in a pan
~ **rosolate** roasted
~ **saltate** sliced and sautéed
patatine small, new potatoes
pecorino a hard cheese made from sheep's milk
pepato peppered
pepe pepper
peperonata stew of peppers, tomatoes and sometimes onions
peperone green or red sweet pepper
~ **arrostito** roasted sweet pepper
~ **ripieno** stuffed, usually with rice and chopped meat
pera pear
pernice partridge
pesca peach
~ **melba** peach-halves poached in syrup over vanilla ice-cream, topped with raspberry sauce and whipped cream
pescatrice angler fish, frog fish
pesce fish
~ **spada** swordfish
pesto sauce of basil leaves, garlic, cheese and sometimes with pine kernels and majoram; used in *minestrone* or with *pasta*
petto breast
(a) piacere to your own choosing
piatto dish
~ **del giorno** the day's speciality
~ **principale** main course
primo ~ first course
piccante highly seasoned
piccata thin veal scallop
~ **al marsala** braised in Marsala sauce
piccione pigeon (US squab)
piede trotter (US foot)
(alla) piemontese Piedmontese style; with truffles and rice
pignoli pine kernels
pinoccate pine kernel and almond cake
pisello pea
pistacchi pistachio nuts
piviere plover (bird)
pizza flat, open(-faced) pie, tart, flan; bread dough bottom with any of a wide variety of toppings
pizzetta small *pizza*
polenta pudding of maizemeal (US cornmeal)
~ **pasticciata** *polenta*, sliced and served with meat sauce, mushrooms, white sauce, butter and cheese
~ **e uccelli** small birds spit-roasted and served with *polenta*
pollame fowl
pollo chicken
~ **alla diavola** highly spiced and grilled
~ **novello** spring chicken
polpetta di carne meatball
polpettone meat loaf of seasoned beef or veal
polpo octopus
~ **in purgatorio** sautéed in oil with tomatoes, parsley, garlic and peppers
(salsa di) pommarola tomato sauce

for *pasta*
pomodoro tomato
pompelmo grapefruit
popone melon
porchetta roast suck(l)ing pig
porcini boletus mushrooms
porro leek
pranzo lunch or dinner
prezzemolo parsley
prezzo price
~ **fisso** fixed price
prima colazione breakfast
primizie spring fruit or vegetables
profiterole filled cream puff
~ **alla cioccolata** with chocolate frosting
prosciutto ham
~ **affumicato** cured, smoked
~ **di cinghiale** smoked wild boar
~ **di Parma** cured ham from Parma
provatura soft, mild and slightly sweet cheese made from buffalo's milk
provolone white, medium-hard cheese
prugna plum
~ **secca** prune
punte di asparagi asparagus tips
purè di patate mashed potatoes
quaglia quail
rabarbaro rhubarb
rafano horse-radish
ragù meat sauce for *pasta*
ragusano hard and slightly sweet cheese
rapa turnip
ravanello radish
raviggiolo cheese made from sheep's or goat's milk
razza ray
ribes currants
~ **neri** blackcurrants
~ **rossi** redcurrants
riccio di mare sea urchin
ricotta soft cow's or sheep's milk cheese
rigaglie giblets
rigatoni 1) type of *pasta* similar to *cannelloni* 2) type of macaroni
ripieno stuffing, stuffed
risi e bisi rice and peas cooked in chicken bouillon
riso rice
~ **in bianco** white rice with butter
risotto dish made of boiled rice served as a first course, with various ingredients according to the region
(brodo) ristretto consommé
robiola soft, rich and sweet sheep's milk cheese
robiolina goat's or sheep's milk cheese
rognoni kidneys
(alla) romana with vegetables, particularly onions, mint and sometimes anchovies
rombo turbot, brill
rosbif roast beef
rosmarino rosemary
rotolo rolled, stuffed meat
salame salami
salato salted
sale salt
salmone salmon
salsa sauce
salsiccia any spiced pork sausage to be served cooked
saltimbocca veal slices with ham, sage, herbs and wine
~ **alla romana** veal cutlet flavoured with ham and sage, sautéed in butter and white wine
(al) sangue underdone (US rare)
sarda pilchard, sardine

sardina small sardine
sardo sheep's milk cheese, hard, pungent and aromatic
sartù oven-baked rice with tomatoes, meat balls, chicken giblets, mushrooms and peas
scalogno shallot
scaloppa, scaloppina veal scallop
~ **alla fiorentina** with spinach and white sauce
scamorza aged *mozzarella*, firmer and saltier
scampi Dublin Bay prawns
scapece fried fish preserved in white vinegar with saffron
(allo) sciroppo in syrup
scorfano rascasse, a Mediterranean fish, used for fish soup
scorzonera salsify
sedano celery
selvaggina game
senape mustard
seppia cuttlefish, squid
servizio (non) compreso service (not) included
sfogliatelle puff pastry with custard or fruit-preserve filling
sgombro mackerel
silvano chocolate meringue or tart
soffritto sautéed
sogliola sole
~ **arrosto** baked in olive oil, herbs and white wine
~ **dorata** breaded and fried
~ **ai ferri** grilled
~ **alla mugnaia** sautéed in butter with lemon juice and parsley
soppressata 1) sausage 2) preserved pig's head with pistachio nuts
sottaceti pickled vegetables
sottaceto pickled
spaghetti spaghetti
~ **aglio e olio** with olive oil and fried garlic
~ **all'amatriciana** with tomato sauce, garlic and parmesan cheese
~ **alla carbonara** with oil, cheese, bacon and eggs
~ **pomodoro e basilico** fresh tomatoes and basil leaves
~ **alle vongole** with clam or mussel sauce, tomatoes, garlic and pimento
spalla shoulder
specialità speciality
spezzatino meat or fowl stew
spiedino pieces of meat grilled or roasted on a skewer
~ **di mare** pieces of fish and seafood skewered and roasted
(allo) spiedo (on a) spit
spigola sea bass
spinaci spinach
spugnola morel mushroom
spumone foamy ice-cream dessert with crystallized fruit, whipped cream and nuts
(di) stagione (in) season
stellette star-shaped *pasta*
stinco knuckle (of veal), shin (of beef)
stoccafisso stockfish, dried cod
storione sturgeon
stracchino creamy, soft to medium-soft cheese
stracciatella consommé with semolina or breadcrumbs, eggs and grated cheese
stracotto meat stew, slowly cooked for several hours
strascinati shell-shaped fresh *pasta* with different sauces
stufato 1) stew(ed) 2) beef stew
succu tunnu soup with semolina and saffron dumplings

sufflé soufflé
sugo sauce, gravy
(carne di) suino pork
suppli rice croquettes with *mozzarella* cheese and meat sauce
suprema di pollo in gelatina chicken breast in aspic jelly
susina plum
tacchino turkey
tagliatelle flat noodles
tagliolini thin flat noodles
taleggio medium-hard cheese with a mild flavour
tartaruga turtle
tartina open(-faced) sandwich
tartufo truffle
tartufi di mare cockles or small clams
(al) tegame sautéed
(alla) teglia fried in a pan
testa di vitello calf's head
timo thyme
tinca tench (fish)
tonnato in tunny (tuna) sauce
tonno tunny (US tuna)
topinambur Jerusalem artichoke
tordo thrush
torrone nougat
torta pie, tart, flan
tortelli small fritters
tortellini ringlets of dough filled with seasoned minced meat
tortiglione almond cake
tortino savoury tart filled with cheese and vegetables
~ **di carciofi** fried artichokes mixed with beaten eggs
(alla) toscana with tomatoes, celery and herbs
tostato toasted
totano young squid
tramezzino small sandwich
trenette noodles
triglia red mullet
trippe alla fiorentina slowly braised tripe and minced beef with tomato sauce, marjoram, parmesan cheese
trippe alla milanese tripe stewed with onions, leek, carrots, tomatoes, beans, sage and nutmeg
trippe alla romana cooked in sweet-and-sour sauce with cheese
tritato minced
trota trout
~ **alle mandorle** stuffed, seasoned, baked in cream and topped with almonds
~ **di ruscello** river trout
tutto compreso everything included
uccelletti, uccelli small birds, usually spit-roasted
~ **in umido** stewed
uovo egg
~ **affogato nel vino** poached in wine
~ **al burro** fried in butter
~ **in camicia** poached
~ **alla coque** boiled
~ **alla fiorentina** fried, served on a bed of spinach
~ **(al) forno** baked
~ **fritto** fried
~ **molle** soft-boiled
~ **ripieno** stuffed
~ **sodo** hard-boiled
~ **strapazzato** scrambled
uva grape
vaniglia vanilla
vario assorted
(alla) veneziana with onions or shallots, white wine and mint
verdura green vegetables
vermicelli thin noodles
verza green cabbage
vitello veal

~ **all'uccelletto** diced veal, sage, simmered in wine
vongola small clam
zaba(gl)ione dessert of egg-yolks, sugar and Marsala wine; served warm
zampone pig's trotter filled with seasoned pork, boiled and served in slices
zèppola fritter, doughnut
zimino fish stew
zucca pumpkin, gourd
zucchero sugar
zucchino small vegetable marrow (US zucchini)
zuppa soup
~ **fredda** cold
~ **di frutti di mare** seafood
~ **inglese** sponge cake steeped in rum with candied fruit and custard or whipped cream
~ **alla pavese** consommé with poached egg, croutons and grated cheese
~ **di vongole** clam soup with white wine

Drink

abboccato medium dry (wine)
acqua water
~ **fredda** ice-cold
~ **gasata** soda water
acquavite brandy, spirits
Aleatico a dessert wine made from muscat grapes
amabile slightly sweet (wine)
Americano a popular aperitif made with *Campari*, vermouth, angostura and lemon peel
aperitivo aperitif
aranciata orangeade
asciutto dry (wine)
Asti Spumante the renowned sparkling white wine from Piedmont
Aurum an orange liqueur
Barbaresco a red wine from Piedmont resembling *Barolo*, but lighter and slightly drier
Barbera a dark red, full-bodied wine from Piedmont and Lombardy with a rich bouquet
Bardolino a very pale red wine, from the Lago di Garda near Verona
Barolo a high quality red wine from Piedmont, can be compared to wines from the Rhone Valley
bibita beverage, drink
birra beer
~ **di barile** draught (US draft)
~ **chiara** lager, light
~ **scura** dark
~ **alla spina** draught (US draft)
caffè coffee
~ **corretto** espresso laced with a shot of liquor or brandy
~ **freddo** iced
~ **macchiato** with a few drops of warm milk
~ **nero** black

~ **ristretto** small and concentrated
caffellatte coffee with milk
Campania the region around Naples is noted for its fine red and white wines like *Capri*, *Falerno* and *Lacrima Christi*
Campari a reddish bitter aperitif with a quinine taste
cappuccino black coffee and whipped milk, sometimes with grated chocolate
caraffa carafe
Castelli Romani a common dry white wine from south-east of Rome
Centerbe a strong, green herb liqueur
Cerasella a cherry liqueur
Certosino a yellow or green herb liqueur
Chianti the renowned red and white table wines of Tuscany, traditionally bottled in a *fiasco;* there are many different qualities depending on the vineyards
Chiaretto one of Italy's most famous rosé wines; best when drunk very young; produced south of Lago di Garda
Cortese a dry white wine from Piedmont with limited production
dolce sweet (wine)
Emilia-Romagna the region around Bologna produces chiefly red wine like *Lambrusco*, which is sparkling and has a certain tang, and *Sangiovese*, a still type
Est! Est! Est! a semi-sweet white wine from the region north of Rome
Etna wines from the west slopes of Mount Etna (Sicily)
Falerno red and white dry wines produced in Campagnia
Fernet-Branca a bitter digestive
fiasco a straw-covered flask
frappè milk shake
Frascati a *Castelli Romani* white wine which can be dry or slightly sweet
Freisa red wines from Piedmont; one type is dry and fruity, the other is lighter and can be slightly sweet or semi-sparkling; one of Italy's best red wines produced south-west of Lago Maggiore
frizzante semi-sparkling (wine)
Gattinara a red, high-quality full-bodied wine from Piedmont, south-east of Lago Maggiore
granatina, granita fruit syrup or coffee served over crushed ice
grappa spirit distilled from grape mash
Grignolino good quality red wine with a special character and scent; often with a high alcoholic content
Lacrima Christi the most well-known wine from the Vesuvian slopes (Campania); the white wine is the best, but there are also red and rosé versions
Lago di Caldaro light red wine produced in the Italian Tyrol
Lagrein Rosato a good rosé from the region around Bolzano in the Italian Tyrol
Lambrusco a sparkling and tingling red wine from Emilia-Romagna
latte milk
~ **al cacao** chocolate drink
Lazio Latium; the region princi-

pally to the south of Rome produces chiefly white wine like *Castelli Romani, Est! Est! Est!* and *Frascati*

limonata lemonade

Lombardia Lombardy; the region around Milan produces various red wines like the *Bonarda, Inferno, Spanna* and *Valtellina*, the rosé *Chiaretto* and the white *Lugana*

Lugana a good dry white wine from the region of Lago di Garda

Marsala the renowned red dessert wine from Sicily

Martini a brand-name of white and red vermouth

Millefiori a liqueur distilled from herbs and alpine flowers

Moscatello, Moscato muscatel; name for different dessert and table wines produced from the muscat grapes; there are some red, but most are white

Orvieto light, white wine from Umbria; three versions exist: dry, slightly sweet and sweet

Piemonte Piedmont; the north-western region of Italy reputedly produces the highest quality wine in the country and is best known for its sparkling wine *Asti Spumante;* among its red wines are *Barbaresco, Barbera, Barolo, Dolcetto, Freisa, Gattinara, Grignolino, Nebbiolo; Cortese* is a light white wine

porto port (wine)

Puglia Apulia; at the south-eastern tip of Italy, this region produces the greatest quantity of the nation's wine, mainly table wine and some dessert wine

Punt e Mès a brand-name ver mouth

Sangiovese a red table wine fron Emilia-Romagna

Santa Giustina a good red tabl wine from the Italian Tyrol

Santa Maddalena a good qualit red wine from the Italian Tyro light in colour and rather fruit

sciroppo fruit syrup diluted wit water

secco dry (wine)

Sicilia Sicily; this island is note for its dessert wine, particularl the celebrated *Marsala;* amon many table wines the red, whit and rosé *Etna* wines are the bes known

sidro cider

Silvestro a herb and mint liqueu

Soave very good dry white wine which is best when drunk youn (from the east ov Verona)

spremuta fresh fruit drink

spumante sparkling

Stock a wine-distilled brandy

Strega a strong herb liqueur

succo juice

tè tea

~ **al latte** with milk

~ **al limone** with lemon

Terlano Tyrolean white wine, re nowned, well balanced, green ish yellow in colour and with delicate taste

Toscana Tuscany; the regio around Florence is particularl noted for its red and whit *Chianti*, a good table wine, an the dessert wines *Aleatico* an *Vin Santo*

Traminer a Tyrolean white win from the region which gave th grape and the name to the re

ITALIAN

nowned Alsatian *Traminer* and *Gewürztraminer* white wines

Trentino-Alto Adige the alpine region produces red wines like *Lago di Caldaro, Santa Giustina, Santa Maddalena; Terlano* and *Traminer* are notable white wines; *Lagrein Rosato* is a rosé to remember while *Vin Santo* is a good dessert wine

Valpolicella a light red wine with a rich cherry colour and a trace of bitterness; it is best when drunk young

Valtellina region near the Swiss border which produces good, dark red wine

Vecchia Romagna a wine-distilled brandy

Veneto the north-eastern region of Italy produces high quality wines; among its red wines are *Amarone, Bardolino, Merlot, Pinot Nero, Valpolicella;* among the whites, *Pinot Grigio, Soave. Recioto* is a sparkling red wine

Vin Santo (Vinsanto) a fine dessert wine produced chiefly in Tuscany but also in Trentino, the Italian Tyrol

vino wine

~ **aperto** open
~ **bianco** white
~ **del paese** local
~ **rosatello, rosato** rosé
~ **rosso** red

ITALIAN

Norwegian

Guide to pronunciation

Letter	Approximate pronunciation
Consonants	
b, d, f, h, m, n, p, t, v	as in English
g	1) before **i, y** or **ei,** like **y** in **y**et 2) otherwise, like **g** in **g**o
j, gj, hj, lj	like **y** in **y**et
k	1) before **i, y** or **j,** like **ch** in German i**ch** or something like **ch** in Scottish lo**ch;** it's similar to the first sound of **h**uge 2) otherwise, like **k** in **k**it
l	always as in **l**ee, never as in be**ll**
r	in southwestern Norway, it's pronounced in the back of the mouth (as in French), elsewhere it's slightly rolled in the front of the mouth
rs	is generally pronounced like **sh** in **sh**ut in eastern Norway

s	always as in so
sj, skj, sk	when followed by **i, y** or **øy,** like **sh** in **sh**ut

Notice that in groups **rd, rl, rn** and **rt,** the **r** tends not to be pronounced but influences the pronunciation of the following consonant, which is then pronounced with the tongue behind the upper teeth ridge (turned upwards at the front). The letters **c, q, w, z** are only found in foreign words and tend to be pronounced as in the language of origin.

Vowels

A vowel is generally long in stressed syllables when it's the final letter or followed by only one consonant. If followed by two or more consonants, or in unstressed syllables, the vowel is generally short.

a	1) when long, like **a** in c**a**r 2) when short, very much like **u** in c**u**t
e	1) when long, like **ay** in s**ay,** but a pure sound, *not* a diphthong 2) when short, like **e** in g**e**t 3) when followed by **r,** like **a** in b**a**d; long or short 4) when unstressed, like **er** in oth**er**
i	1) when long, like **ee** in s**ee,** but with the tongue more raised and the lips more drawn back at the sides 2) when short, like **ee** in m**ee**t
o	1) when long, like **oo** in s**oo**n, but with the lips more rounded (when followed by **-rt, -st, -m** and **-nd,** it can be short) 2) when short, generally like **o** in h**o**t
u	a difficult sound; something like the **ew** in f**ew** or Scottish **oo** in g**oo**d; you'll find it very hard to distinguish from Norwegian **y**
y	put your tongue in the position for the **ee** in b**ee** and then round your lips as for the **oo** in p**oo**l; the vowel you pronounce like this should be more or less correct
æ	1) before **r,** like **a** in b**a**d; usually long but sometimes short 2) otherwise, like **ay** in s**ay**
å	1) when long, like **aw** in s**aw** 2) when short (which is rare), more like **o** in h**o**t
ø, ö	like **u** in f**u**r; either long or short

NORWEGIAN

Diphthongs

au	this sounds like **ow** in n**ow,** but in fact the first part is a Norwegian **ø** sound
ei	like **ay** in s**ay** but often reminiscent of **igh** in s**igh**
øy	fairly like **oy** in b**oy**

Silent letters

1) The letter **g** is generally silent in the endings **-lig** and **-ig.**
2) The letter **d** is generally silent after **l** or **n** or after **r** at the end of a word (with lengthening of the vowel) or often after a long vowel, e.g., ho**ld**e, la**nd,** gå**rd.**
3) The letter **v** is silent in a few words, e.g., sel**v,** tol**v,** hal**v,** søl**v.**

Some useful expressions

Hungry

I'm hungry/I'm thirsty.	**Jeg er sulten/Jeg er tørst.**
Can you recommend a good restaurant?	**Kan De anbefale en bra restaurant?**
Are there any good, cheap restaurants around here?	**Finnes det en bra og rimelig restaurant i nærheten?**
I'd like to reserve a table for ... people.	**Jeg vil gjerne bestille et bord til ...**
We'll come at ... o'clock.	**Vi kommer klokken ...**

Asking

Good evening. I'd like a table for ... people.	**God aften, jeg vil gjerne ha et bord til ...**
Could we have a table...?	**Kan vi få et bord...?**
in the corner	**i hjørnet**
by the window	**ved vinduet**
outside	**ute**
on the terrace	**på terrassen**
May I please have the menu?	**Kan jeg få se spisekortet?**
What's this?	**Hva er dette?**

Do you have...?	**Har De...?**
a set menu	**en fast meny**
local dishes	**stedets spesialiteter**
a children's menu	**en barnemeny**
Waiter/Waitress!	**Kelner/Frøken!**
What do you recommend?	**Hva kan De anbefale?**
Could I have (a/an/some) ... please?	**Kunne De gi meg...?**
ashtray	**et askebeger**
another chair	**en stol til**
finger bowl	**en skylleskål**
fork	**en gaffel**
glass	**et glass**
knife	**en kniv**
napkin	**en serviett**
plate	**en tallerken**
pepper mill	**en pepperkvern**
serviette	**en serviett**
spoon	**en skje**
toothpicks	**noen tannpirkere**

Ordering

I'd like a/an/some...	**Jeg vil gjerne ha...**
aperitif	**en aperitiff**
appetizer	**en forrett**
beer	**en øl**
bread	**brød**
butter	**smør**
cheese	**ost**
chips	**pommes frites**
coffee	**kaffe**
dessert	**en dessert**
fish	**fisk**
french fries	**pommes frites**
fruit	**frukt**
game	**vilt**
ice-cream	**en iskrem**
lemon	**sitron**
lettuce	**en salat**

meat	**kjøtt**
mineral water	**mineralvann**
milk	**melk**
mustard	**sennep**
noodles	**nudler**
oil	**olje**
olive oil	**olivenolje**
pepper	**pepper**
potatoes	**poteter**
poultry	**fugl**
rice	**ris**
rolls	**rundstykker**
saccharin	**sakkarin**
salad	**en salat**
salt	**salt**
sandwich	**et smørbrød**
seafood	**fisk og skalldyr**
seasoning	**krydder**
soup	**en suppe**
starter	**en forrett**
sugar	**sukker**
tea	**te**
vegetables	**grønnsaker**
vinegar	**eddik**
(iced) water	**(is)vann**
wine	**vin**

VELBEKOMME!
ENJOY YOUR MEAL!

baked	**ovnsbakt**
baked in parchment	**ovnsbakt i smørpapir**
boiled	**kokt**
braised	**stekt**
cured	**spekt**
fried	**stekt**
grilled	**grillstekt, griljert**
marinated	**marinert**
poached	**pochert**

roasted	**stekt**
sautéed	**ristet**
smoked	**røkt**
steamed	**dampkokt**
stewed	**surret i gryte**
underdone (rare)	**råstekt**
medium	**medium stekt**
well-done	**godt stekt**

SKÅL!
CHEERS!

glass	**glass**
bottle	**flaske**
red	**rød**
white	**hvit**
rosé	**rosé**
very dry	**ekstra tørr**
dry	**tørr**
sweet	**søt**
light	**lett**
full-bodied	**fyldig**
sparkling	**musserende**
neat (straight)	**bar**
on the rocks	**med is**

The bill

I'd like to pay.	**Jeg vil gjerne betale.**
We'd like to pay separately.	**Vi vil gjerne betale hver for oss.**
You've made a mistake in this bill, I think.	**Jeg tror De har gjort en feil på regningen.**
What's this amount for?	**Hva står dette beløpet for?**
Is service included?	**Er service inkludert?**
Is everything included?	**Er alt inkludert?**
Do you accept traveller's cheques?	**Tar De reisesjekker?**

Thank you. This is for you.	**Takk skal De ha, dette er til Dem.**
Keep the change.	**Behold resten.**
That was a very good meal.	**Det var et deilig måltid.**
We enjoyed it, thank you.	**Det smakte meget godt.**

Complaints

That's not what I ordered. I asked for…	**Det er ikke det jeg bestilte, jeg ba om…**
May I change this?	**Kan jeg få byttet dette?**
The meat is…	**Kjøttet er…**
overdone	**for mye stekt**
underdone	**for lite stekt**
too rare	**for rått**
too tough	**for seigt**
This is too…	**Dette er for…**
bitter/salty/sweet	**bittert/salt/søtt**
The food is cold.	**Maten er kald.**
This isn't fresh.	**Dette er ikke ferskt.**
What's taking you so long?	**Hvorfor tar det så lang tid?**
Where are our drinks?	**Har De glemt drinkene våre?**
This isn't clean.	**Dette er ikke rent.**
Would you ask the head waiter to come over?	**Vil De be hovmesteren komme hit?**

Numbers

1	**en**	11	**elleve**
2	**to**	12	**tolv**
3	**tre**	13	**tretten**
4	**fire**	14	**fjorten**
5	**fem**	15	**femten**
6	**seks**	16	**seksten**
7	**sju**	17	**sytten**
8	**åtte**	18	**atten**
9	**ni**	19	**nitten**
10	**ti**	20	**tjue**

NORWEGIAN

Food

Please note that Norwegian alphabetical order is **a-z, æ, ø, å.**

agurk cucumber
ananas pineapple
and duck
ansjos marinated sprats
appelsin orange
aprikos apricot
arme riddere French toast; slices of bread dipped in batter and fried, served with jam
asparges asparagus
~**bønne** French bean (US green bean)
~**topp** asparagus tip
bakt baked
banan banana
bankebiff slices or chunks of beef simmered in gravy
bekkørret river trout
benløse fugler rolled slices of veal stuffed with minced meat
betasuppe thick soup of meat, bone marrow and vegetables
biff beefsteak
~ **med løk** with fried onions
~**tartar** steak tartare, minced raw beef
bjørnebær blackberry
blandede grønnsaker mixed vegetables
blodpudding black pudding (US blood sausage)
blomkål cauliflower
bløtkake rich sponge layer cake
blåbær bilberry (US blueberry)
blåskjell mussel
brekkbønne French bean (US green bean)
bringebær raspberry
brisling sprat
broiler specially fed 2-months-old chicken
brød bread
buljong broth, consommé
bønne bean
daddel (pl **dadler**) date
dagens meny day's menu
dagens rett day's special
drue grape
dyrestek roast venison
eddik vinegar
egg egg
~ **og bacon** bacon and eggs
bløtkokt ~ soft-boiled
forlorent ~ poached
hårdkokt ~ hard-boiled
kokt ~ boiled
speil~ fried (US sunny side up)
eggerøre scrambled eggs
elgstek roast elk (US moose)
eple apple
~**kake** apple cake
ert pea
ertesuppe pea soup

estragon tarragon
fasan pheasant
fenalår cured leg of mutton
fersken peach
ferskt kjøtt og suppe meat-and-vegetable soup
fiken fig
fisk fish
fiskebolle fish ball
fiskegrateng fish casserole
fiskekabaret fish and shellfish in aspic
fiskekake fried fish ball
fiskepudding fish pudding
fiskesuppe fish soup
flatbrød thin wafer of rye and sometimes barley
fleskepannekake thick oven-baked pancake with bacon
fleskepølse pork sandwich spread
flyndrefilet fillet of flounder
fløte cream
~**ost** cream cheese
~**vaffel** cream-enriched waffle often served with Arctic cloudberries or jam
forrett first course, starter
frokost breakfast
fromasj mousse, blancmange
frukt fruit
~**is** water-ice, sherbet
~**salat** fruit salad
~**terte** fruit tart
fugl fowl
fyll stuffing, forcemeat
fårefrikassé mutton or lamb fricassee
fårekjøtt mutton
fårestek leg of lamb
fårikål mutton or lamb in cabbage stew
gaffelbiter salt- and sugar-cured herring fillets
gammelost a semi-hard cheese with grainy texture and strong flavour
geitekilling kid
geitost a bitter-sweet brown cheese made from goat's milk
gjedde pike
grapefrukt grapefruit
gravet ørret salt-cured trout flavoured with dill
gravlaks salt- and sugar-cured salmon flavoured with dill, often served with creamy dill-and-mustard sauce
gressløk chive
griljert breaded
grillet grilled
grovbrød brown bread
grønnsak vegetable
grøt porridge, cereal
gudbrandsdalsost a slightly sweet brown cheese made from goat's and cow's milk
gulrot (pl **gulrøtter**) carrot
gås goose
gåselever(postei) goose liver (paste)
gåsestek roast goose
hasselnøtt hazelnut
havre oats
~**grøt** oatmeal (porridge)
~**kjeks** oatmeal biscuit (US oatmeal cookie)
helkornbrød wholemeal (US whole-wheat) bread
hellefisk halibut
helstekt roasted whole
hjemmelaget home-made
hoffdessert layers of meringue and whipped cream, topped with chocolate sauce and toasted almonds
honning honey
hummer lobster
hvalbiff steak of whale

hvetebolle sweet roll, bun
~ **med rosiner** with raisins
hvitløk garlic
hvitting whiting
hønsefrikassé chicken fricassée
is ice, water ice (US sherbet)
~**krem** ice-cream
italiensk salat salad of diced cold meat or ham, apples, potatoes, gherkins and other vegetables in mayonnaise
jordbær strawberry
julekake rich fruit cake (Christmas speciality)
kake cake, tart
kalkun turkey
kalvekjøtt veal
kalvekotelett veal chop
kalvemedaljong a small round fillet of veal
kalvetunge calf's tongue
kanel cinnamon
karamellpudding caramel blancmange (US pudding)
karbonadekake hamburger steak
kardemomme cardamom
karri curry
karve caraway seed
kastanje chestnut
kirsebær cherry
kjeks biscuit (US cracker or cookie)
kjøtt meat
~**bolle** meat ball
~**deig** minced meat
~**kake** small hamburger steak
~**pudding** meat loaf
~**suppe** broth with diced meat or sausage
klippfisk salted and dried cod
knekkebrød crisp bread (US hardtack)
kokosmakron coconut macaroon
kokosnøtt coconut
kokt cooked, boiled
koldtbord a buffet of cold dishes such as fish, meat, salad, cheese and dessert
kolje haddock
korint currant
kotelett chop, cutlet
krabbe crab
kransekake cone-shaped pile of almond-macaroon rings
krem whipped cream
kreps crayfish
kringle ring-twisted bread with raisins
kryddersild soused herring
kumle potato dumpling
kylling chicken
~**bryst** breast
~**lår** leg, thigh
~**vinge** wing
kål cabbage
~**ruletter** cabbage leaves stuffed with minced meat
laks salmon
lammebog shoulder of lamb
lammebryst brisket of lamb
lammekotelett lamb chop
lapskaus thick stew of diced or minced meat (generally beef, lamb or pork), potatoes, onions and other vegetables
lefse thin pancake (without eggs)
lettstekt sautéed
lever liver
~**postei** liver paste
loff white bread
lompe kind of potato pancake
lungemos hash of pork lungs and onions
lutefisk boiled stockfish, served with white sauce or melted butter and potatoes
løk onion
makrell mackerel

mandel (pl **mandler**) almond
marengs meringue
marinert marinated
medisterkake hamburger steak made of pork
meny bill of fare, menu
middag dinner
morell morello cherry
morkel (pl **morkler**) morel mushroom
multe Arctic cloudberry
musling mussel
mysost a brown whey cheese similar to *gudbrandsdalsost*
mørbrad rumpsteak
napoleonskake custard slice (US napoleon)
normannaost blue cheese
nype rose hip
nyre kidney
nøtt nut
oksefilet fillet of beef
oksehalesuppe oxtail soup
oksekjøtt beef
okserull rolled stuffed beef, served cold
oksestek roast beef
omelett med sjampinjonger button mushroom omelet
ost cheese
pai pie
pale young coalfish
panert breaded
pannekake pancake
pepperkake ginger biscuit (US ginger snap)
pepperrot horse-radish
~**saus** horse-radish sauce
persille parsley
pinnekjøtt salted and fried ribs of mutton roasted on twigs (Christmas speciality)
pir small mackerel
pisket krem whipped cream
plomme plum
~**grøt med fløtemelk** stewed plums and cream
plukkfisk poached fish (usually dried cod or haddock) in white sauce
pommes frites potato chips (US French fries)
postei 1) vol-au-vent 2) meat or fish pie
potet potato
~**chips** crisps (US chips)
~**gull** crisps (US chips)
~**kake** potato fritter
pultost a soft, sometimes fermented cheese, usually flavoured with caraway seeds
purre leek
pyttipanne diced meat and potatoes fried with onions, sometimes topped with a fried egg
pære pear
pølse sausage
rabarbra rhubarb
rakørret salt-cured trout
rapphøne partridge
reddik radish
regnbueørret rainbow trout
reinsdyrstek roast reindeer
reke shrimp
remuladesaus mayonnaise mixed with cream, chopped gherkins and parsley
rips redcurrant
ris rice
risengrynsgrøt rice pudding sprinkled with cinammon and sugar, served warm
riskrem boiled rice mixed with whipped cream, served with raspberry or strawberry sauce
rislapp small sweet rice cake
ristet grilled, sautéed, toasted

rogn roe
rosenkål brussels sprout
rosin raisin
rundstykke roll
rype ptarmigan, snow grouse
rødbete beetroot
rødgrøt fruit pudding served with vanilla custard or cream
rødkål red cabbage
rødspette plaice
røkelaks smoked salmon
røkt smoked
rømme thick sour cream
~**grøt** boiled and served with sugar
rørte tyttebær cranberry jam made without cooking
rå raw
~**stekt** underdone
saus sauce
sei coalfish
selleri celery
sennep mustard
service inkludert service included
sild herring
sildekake herring patty
sildesalat salad of diced salt herring, cucumber, onions, vegetables, spices and mayonnaise
sirupssnipp ginger biscuit (US ginger snap)
sitron lemon
~**fromasj** lemon blancmange (US lemon custard)
sjampinjong button mushroom, champignon
sjokolade chocolate
sjøtunge sole
sjøørret sea trout
skalldyr shellfish
skilpaddesuppe turtle soup
skinke ham
skive slice
slangeagurk cucumber
smør butter
~**brød** open-faced sandwich
småkake biscuit (US cookie)
snittebønner sliced French beans
solbær blackcurrant
sopp mushroom
speilegg fried egg
spekemat cured meat (beef, mutton, pork, reindeer), often served with scrambled eggs an chives
spekepølse large air-dried sausag
spekesild salted herring, often served with cabbage, potatoes and pickled beetroot
spekeskinke cured ham
spinat spinach
stangselleri branch celery
stek roast
stekt fried, roasted
stikkelsbær gooseberry
stuet 1) stewed (of fruit) 2) creamed (of vegetables)
sukker sugar
~**brød** sponge cake
~**ert** sugar pea
suppe soup
surkål boiled cabbage flavoured with sugar, vinegar and caraway seeds
sursild soused herring
svinekjøtt pork
svinekotelett pork chop
svineribbe spare-rib
svinestek roast pork
sviske prune
~**grøt** stewed prunes
sylte brawn (US head cheese)
~**agurk** pickled gherkin (US pickle)
syltelabb boiled and salt-cured pig's trotter (US pig's foot)
syltetøy jam
terte tart, cake

tilslørte bondepiker dessert made from layers of apple sauce and bread-crumbs, topped with whipped cream
timian thyme
torsk cod
torskerogn cod roe
torsketunge cod tongue
trøffel (pl **trøfler**) truffle
tunfisk tunny (US tuna)
tunge tongue
yttebær kind of cranberry
vaffel waffle
vaktel quail
valnøtt walnut
vannbakkels cream puff
vannis water-ice (US sherbet)
vilt game
voksbønne butter bean (US wax bean)
vørterkake spiced malt bread
wienerbrød Danish pastry
ørret (salmon) trout
østers oyster
ål eel
årfugl black grouse

Drink

kevitt spirits distilled from potatoes or grain, often flavoured with aromatic seeds and spices
lkoholfri non-alcoholic
peritiff aperitif
ppelsinbrus orangeade
ar neat (US straight)
rennevin brandy, spirit
rus fizzy (US carbonated) fruit drink
obbel double
ram shot of spirit
plemost applejuice
øte cream
uktsaft fruit juice
løgg similar to mulled wine, with spirits and spices
ice
med ~ on the rocks
affe coffee
~ **med fløte** with cream
~ **uten fløte** black
~ **likør** coffee-flavoured liqueur
is~ iced
kakao cocoa
kefir kefir, a kind of yoghurt
konjakk cognac
likør liqueur
linjeakevitt *akevitt* which is stored in oak casks in the holds of Norwegian ships; the rolling motion of the ship is said to produce a unique taste
melk milk
kald ~ cold
varm ~ warm
mineralvann mineral water
pils lager
pjolter long drink of whisky or brandy and soda water
portvin port (wine)
rom rum

rødvinstoddi mulled wine
saft squash (US fruit drink)
sjokolade chocolate drink
te tea
  ~ **med sitron** with lemon
vann water
vin wine
  het~ fortified
  hvit~ white
  musserende ~ sparkling
  rød~ red
  tørr ~ dry
øl beer
  bayer~ medium-strong, dark
  bokk~ bock
  export~ strong, light coloured
  lager~ light lager
  vørter~ non-alcoholic beer

Polish

Guide to pronunciation

Letter	Approximate pronunciation
Consonants	
b, f, k, l, m, p, z	are pronounced as in English
cz	like **ch** in **ch**urch
dż	like **j** in **j**am
g	as in **g**irl
j	like **y** in **y**et
ł	like **w** in **w**in
n	as in English but put your tongue against the front teeth and not the teeth ridge
s	as in **s**it
sz	like **sh** in **sh**ine
t, d	as in English but put your tongue against the front teeth and not against the teeth ridge

w	like **v** in **v**an
ż or **rz**	like **s** in plea**s**ure

Sounds distinctly different

An often recurring phenomenon in the Slavic languages is "softening" or the "softened" pronunciation of consonants. Examples of this in Polish are **ć, dź, ń, ś** and **z.** A similar effect can be produced by pronouncing **y** as in **y**et–but very, very short—after the consonant.

c	like the English sequence **ts** in **tsets**e pronounced quickly
ć	pronounced like the Polish **c** but with "softening"
dz	like the English sequence **ds** in be**ds** pronounced quickly
dź or **dzi**	pronounced like the Polish **dz** but with "softening"
h or **ch**	similar to English **h** but with much more friction
ń or **ni**	pronounced like the English **n** with considerable "softening"
r	like the Scottish **r** (vibration of the tip of the tongue); note that it's also pronounced at the end of words
ś or **si**	pronounced like the English **s** but with "softening"
ź or **zi**	pronounced like the English **z** but with "softening"

Notice that voiced sounds become completely devoiced at the end of a word or in combination with voiceless sounds, i.e., they're pronounced like their voiceless counterparts (e.g., **b** of chle**b** is pronounced like **p; w** of ró**w** is pronounced like **f; rz** and **z** in p**rzez** like **sz** and **s,** etc.).

Vowels

a	like English **u** in c**u**lt
e	like **e** in t**e**n
i	like **ee** in f**ee**t
y	like **i** in f**i**t
o	like **o** in c**o**t
u or **ó**	a sound between the English **u** in p**u**t and **oo** in b**oo**ts
ą	is pronounced **on** before a consonant; when it's the final letter, it's pronounced like French **an** in fi**an**cé
ę	is pronounced **en** before a consonant or like **e** in b**e**d when it's the final letter

POLISH

Some diphthongs

ej	like **a** in t**a**ke
aj	like **i** in l**i**ke

Stress

The stress falls in Polish on the next to the last syllable.

Some useful expressions

Hungry

I'm hungry/I'm thirsty.	**Jestem głodny/Chce mi się pić.**
Can you recommend a good restaurant?	**Czy może pan/pani polecić mi dobrą restaurację?**
Are there any good, cheap restaurants around here?	**Czy jest tu gdzieś blisko tania i dobra restauracja?**
I'd like to reserve a table for ... people.	**Chciałbym zarezerwować stolik dla ... osób.**
We'll come at ... o'clock.	**Przyjdziemy o ...**

Asking

Good evening. I'd like a table for ... people.	**Dobry wieczór. Proszę o stolik dla ... osób.**
Could we have a table...?	**Proszę stolik...**
in the corner	**w rogu**
by the window	**przy oknie**
outside	**na zewnątrz**
on the terrace	**na tarasie**
May I please have the menu?	**Czy mogę prosić o kartę?**
What's this?	**Co to jest?**
Do you have...?	**Czy jest...?**
a set menu	**obiad firmowy**
local dishes	**dania regionalne**
a children's menu	**danie dla dziecka**

Waiter/Waitress!	**Proszę pana/Proszę pani!**
What do you recommend?	**Co pan/pani poleca ?**
Could I have (a/an)... please?	**Proszę...**
ashtray	**popielniczkę**
another chair	**jeszcze jedno krzesło**
finger bowl	**miseczkę do mycia rąk**
fork	**widelec**
glass	**szklankę**
knife	**nóż**
napkin	**serwetkę**
plate	**talerz**
pepper mill	**młynek do pieprzu**
serviette	**serwetkę**
spoon	**łyżkę**
toothpick	**wykałaczkę**
I'd like a/an/some...	**Proszę**
aperitif	**aperitif**
appetizer	**zakąskę**
beer	**piwo**
bread	**chleb**
butter	**masło**
cheese	**ser**
chips	**frytk'**
coffee	**kawę**
dessert	**deser**
fish	**rybę**
french fries	**frytki**
fruit	**owoce**
game	**dziczyznę**
ice-cream	**lody**
lemon	**cytrynę**
lettuce	**sałatę**
meat	**mięso**
mineral water	**wodę mineralną**
milk	**mleko**
mustard	**musztardę**
noodles	**makaron**
oil	**olej**
olive oil	**oliwę**
pepper	**pieprz**

potatoes	**ziemniaki**
poultry	**drób**
rice	**ryż**
rolls	**bułeczki**
saccharin	**sacharynę**
salad	**sałatkę**
salt	**sól**
sandwich	**kanapkę**
seafood	**frutti di mare**
seasoning	**przyprawy**
soup	**zupę**
starter	**zakąskę**
sugar	**cukier**
tea	**herbatę**
vegetables	**jarzynę**
vinegar	**ocet**
(iced) water	**wodę (z lodem)**
wine	**wino**

SMACZNEGO!
ENJOY YOUR MEAL!

baked	**zapiekane**
baked in parchment	**pieczone w pergaminie**
boiled	**gotowane**
braised	**gotowane**
cured	**peklowane**
fried	**smażone**
grilled	**z rusztu**
marinated	**marynowane**
poached	**z wody**
roasted	**pieczone**
sautéed	**sauté**
smoked	**wędzone**
steamed	**gotowane**
stewed	**duszone**
underdone (rare)	**po angielsku**
medium	**średnio wysmażone**
well-done	**mocno wysmażone**

NA ZDROWIE!
CHEERS!

glass	**lampka**
bottle	**butelka**
red	**czerwone**
white	**białe**
rosé	**rosé**
very dry	**wytrawne**
dry	**półwytrawne**
sweet	**słodkie**
light	**jasne**
full-bodied	**wytrawne**
sparkling	**musujące**
neat (straight)	**czysta**
on the rocks	**z lodem**

The bill

I'd like to pay.	**Chciałbym zapłacić.**
We'd like to pay separately.	**Chcielibyśmy zapłacić oddzielnie.**
You've made a mistake in this bill, I think.	**Chyba się pan pomylił w rachunku.**
What's this amount for?	**Czego dotyczy ta suma?**
Is service included?	**Czy obsługa jest wliczona?**
Is everything included?	**Czy rachunek obejmuje wszystko?**
Do you accept traveller's cheques?	**Czy pan/pani przyjmuje czeki podróżne?**
Thank you. This is for you.	**Dziękuję, to dla pana/pani.**
Keep the change.	**Reszty nie trzeba.**
That was a very good meal.	**Jedzenie było bardzo dobre.**
We enjoyed it, thank you.	**Smakowało nam. Dziękuję.**

Complaints

That's not what I ordered. I asked for...	**Tego nie zamawiałem. Prosiłem o...**
May I change this?	**Czy mogę to zamienić?**
The meat is...	**Mięso jest...**
overdone	**przesmażone**
underdone	**niedosmażone**
too rare	**za surowe**
too tough	**za twarde**
This is too...	**To jest za...**
bitter/salty/sweet	**gorzkie/słone/słodkie**
The food is cold.	**To danie jest zimne.**
This isn't fresh.	**To nie jest świeże.**
What's taking you so long?	**Dlaczego to trwa tak długo?**
Where are our drinks?	**Gdzie są nasze napoje?**
This isn't clean.	**To nie jest czyste.**
Would you ask the head waiter to come over?	**Czy można prosić kierownika sali?**

Numbers

1	**jeden**	11	**jedenaście**
2	**dwa**	12	**dwanaście**
3	**trzy**	13	**trzynaście**
4	**cztery**	14	**czternaście**
5	**pięć**	15	**piętnaście**
6	**sześć**	16	**szesnaście**
7	**siedem**	17	**siedemnaście**
8	**osiem**	18	**osiemnaście**
9	**dziewięć**	19	**dziewiętnaście**
10	**dziesięć**	20	**dwadzieścia**

Food

Please note that Polish alphabetical order is **a, ą, b, c, ć, d, e, ę, f, g, h, i, j, k, l. ł, m, n, ń, o, ó, p, r, s, ś, t, u, w, y, z, ź, ż.**

agrest gooseberries
ananas pineapple
antrykot rib steak
arbuz watermelon
(w) auszpiku (in) gelatine
babka drożdżowa a yeast cake with a hole in the centre
~ **piaskowa** a yeast cake with a hole in the centre, usually with raisins and almonds added
bakalie exotic or non-Polish fruits such as raisins, almonds
bakłażany eggplant, aubergine
~ **faszerowane mięsem** stuffed with meat
baleron large ham sausage
banany bananas
baranina mutton
~ **duszona w kapuście** stewed mutton with cabbage
~ **duszona z kminkiem** stewed mutton with cumin
barszcz czerwony borsch, beetroot soup; served hot
~ **ukraiński** Ukrainian-style borsch, soup with vegetables
bażant pheasant
~ **pieczony** broiled pheasant
befsztyk beefsteak
~ **tatarski** raw chopped meat, anchovies, egg, onion, oil, pepper, salt
~ **z cebulą** beefsteak with fried onions
bezy meringue
biała kiełbasa pork sausage
białko egg white
bigos a mixture of cabbage and sauerkraut with a variety of boiled meats
~ **z dorsza** browned slices of cod, mixed with cabbage, boiled mushrooms, tomato paste, paprika and other seasonings
biszkoptowe ciasto sponge cake
biszkopty fancy biscuits (US cookies)
bita śmietana whipped cream
~ **z rodzynkami** whipped cream with raisins
bliny Russian-style pancakes; small and thick yeast pancakes
boczek bacon
~ **wędzony** smoked bacon
boeuf Stroganoff beef stroganoff; thin slices of beef braised in a sour-cream sauce
borowiki boletus mushrooms
borówki bilberries, blueberries
~ **z chrzanem** bilberries with horseradish
botwina beet greens
bób broad beans
~ **z wody** stewed broad beans
brizol grilled beefsteak
brukiew turnips

rukselka brussels sprouts
ryndza kind of sheep's milk cheese, strong flavour and salty
rzoskwinie peaches
udyń milk pudding
ukiet z jarzyn mixed vegetables
ulion z diablotką consommé with meat-fillet, ravioli-type noddles
~ **z żółtkiem** consommé with raw egg
ułki rolls
~ **mleczne** bread rolls or sweet rolls
uraczki beetroot
amembert imitation camembert; a soft cheese with a tangy flavour
ebula onion
ebulka marynowana pickled onion
ena price
hałwa halvah; a sugary loaf, made with honey and often pistachio nuts
hińska półsurówka z selerem half raw and half cooked salad of celery root, seasoned with oil and mustard
hleb bread
~ **czerstwy** stale bread
~ **pszenny** wholemeal (US wholewheat) bread
~ **razowy** black bread (US pumpernickel)
~ **świeży** fresh bread
~ **żytni** rye bread
hłodnik chilled cream of beetroot soup with vegetables
hrzan horseradish
iastka kruche biscuits (US cookies)
~ **drożdżowe** yeast cake
~ **tortowe** layer cake with flavoured butter-cream filling
ciastko cake
cielęcina veal
~ **duszona w jarzynach** veal and vegetable stew
(w) cieście 1) pasty 2) pastry
cietrzew duszony w śmietanie black grouse braised in sour cream
comber barani saddle of mutton
comber sarni loin of venison
cukier sugar
cukierki sweets (US candy)
cykoria endive (US chicory)
cynaderki kidneys
~ **cielęce** veal kidneys
cynamon cinnamon
cytryna lemon
czarna rzepa black radish
czarne porzeczki blackcurrants
czekolada chocolate
czekoladki chocolate biscuits (US chocolate sandwich cookies) with different fillings
czereśnie cherries
czernina soup made of duck blood broth and vinegar
czosnek garlic
ćwikła salad of beetroot with horseradish
daktyle dates
danie meal
deser dessert
diablotka a kind of dumpling or meatball served with soup
dorsz cod
~ **po grecku** cod, marinated with vegetables; grilled
~ **w galarecie** cod in gelatine
drożdże yeast
drożdżowe ciastko sugared tea cake (US Danish pastry)
drób fowl
~ **w kokilce** dressed with white sauce
duszone stewed, braised

dynia pumpkin
dziczyzna game
dzik boar
dzika kaczka pieczona roast wild duck
dżem jam
~ **owocowy** fruit jam
~ **śliwkowy** plum jam
edamski ser imitation edam cheese; mild flavour, yellow colour
eklerka chocolate cake with whipped-cream filling
ementalski ser swiss cheese; imitation *Emmental,* with holes and mild, nutty flavour
eskalop schabowy loin of pork
estragon tarragon
fasola beans
~ **po bretońsku** butter (US navy) beans in tomato sauce
~ **szparagowa** haricot beans
faworki a kind of light, sugared fritter
figi figs
filet fillet
~ **cielęcy** veal scallop
~ **wieprzowy** pork fillet
~ **z polędwicy** beef fillet
~ **z ryby** fish fillet
flaki tripe with seasoning
~ **cielęce** veal tripe
~ **po warszawsku** Warsaw-style tripe with marjoram and pepper seasoning
flaki jarskie "vegetable tripe"; different kinds of spiced, stewed vegetables
flądra flounder
~ **wędzona** smoked flounder
forszmak veal in tomato sauce
fricassée z dorsza oven-browned cod, with mushrooms, cauliflower, french beans
frytki chips (US french fries)
(w) galarecie (in) gelatine
galaretka owocowa jam
galaretka z nóżek cielęcych calf's trotters (US feet) in gelatine
galaretka z nóżek wieprzowych pig's trotters (US feet) in gelatine
gąski marynowane marinated chanterelle mushrooms
gęś goose
~ **pieczona z jabłkami** roast goose with apples
~ **w maladze** goose braised in red dessert wine
gicz leg
główka cielęca calf's head
golonka shoulder of pork
~ **gotowana** boiled
~ **peklowana** pickled
~ **z kapustą** with sauerkraut
gołąbki cabbage
~ **z kaszą i mięsem** stuffed cabbage with cooked groats and meat
~ **z ryżu i grzybami** stuffed with rice and mushrooms
gołębie pieczone roast pigeon
gorące hot
gorczyca Russian mustard, sharp
gotowane braised
Gouda imitation Dutch-style cheese, mild
goździki cloves
grejpfrut grapefruit
grochówka pea soup
groszek green peas
~ **w majonezie** green peas in mayonnaise
gruszki pears
~ **w czekoladzie** pears in chocolate sauce
grzanki toast
~ **do zupy** sippets, croutons

grzyby mushrooms
gulasz goulash; chunks of beef braised in a savoury paprika sauce
~ **po węgiersku** a hotter and spicier goulash dish
halibut halibut
~ **w sosie śliwkowym** halibut in plum sauce
herbatniki biscuits (US cookies)
homar lobster
imbir ginger
indyk turkey
~ **nadziewany** stuffed turkey braised in dessert wine
~ **pieczony** roast turkey
jabłka apples
~ **nadziewane z konfiturami** apples filled with jam
~ **pieczone** baked apples
~ **w cieście** apple fritters
jadłospis set menu
jagody bilberries, blueberries
jajecznica scrambled eggs
~ **na boczku** with bacon
~ **z szynką** with ham
jajka eggs
~ **faszerowane** stuffed eggs
~ **na miękko** soft-boiled eggs
~ **na twardo** hard-boiled eggs
~ **sadzone** soft-boiled eggs, shelled, served in a glass
~ **w galarecie** eggs lightly poached and served in gelatine
~ **w majonezie** egg salad
~ **w sosie chrzanowym** hard-boiled eggs with horseradish sauce
~ **w sosie musztardowym** hard-boiled eggs with mustard sauce
~ **w szklance (po wiedeńsku)** soft-boiled eggs, shelled, served in a glass
jarzyny vegetables
jeleń venison
jesiotr sturgeon
jeżyny blackberries
kabaczki vegetable marrow (US zucchini)
kabanosy very thin dried pork sausage
kaczka duck
~ **pieczona** roast duck
~ **z jabłkami** duck stuffed with apples
kajzerka bread roll
kalafior cauliflower
kalamary squid
~ **w majonezie** squid with mayonnaise
kalarepka kohlrabi
kanapka sandwich
~ **z serem** cheese
~ **z szynką** jam
kaparki capers
kapusta cabbage
~ **czerwona** red cabbage
~ **kiszona** sauerkraut
~ **na słodko z kminkiem** cabbage seasoned with cumin
~ **włoska** savoy
kapuśniak sauerkraut and cabbage soup
karaś crucian, a freshwater fish
karmazyn haddock
karp carp
~ **na słodko z migdałami** carp in almond sauce
~ **po królewsku** "king's carp"; baked carp balls with almonds and raisins
~ **w szarym sosie z grzybami** carp in sweet-and-sour sauce with mushrooms
kartoflanka potato soup
kartofle potatoes
~ **w mundurkach** boiled potatoes in their jackets

kasza groats, porridge
~ **gryczana** buckwheat groats
~ **jaglana** millet groats
~ **manna** wheat groats
~ **perłowa** pearl barley
~ **ze słoniną** groats with bacon bits

kaszanka z cebulą black pudding (US blood sausage) braised with onions
kasztany chestnuts
kawior caviar
ketchup ketchup
kiełbasa sausage
~ **na gorąco** hot sausage
~ **na rożnie** grilled sausage
~ **parówkowa** kind of frankfurter, wiener

kisiel jam
~ **żurawinowy** cranberry sauce

kiszka krwawa black pudding (US blood sausage)
~ **wątrobiana** liver sausage

kleik gruel, porridge
klops z cielęciny veal meatballs
kluski dumplings
~ **kładzione** poached dumplings
~ **lane** dumplings
~ **śląskie ze słoniną** bacon dumplings
~ **z makiem** poppy seed dumplings
~ **z serem** cream cheese dumplings

kminek cumin
knedle dumplings
~ **czeskie ze słoniną** a type of dumpling made of white rolls and bacon
~ **ze śliwkami** plum dumplings

kogel-mogel beaten egg yolk with sugar; especially given to children as a tonic
kolacja supper
kołduny litewskie dumpling of meat, suet, marjoram and onions
kompot stewed fruit
~ **z gruszek** stewed pears
~ **z jabłek** stewed apples
~ **z wiśni** stewed cherries
~ **ze śliwek** stewed plums

koncentrat pomidorowy tomato paste
konfitura jam
konina horse meat
konserwa tin (US can)
koper dill
kopytka potato dumplings, served with bacon bits
korki ze śledzia small rolled herring
korniszony gherkins
kości bones
kotlet chop, hamburger, chicken breast
~ **de volaille** chicken breast filled with melted butter
~ **mielony** hamburger steak
~ **schabowy** pork chop

krem 1) whipped cream 2) a kind of dessert made of whipped cream with the addition of other ingredients, e.g. raisins, fruit, etc.
~ **czekoladowy** whipped cream with chocolate
~ **pomarańczowy** whipped cream with orange
~ **sułtański** whipped cream with raisins

krewetki shrimp
królik rabbit
~ **w śmietanie** rabbit braised in sour cream

krupnik barley soup
kukurydza maize (US corn)

kulebiak pasty, pie
~ **z grzybami** mushroom pasty
~ **z kapustą** cabbage pasty
~ **z rybą** fish pasty
kura w potrawce chicken fricassee
~ **w rosole** stewed chicken
kurczę chicken
~ **po polsku** roast chicken stuffed with chicken livers and white bread
kurki chanterelle mushrooms
kwaśne sour
leniwe pierogi white-cheese dumpling
leszcz bream
~ **w galarecie** bream in gelatine
lin tench
listek laurowy laurel
lody ice-cream
~ **bakaliowe** tutti-frutti ice-cream
~ **mieszane** mixed ice-cream
~ **truskawkowe** strawberry ice-cream
~ **waniliowe** vanilla ice-cream
łazanki thin noodles, often served with soup on special occasions, e.g. Christmas
łopatka shoulder
łosoś salmon
~ **wędzony** smoked salmon
majeranek marjoram
majonez mayonnaise
mak poppy seed
makaron macaroni, noodles
~ **z jajkami** noodles with fried eggs
~ **z serem** macaroni and cheese
makowiec poppy seed cake
makrela mackerel
maliny raspberries
mała small
mandarynki tangerines
manna kasza cream of wheat
Marago a brand-name instant coffee
marchewka carrot
marmolada jam
marynowane marinated
marynowane grzyby marinated mushrooms
masło butter
maślaki boletus mushrooms
~ **ze śmietaną** with sour cream
mazurek a square cake
~ **bakaliowy** usually with raisins, almonds
~ **figowy** with figs
~ **orzechowy** with chestnuts
mąka flour
medalion small, round or oval cut of meat
~ **cielęcy** small, round or oval cut of veal
melba ice-cream with fruit
melon melon
mieszane (a), (y) mixed
mięso meat
~ **mocno wysmażone** well-done
~ **po angielsku** underdone (US rare)
~ **wysmażone** medium
~ **zimne w galarecie** cold meat in gelatine
mięta peppermint
migdały almonds
miód pszczeli honey
mirabelki yellow plums
mizeria chopped cucumbers with sour cream and dill
mleczko waniliowe vanilla custard pudding
młode young, spring
~ **kartofle** spring potatoes
morele apricots
mortadela bologna sausage
mostek breast portion of meat with a savoury stuffing

~ **barani** stuffed breast of mutton
~ **cielęcy** stuffed breast of veal
móżdżek cielęcy calf's brains
~ **w cieście** pasty of calf's brains
mus z jabłek apple sauce
musztarda mustard
myśliwska kiełbasa kind of dry pork sausage
nabiał dairy products
nadzienie stuffing
naleśniki pancakes
~ **z kapustą i grzybami** filled with cabbage and mushrooms
~ **z marmoladą** with jam
~ **z mięsem** with meat
~ **z serem** with cottage cheese
~ **ze szpinakiem** with spinach
napoleonka napoleon
nerki kidney
~ **cielęce duszone** stewed veal kidneys
nerkówka cielęca nadziewana roast veal stuffed with kidneys
nerkówka cielęca pieczona roast veal with kidneys
Neska a brand-name instant coffee
nóżki cielęce calf's trotters (US feet)
~ **w cieście** calf's trotters (US feet) in pasty
~ **w galarecie** calf's trotters (US feet) in gelatine
obiad dinner
~ **firmowy** menu
obsługa wliczona service included
ocet vinegar
ogórek cucumber
~ **kiszony** pickled cucumber
~ **konserwowy** gherkins
olej oil
oliwa olive oil
oliwki olives
omlet omelet
~ **z dżemem** jam
~ **z groszkiem** peas
~ **z grzybami** mushrooms
~ **z szynką** ham
~ **ze szczawiem** sorrel
orzechy chestnuts
~ **laskowe** hazelnuts
~ **włoskie** walnuts
ostrygi oysters
oszczypek smoked sheep's milk cheese
owoce fruit
ozór tongue
~ **cielęcy** veal tongue
~ **po polsku** in sweet-and-sour sauce
~ **wołowy** beef tongue
panierowane breaded
parmezan parmesan cheese
parówki wiener, frankfurter
papryka pepper, sweet pepper, pimento
~ **czerwona** red sweet pepper
~ **zielona** green pepper
paprykarz stew
~ **cięlecy** veal stew
~ **z królika** rabbit stew
~ **z ryby** fish stew
paszteciki rissole (US patty), croquette
~ **z kapustą** cabbage rissole
~ **z mięsem** meat croquette
~ **z ryby** fish croquette
pasztet moulded pâté; meatloaf
~ **w auszpiku** meatloaf in gelatine
~ **z cielęciny** veal
~ **z drobiu** chicken
~ **z dziczyzny** game
~ **z gęsich wątróbek** goose-liver pâté
~ **z indyka** turkey
~ **z królika** rabbit

POLISH

~ **z zająca** hare
pączki doughnut
perliczki pieczone roast guinea fowl
pieczarki button mushrooms
~ **w śmietanie** in sour-cream
~ **z patelni** sautéed
pieczeń barania roast mutton
~ **cielęca** roast veal
~ **wieprzowa** roast pork
~ **wołowa** roast beef
~ **z dzika** roast wild boar
pieczeń z ryb morskich a loaf of saltwater fish, served with potatoes and salad, or cold with marinated mushrooms and plums
pieczone roasted
pieczywo bread and rolls
pieprz pepper
piernik spice cake
pierogi dumplings
~ **ruskie ze słoniną** dumplings with bacon bits
~ **z grzybami** mushroom dumplings
~ **z jagodami** bilberry, blueberry dumplings
~ **z kiszonej kapusty** sauerkraut dumplings
~ **z mięsem** meatballs
~ **z serem** cheese dumplings
~ **z wiśniami** cherry dumplings
pieróg pasty
~ **ruski ze słodką kapustą** cabbage pasty
~ **z mięsem** meat pasty
pietruszka parsley
pigwa quince
pilaw steamed rice
piwna zupa beer soup with cinnamon, cloves and sometimes cream
placek drożdżowy z owocami yeast cake with fresh fruit
placki ziemniaczane potato fritters
płastuga dab
~ **pieczona w słoninie** baked dab with salt bacon
płatki owsiane z mlekiem porridge
płucka cielęce z winem veal lights in wine
podroby giblets
polewka buttermilk soup
polędwica beef
~ **duszona ze śmietaną** braised with sour cream
~ **po angielsku** roast
~ **wędzona** smoked
pomarańcze oranges
pomidory tomatoes
ponczowe ciastko sponge cake steeped in rum
pory leeks
porzeczki currants
powidła damson (plum) jam
poziomki wild strawberries
przepiórka quail
przyprawy seasoning, spices
przystawki appetizers
pstrąg trout
~ **sauté** sautéed trout
ptysie z bitą śmietaną cream puff
pulardy fattened pullet
pulpety croquette of meat, fish, vegetables or dough, coated with breadcrumbs or butter and deep-fried
pumpernikiel black bread (US pumpernickel)
purée purée, mashed
~ **z jarzyn** purée of vegetables
~ **z ziemniaków** mashed potatoes
pyzy meat pie
rabarbar rhubarb
racuszki drożdżowe a kind of yeast doughnut

ragout z baraniny mutton stew
raki freshwater crayfish
~ **z wody** poached crayfish
rakowa zupa crayfish soup
renklody greengage
rizotto rice casserole
~ **z baraniny** mutton and rice casserole
~ **z drobiu** chicken and rice casserole
rodzynki raisins
rogaliki crescent roll
roladą a slice of meat rolled around minced meat or other stuffing
rolmops marinated herring rolled around chopped onions or gherkins
rosół broth
~ **z cielęciny** veal
~ **z kury** chicken
~ **z wołowiny** beef
rostbef roast beef
roztrzepaniec sour milk
(z) rożna grilled
rumsztyk rumpsteak
rurki francuskie z bitą śmietaną tube-like waffles filled with whipped cream
(z) rusztu grilled
ryba fish
~ **po grecku** fish marinated with vegetables in tomato sauce, grilled and served chilled
rydze orange agaric or meadow mushrooms
~ **z patelni** fried orange agaric mushrooms
ryż rice
~ **z masłem** with butter
~ **zapiekany z jabłkami** baked with apples
~ **z mlekiem** with milk

rzodkiewki radishes
sago sago
salami salami
salceson brawn (US headcheese)
sałata lettuce
sałatka salad
~ **jarzynowa** cooked vegetables in mayonnaise
~ **śledziowa** cooked vegetables in mayonnaise with herring
~ **z ryby** fish salad
sałatki z ryb wędzonych smoked-fish salad with marinated plums, mayonnaise, paprika
sandacz perch
~ **polski** with eggs
~ **w galarecie** in gelatine
~ **z pieczarkami** perch-pike with mushrooms
sardynki sardines
~ **w oliwie** sardines in oil
sarna roe deer, venison
sarnina venison
schab pieczony roast pork tenderloin steak
schab po wiedeńsku breaded pork chop
seler celery
ser cheese
~ **biały** fresh curd cheese
~ **owczy** cheese from sheep's milk
~ **żółty** semi-hard, robust yellow cheese
serce heart
sernik wiedeński cheesecake
sękacz a layer cake
siekane minced, hashed
sielawa whiting
słodkie sweet
słodycze sweets (US candy)
słodzone sweetened
słonina salt bacon
smalec lard

POLISH

~ **gęsi** goose fat
smażone fried
soja soya beans
sola sole
~ **zapiekana z pomidorami** baked in tomatoes
solone salted
solone śledzie salted herring
sos sauce
~ **cebulowy** onion
~ **chrzanowy** horseradish
~ **cumberland** sauce of orange juice and redcurrant jelly
~ **grzybowy** mushroom
~ **holenderski** tangy mayonnaise
~ **koperkowy** dill
~ **musztardowy** mustard
~ **pomidorowy** tomato
~ **sojowy** soy
~ **szary** sweet-and-sour sauce with raisins, almonds; served with fish
~ **tatarski** mayonnaise with gherkins, chives, capers
~ **węgierski** hot tomato sauce with paprika
sól salt
stefanka a long layer cake with butter-cream filling
stek steak, fillet
~ **barani** mutton fillet
~ **cielęcy** veal fillet
~ **wieprzowy** pork fillet
~ **z polędwicy** beefsteak
strucla long white plain cake (US coffee cake); Christmas speciality
strudel thin layers of pastry alternating with apples, nuts, raisins
sucha kiełbasa dried pork sausage
sucharki crackers
sułtanki sultanas, raisins
sum sheatfish (type of large catfish)
~ **duszony** stewed sheatfish
surowe raw
surówka salad
~ **z cykorii** chicory (US endive)
~ **z kapusty kiszonej** sauerkraut
~ **z marchwi** carrot
~ **z ogórków** cucumber
~ **z pomidorów** tomato
~ **z rzodkiewki** radish
suszone grzyby dried mushrooms
suszone owoce dried fruit
szafran saffron
szarlotka apple cake
szaszłyk shashlik; grilled chunks of meat on a skewer
~ **barani** mutton shashlik
~ **z polędwicy** beef shashlik with onions
szczaw sorrel
szczupak pike
~ **gotowany z jajami** poached with hard-boiled eggs
~ **w galarecie** in gelatine
szczypiorek chives
sznycel cielęcy veal scallop
sznycel jarski "vegetarian scallop"; a kind of potato fritter
szparagi asparagus tips
szpinak spinach
~ **zasmażany** spinach thickened with browned butter
szprotki sprats
sztufada marinated and larded roast beef
sztuka mięsa boiled beef
szynka ham
~ **gotowana** boiled
~ **konserwowa** tinned (US canned)
~ **wędzona** smoked
szynkowa sausage which resembles ham in taste

śledź herring
~ **marynowany** marinated
~ **po śląsku** a paste of herring, sausage and apples
~ **po wileńsku** marinated herring, served with a sauce made of onions, mushrooms, gherkins, sprats, tomato paste and pepper
~ **w oleju** in oil
~ **w śmietanie** in sour cream
śliwki plums
~ **suszone** prunes
śmietana cream
~ **bita** whipped and sweetened cream
~ **kwaśna** sour
~ **słodka** fresh
śniadanie breakfast
świeży fresh
talerz plate
tapioka tapioca
tłuste fat (adj)
topiony ser melted cheese
torcik waflowy waffle sandwich; two waffles with a sweet filling
tort layer cake
~ **czekoladowy** chocolate
~ **kawowy** mocha
~ **makowy** poppy-seed
~ **marcepanowy** marzipan
~ **orzechowy** walnut
~ **pomarańczowy** orange
trufle truffles
truskawki strawberries
~ **ze śmietaną** with cream
tuńczyk tunny (US tuna)
twaróg fresh curd cheese
~ **z kminkiem** flavoured with cumin
~ **ze słodką śmietaną** flavoured with sweet cream
~ **ze szczypiorkiem i rzodkiewką** flavoured with chives and radishes
tylżycki ser firm, pale yellow cheese with mild taste
tymianek thyme
udziec leg
~ **sarni** leg of venison
uszka do barszczu dough envelopes served in hot borsch (beetroot soup)
~ **z grzybami** with mushroom filling
~ **z mięsem** with meat filling
wafelki waffles
wanilia vanilla
warzywa vegetables
wątróbka liver
~ **cielęca duszona** sautéed calf's liver
~ **z dorsza w oliwie** cod liver in oil
wędliny cured pork sausages and beef products
wędzone smoked
wędzonka smoked bacon
węgorz eel
~ **w marynacie** eel in vegetable gelatine
~ **wędzony** smoked eel
wieprzowina pork
winogrona grapes
wiśnie cherries
(z) wody poached
wołowina beef
W–Z (wuzetka) a small cake, with a filling of chocolate, jam and custard
zając hare
~ **duszony po myśliwsku** stewed in wine with mushrooms and sour cream
~ **pieczony** roast hare
~ **po polsku** braised in sour cream
~ **w śmietanie** roast hare served

in sour cream
akąska appetizer
apiekane baked
iemniaki potatoes
~ **purée** creamed
~ **smażone** roast
~ **z wody** boiled
imne cold
razy chop, slice of meat
~ **baranie** mutton chop
~ **bite** pounded fillet
~ **siekane** chop, cutlet
~ **w sosie pomidorowym** in tomato sauce
~ **wieprzowe z ryżem** pork chop with rice
~ **z grzybami i ze śmietaną** with mushrooms and sour cream
~ **zawijane** an escalope of meat which has been filled and rolled
upa soup
~ **fasolowa** bean
~ **grzybowa** mushroom
~ **jarzynowa** vegetable
~ **ogórkowa** cucumber
~ **pomidorowa** tomato
~ **rybna** fish
~ **szczawiowa** sorrel
~ **szparagowa** asparagus
~ **w proszku** packaged soup
zupa mleczna cream soup
~ **z kaszki manny** cream of semolina soup
~ **z płatków owsianych** porridge
~ **z ryżu** cream of rice soup
zupa owocowa fruit soup
~ **śliwkowa** plum
~ **z rabarbaru** rhubarb
~ **z wiśni** cherry
żeberka wieprzowe spare ribs
~ **duszone** stewed
~ **w jarzynach** with vegetables
żurawiny cranberries
żurek sour rye-flour soup, usually with cream
żytni chleb rye bread

POLISH

Drink

dvocat egg brandy
lkoholowe napoje spirits
nyżówka aniseed-flavoured vodka
peritif aperitif
utelka bottle
Cassis blackcurrant liqueur
octail mleczny milkshake
~ **jabłkowy** apple
~ **jagodowy** blackberry
~ **kawowy** mocha
~ **truskawkowy** strawberry
ytrynówka lemon-flavoured vodka
wiartka wódki a quarter of a litre (about ½ pint) of vodka
Egri-Bikaver "bull's blood"; a full-bodied red wine from Hungary
eierkoniak egg brandy
gazowane sparkling
gorąca czekolada hot chocolate, often with the addition of a beaten egg, topped with whipped cream
grog toddy, hot tea to which rum and spices are added
grzane mulled
~ **piwo** ale
~ **wino** wine

herbata tea
 ~ **z cytryną** with lemon
jabłecznik cider
jałowcówka home-distilled liquor
jarzębiak vodka flavoured with rowanberries (mountain ashberries)
jogurt yoghurt
kakao cocoa
karafka carafe
kawa coffee
 ~ **duża** large cup
 ~ **mała** small cup
 ~ **mrożona** iced coffee
 ~ **po arabsku** a strong, boiled coffee flavoured with cinnamon
 ~ **po malajsku** a strong, boiled coffee flavoured with vanilla
 ~ **po staropolsku** coffee with whipped cream and cinnamon, and laced with brandy
 ~ **po turecku** a strong, boiled coffee
 ~ **z mlekiem** white coffee
 ~ **zbożowa** coffee substitute, like Postam
 ~ **ze śmietanką** coffee with cream
kefir sour milk
koniak brandy, cognac
krupnik liqueur made from mead (a fermented mixture of water, honey, malt and yeast)
kryniczanka a mineral water
lampka wina a glass of wine
lemoniada soft drink
likier liqueur
(z) lodem on the rocks
lód ice
Madera imitation madeira wine
maślanka buttermilk
mineralna woda mineral water
miód pitny mead, a fermented drink of water, malt, honey, yeast
 ~ **grzany** mulled mead
mleko milk
 ~ **gorące** hot
 ~ **kwaśne** sour
 ~ **zimne** cold
Myśliwska wódka "hunter's vodka"; has a flavour rather lik gin
nalewka na świerzych owocac fruit liqueur
napoje drinks
 ~ **alkoholowe** alcoholic drink
 ~ **mleczne** dairy drinks
 ~ **niealkoholowe** soft drinks
 ~ **orzeźwiające** refreshments
napój juice, nectar
 ~ **firmowy** home-made
 ~ **jabłeczny** apple
 ~ **malinowy** raspberry
 ~ **z porzeczek** raisin
okocimskie piwo full, light bee (Okocim)
oranżada orangeade
Ovomaltina Ovaltine
pieprzówka pepper-flavoured vodka
Pilsner beer from Pilsen, Czechos lovakia; a light beer with strong hops flavour
piwo beer
 ~ **beczkowe** draught (draft) be
 ~ **ciemne** dark beer
 ~ **grzane** mulled beer
 ~ **jasne** light beer
 ~ **z jajkiem** with an egg yolk
 ~ **z sokiem** with syrup
poncz punch, usually a mulled ru drink diluted with water
porter strong, stout beer; 12% a coholic content
Radeberger East German ligh beer from Radeberg
Rizling imitation Riesling; dr

POLISH

white wine from Hungary or Yugoslavia
ım kubański Cuban rum
ɔk juice
~ **ananasowy** pineapple
~ **grejpfrutowy** grapefruit
~ **jabłkowy** apple
~ **naturalny** fruit
~ **pomarańczowy** orange
~ **pomidorowy** tomato
~ **z czarnej porzeczki** blackcurrant
ɔplica a dry and fine golden-coloured vodka
pirytus distilling alcohol
yrop syrup
zampan champagne, sparkling wine
liwowica plum brandy
~ **paschalna** strong plum brandy, especially drunk during Jewish passover
okaj sweet golden or dry white wine from Hungary
ɔnic tonic water
rójniak a very popular mead (a mixture of water, honey, malt, yeast) liqueur

vermouth vermouth
winiak brandy, distilled from grapes, like cognac
wino wine
~ **białe** white wine
~ **czerwone** red wine
~ **grzane** mulled wine
~ **musujące** sparkling wine
~ **owocowe** apple cider
~ **półwytrawne** slightly dry
~ **słodkie** sweet wine
~ **w temperaturze pokojowej** wine at room temperature
~ **wytrawne** dry wine
~ **zimne** chilled wine
wiśniówka cherry liqueur
woda water
~ **mineralna** mineral water
~ **sodowa** soda water
wódka vodka
~ **wyborowa** the finest clear vodka
żubrówka vodka flavoured with the grass the bison feeds on
żytnia wódka top-quality rye vodka
Żywieckie piwo full light beer from Zywiec

POLISH

Portuguese

Guide to pronunciation

Letter	Approximate pronunciation
Consonants	
f, k, l, p, t, v	as in English
b	as in English, but often less decisive (more like **v**)
c	1) before **e** and **i**, like **s** in **s**it 2) elsewhere, like **k** in **k**ill
ç	like **s** in **s**it
ch	like **sh** in **sh**ut
d	as in English, but often less decisive (more like **th** in **th**is)
g	1) before **a**, **o** and **u** or a consonant or after **l**, **n** and **r**, like **g** in **g**o 2) between vowels, like a soft version of the **ch** in Scottish lo**ch** 3) before **e** and **i**, like **s** in plea**s**ure
h	always silent
j	like **s** in plea**s**ure

lh like **lli** in mi**lli**on

m 1) between a vowel and a consonant or at the end of a word, it indicates that the vowel is nasalized (see "Nasal vowels")
2) elsewhere, like **m** in **m**et

n 1) when the initial letter or between vowels, like **n** in **n**o
2) in a consonant group and in plural endings it nasalizes the preceding vowel, but is generally silent

nh like **ni** in o**ni**on

q like **k** in **k**ill

r strongly trilled as in Scottish speech

s 1) when the initial letter, after a consonant or written **ss,** like **s** in **s**it
2) between vowels (not necessarily in the same word), like **z** in ra**z**or
3) when final or before **c, f, p, q, t,** like **sh** in **sh**ut
4) elsewhere, like **s** in plea**s**ure

x 1) generally, like **sh** in **sh**ut
2) in **ex-** before a vowel, like **z** in ra**z**or
3) sometimes like **x** in e**x**it

z 1) when the initial letter, or between vowels, like **z** in ra**z**or
2) when final or before **c, f, p, q, s** or **t,** like **sh** in **sh**ut
3) elsewhere, like **s** in plea**s**ure

Vowels

a 1) when stressed (see under "Stress"), it's like a blend of the **u** in c**u**t and the **a** in p**a**rty
2) when unstressed or before **m, n** or **nh** but not in the same syllable, like **a** in **a**bout

e 1) when stressed, generally like **e** in g**e**t
2) when stressed, sometimes like **a** in l**a**te
3) when unstressed, like **er** in oth**er**
4) at the beginning of a word and in certain other cases, like **i** in h**i**t

é like **e** in g**e**t

ê like **a** in l**a**te

i 1) when stressed, like **ee** in s**ee**d
2) when unstressed, like **i** in com**i**ng

o 1) when stressed, like **o** in r**o**d
2) when unstressed, usually like **oo** in f**oo**t
3) sometimes, either stressed or unstressed like **o** in n**o**te (most common **o** sound)

ô	like **o** in n**o**te
u	1) generally like **oo** in s**oo**n 2) silent in **gu** and **qu** before **e** or **i**

Diphthongs

A diphthong is two vowels pronounced as a single vowel sound, e.g., in English **boy** there is a diphthong consisting of **o** plus a weak **i** sound. In Portuguese diphthongs, **a, e** and **o** are strong vowels and **i** and **u** are weak vowels. In diphthongs the strong vowels are pronounced with more stress (louder) than the weak ones, e.g., **ai** is pronounced like **igh** in s**igh,** and **au** like **ow** in h**ow.** Sometimes the weak vowels can combine to make a diphthong. Apart from these generalizations the exact pronunciation of Portuguese diphthongs isn't easy to predict.

Nasal vowels

These are pronounced through the mouth and through the nose at the same time, just as in the French nasal vowels (e.g., in the French **bon**) and quite similar to the nasal twang heard in some areas of America and Britain.

ã, am, an	something like **ung** in l**ung** or like **an** in French d**an**s
em, en	something like **ing** in s**ing,** but recalling also the **a** in l**a**te
im, in	a nasalized version of the **ea** in l**ea**rn
om, on	like **orn** in c**orn**cob or like **on** in French b**on**
um, un	something like the pronunciation in the North of England of **ung** in l**ung** (a nasalized version of **u** in p**u**t)

Semi-nasalized diphthongs

In these, the first element is nasalized and combined with a weak **i** (pronounced like **y** in **y**et) or **u** pronounced like **w** in **w**as).

ãe, ãi, êm, final **en,** usually final **em**
pronounced as **ã** followed by **y** in **y**et

ão, final unstressed **am**
pronounced as **ã** followed by **w** in **w**as

õe, oi	like **orn** in c**orn**cob or like **on** in French b**on,** followed by **y** in **y**et
ui	like nasal vowel **u** followed by **y** in **y**et

Stress

1) If a word ends with **a, e** or **o,** the stress falls on the next to the last syllable. Plural endings **m** and **s** are generally disregarded.
2) All other words are stressed on the last syllable.

Words not stressed in accordance with these rules have an accent (′or`) over the vowel of the stressed syllable.

Some useful expressions

Hungry

I'm hungry/I'm thirsty.	**Tenho fome/Tenho sede.**
Can you recommend a good restaurant?	**Pode aconselhar um bom restaurante?**
Are there any good, cheap restaurants around here?	**Há algum restaurante bom, barato por aqui?**
I'd like to reserve a table for ... people.	**Queria reservar uma mesa para ... pessoas.**
We'll come at ... o'clock.	**Chegamos às ...**

Asking

Good evening. I'd like a table for ... people.	**Boa noite. Queria uma mesa para ... pessoas.**
Could we have a table...?	**Podemos ter uma mesa...?**
in the corner	**ao canto**
by the window	**perto da janela**
outside	**ao ar livre/fora**
on the terrace	**no terraço**
May I please have the menu?	**Pode dar-me a ementa [o cardápio]?**
What's this?	**O que é isto?**
Do you have...?	**Tem...?**
a set menu	**uma ementa [cardápio] fixa**
local dishes	**pratos típicos**
a children's menu	**uma ementa [cardápio] para crianças**

(Brazilian variations are shown in brackets)

PORTUGUESE

Waiter/Waitress!	**Por favor [Garçom/Garçonete]!**
What do you recommend?	**O que me aconselha?**
Could I have (a/an)... please?	**Pode dar-me... por favor?**
ashtray	**um cinzeiro**
another chair	**outra cadeira**
finger bowl	**uma taça para os dedos**
fork	**um garfo**
glass	**um copo**
knife	**uma faca**
napkin	**um guardanapo**
plate	**um prato**
pepper mill	**o moinho da pimenta**
serviette	**um guardanapo**
spoon	**uma colher**
toothpick	**um palito**

Ordering

I'd like a/an/some...	**Queria...**
aperitif	**um aperitivo**
appetizer	**uns acepipes [aperitivos]**
beer	**uma cerveja**
bread	**pão**
butter	**manteiga**
cheese	**queijo**
chips	**batatas fritas**
coffee	**café**
dessert	**uma sobremesa**
fish	**peixe**
french fries	**batatas fritas**
fruit	**fruta**
game	**caça**
ice-cream	**um gelado [sorvete]**
lemon	**limão**
lettuce	**alface**
meat	**carne**
mineral water	**uma água mineral**
milk	**leite**

mustard	**mostarda**
noodles	**massa**
oil	**óleo**
olive oil	**azeite**
pepper	**pimenta**
potatoes	**batatas**
poultry	**aves**
rice	**arroz**
rolls	**uns pãezinhos**
saccharin	**sacarina**
salad	**uma salada**
salt	**sal**
sandwich	**uma sanduíche**
seafood	**mariscos**
seasoning	**tempero**
soup	**uma sopa**
starter	**uns acepipes [aperitivos]**
sugar	**açúcar**
tea	**chá**
vegetables	**legumes**
vinegar	**vinagre**
(iced) water	**água (com gelo)**
wine	**vinho**

BOM APETITE!
ENJOY YOUR MEAL!

baked	**no forno**
baked in parchment	**envolto em papel**
boiled	**cozido**
braised	**estufado**
cured	**salgado/curado**
fried	**frito**
grilled	**grelhado**
marinated	**marinado**
poached (of fish or meat)	**cozido**
poached (of eggs)	**escalfado**
roasted	**assado**
sautéed	**salteado**
smoked	**fumado [defumado]**

steamed	**cozido a vapor**
stewed	**guisado**
underdone (rare)	**muito mal passado**
medium	**mal passado**
well-done	**bem passado**

SAÚDE!
CHEERS!

glass	**um copo**
bottle	**uma garrafa**
red	**tinto**
white	**branco**
rosé	**rosé/palhete**
very dry	**extra-seco**
dry	**seco**
sweet	**doce**
light	**ligeiro**
full-bodied	**encorpado**
sparkling	**espumante**
neat (straight)	**puro**
on the rocks	**com gelo**

The bill

I'd like to pay.	**Queria pagar.**
We'd like to pay separately.	**Queríamos pagar cada um separadamente.**
You've made a mistake in this bill, I think.	**Creio que se enganou na conta.**
What's this amount for?	**A que corresponde esta importância?**
Is service included?	**O serviço está incluído?**
Is everything included?	**Está tudo incluído?**
Do you accept traveller's cheques?	**Aceita cheques de viagem?**
Thank you. This is for you.	**Obrigado/a. isto é para si.**

Keep the change.	**Guarde o troco.**
That was a very good meal.	**A refeição estava muito boa.**
We enjoyed it, thank you.	**Apreciámos, obrigado/a.**

Complaints

That's not what I ordered.	**Não é o que eu encomendei.**
I asked for...	**Eu pedi...**
May I change this?	**Posso trocar isto?**
The meat is...	**A carne está...**
overdone	**passada demais**
underdone	**mal passada**
too rare	**mal passada demais**
too tough	**dura demais**
This is too...	**Isto está muito...**
bitter/salty/sweet	**amargo/salgado/doce**
The food is cold.	**A comida está fria.**
This isn't fresh.	**Isto não está fresco.**
What's taking you so long?	**Porque demora tanto?**
Where are our drinks?	**Esqueceu-se de nos trazer as bebidas.**
This isn't clean.	**Isto não está limpo.**
Would you ask the head waiter to come over?	**Pode chamar o Chefe de Mesa [maitre], por favor?**

Numbers

1	**um (fem. uma)**	11	**onze**
2	**dois (fem. duas)**	12	**doze**
3	**três**	13	**treze**
4	**quatro**	14	**catorze**
5	**cinco**	15	**quinze**
6	**seis**	16	**dezasseis**
7	**sete**	17	**dezassete**
8	**oito**	18	**dezoito**
9	**nove**	19	**dezanove**
10	**dez**	20	**vinte**

Food

à, à moda de in the style of
abacate avocado pear
abacaxi pineapple
abóbora pumpkin (US winter squash)
açafrão saffron
acará, acarajé portion of fritters made of black-eyed bean purée, ground, dried shrimps and hot peppers
acelga swiss chard
acepipes hors d'œuvre
acompanhamento vegetables, side dish
açorda thick soup or side dish where bread is a principal ingredient
~ **alentejana** with poached eggs, garlic, coriander leaves and olive-oil
~ **de bacalhau** with dried cod, sliced and fried in garlic-flavoured olive-oil
~ **à moda de Sesimbra** with fish, garlic and coriander leaves
açúcar sugar
agrião watercress
aipim cassava root
aipo celeriac
alcachofra artichoke
fundo de ~ bottom
alcaparra caper
alecrim rosemary
aletria 1) vermicelli, thin noodles 2) dessert made with vermicelli
alface lettuce
alheira garlic sausage made of breadcrumbs and different kinds of minced meat
~ **à transmontana** served with fried eggs, fried potatoes and cabbage
alho garlic
~ **francês/-porro** leek
almoço lunch
almôndega ball of fish or meat
alperce apricot
amargo bitter
amêijoas baby clams
~ **à bulhão pato** fried in olive-oil with garlic and coriander
~ **à espanhola** baked in the oven with onions, tomatoes, peppers, garlic and herbs
~ **ao natural** steamed with herbs and served with melted butter and lemon juice
ameixa plum
~ **seca** prune

amêndoa almond
amendoim peanut
amora blackberry
ananás pineapple
anchova anchovy
angu cassava-root flour or maize boiled in water and salt
ao in the style of
arenque herring
arroz rice
~ **de Cabidela** kind of risotto with giblets and chicken blood, flavoured with vinegar
~ **doce** pudding flavoured with cinnamon
~ **de frango** baked with chicken
~ **de manteiga** cooked in water and butter
~ **de pato no forno** duck cooked with bacon and *chouriço* then baked with rice
~ **tropeiro** with *carne de sol*
aspargo asparagus
assado roast
atum tuna fish
bife de ~ cutlet (US steak) marinated in white wine and fried in olive-oil
aveia oats
avelã hazelnut
aves fowl
azeda sorrel
azedo sour
azeite olive-oil
~ **de dendê** palm-oil
azeitona olive
~ **preta** black
~ **verde (de Elvas)** green
babá de moça dessert made of egg yolks poached in coconut milk and syrup
bacalhau cod, usually dried and salted
~ **à Brás** fried with onions and potatoes, then baked with a topping of beaten eggs
~ **de caldeirada** braised with chopped onions, tomatoes, parsley, garlic and coriander (or saffron)
~ **cozido com todos** poached and served with boiled cabbage, onions, potatoes, chickpeas and eggs
~ **à Gomes de Sá** fried with onions, boiled potatoes, garlic and garnished with hard-boiled eggs and black olives
~ **com leite de coco** poached in coconut milk seasoned with coriander
~ **com natas no forno** boiled, then baked with potatoes in a white sauce with cream
~ **à provinciana** a gratin of poached cod, potatoes and *grelos* (or broccoli), topped with minced hard-boiled eggs, flour and port wine
~ **à transmontana** braised with cured pork or *chouriço,* white wine, parsley, garlic and tomatoes
batata potato
~ **doce** yam, sweet potato
~ **frita** chip (US french fry)
~ **palha** matchstick
baunilha vanilla
berbigão type of cockle
beringela aubergine (US egg-plant)
besugo sunfish, type of sea-bream
beterraba beetroot
bifana slice of pork tenderloin usually served in a bun
bife steak, escalope

~ **a cavalo** of beef topped with a fried egg
~ **à cortador** of beef fried in garlic-flavoured butter
~ **de espadarte** swordfish cutlet (US steak) fried with onions and potatoes
~ **à milanesa** breaded escalope of veal
bifinhos de vitela slices of veal fillet served with a Madeira wine sauce
biscoito biscuit (US cookie)
bobó dish made of dried shrimps, onions, cassava root, fish stock, palm-oil, coconut milk and served with bananas and grated coconut
boi beef
bola de Berlim doughnut
bolacha biscuit (US cookie)
~ **de água e sal** cracker
bolinho de bacalhau deep-fried croquette of dried cod and mashed potatoes flavoured with eggs and parsley
bolo cake
~ **caseiro** home-made
~ **podre** flavoured with honey and cinnamon
borracho young pigeon
borrego lamb
(na) brasa charcoal-grilled
brioche yeast bun
broa 1) thick maize-(US corn-). meal cracker 2) type of ginger-bread
brócolos broccoli
cabrito kid
~**-montês** roebuck
~ **à ribatejana** marinated and roasted with herbs and paprika
caça game
(à) caçador(a) simmered in white wine with carrots, onions, herbs and sometimes tomatoes
cachorro (quente) hot-dog
cachucho small sea-bream
café da manhã breakfast
caju cashew nut
calamar (sliced) squid
caldeirada fish stewed with potatoes, onions, tomatoes, pimentos, spices, wine and olive-oil
~ **de enguias** eel simmered with potatoes, onions, garlic, bay leaf and parsley
~ **à fragateira** fish, shellfish and mussels simmered in a fish stock with tomatoes and herbs; served on toast
~ **à moda da Póvoa** hake, skate, sea-bass and eel simmered with tomatoes in olive-oil
caldo clear soup, consommé
~ **verde** thick soup made from shredded cabbage, potatoes and *chouriço*
camarões shrimps
~ **à baiana** served in a spicy tomato sauce with boiled rice
~ **grandes** Dublin Bay prawns (US jumbo shrimps)
cambuquira tender shoots of pumpkin (US squash) stewed with meat
canapé small open sandwich
canela cinnamon
canja chicken-and-rice soup
canjica dessert made of peanuts and sweet-corn cooked in milk with cloves and cinnamon and served in fresh coconut milk
capão capon
caqui persimmon
caracóis snails
caracol 1) snail 2) a spiral-

shaped bun filled with currants
caranguejo crab
carapau horse mackerel
~ **de escabeche** fried and dipped in a sauce made of vinegar, olive-oil, fried onions and garlic
cardápio menu
caril curry
carne meat
~ **de porco à alentejana** cubes of marinated pork fried with clams
~ **de sol** salted and dried in the sun
carneiro mutton
~ **guisado** stewed with tomatoes, garlic, bay leaf, parsley and often potatoes
carnes frias cold meat (US cold cuts)
caruru 1) green amaranth 2) a dish of minced herbs stewed in oil and spices
castanha chestnut
~ **de caju** cashew nut
(na) cataplana steamed in a copper pan shaped like a big nutshell
cavala mackerel
cebola onion
cebolada fried-onion garnish
cenoura carrot
cereja cherry
cherne black grouper
chicória endive (US chicory)
chispalhada pig's trotters (US feet) stewed with navy beans, cabbage, bacon and blood sausage
chispe pig's trotter (US foot)
chocos com tinta cuttlefish cooked in their own ink
chouriça, chouriço smoked pork sausage flavoured with paprika
chuchu type of marrow (US summer squash)
churrasco charcoal-grilled meat served in Brazil with *farofa* and a hot-pepper sauce
cocada coconut macaroon
coco coconut
codorniz quail
coelho rabbit
coentro coriander
cogumelo (button) mushroom
colorau paprika (used for colouring)
cominho caraway seed
compota compote, stewed fruit
congro conger eel
conta bill (US check)
coração heart
cordeiro lamb
corvina croaker (fish)
costeleta chop, cutlet
couve cabbage
~**-de-bruxelas** brussels sprouts
~**-flor** cauliflower
~ **galega** galician (with a long stem, big dark green leaves and a slightly bitter taste)
~ **lombarda** savoy
~ **portuguesa** portuguese (like the galician but smaller)
~ **roxa** red
cozido 1) boiled stew 2) boiled 3) cooked
~ **em lume brando** simmered
~ **à portuguesa** beef and pork boiled with *chouriço,* carrots, turnips and cabbage *(couve portuguesa)*
creme cream
~ **de leite** fresh
criação fowl
croissant crescent roll
cru raw

PORTUGUESE

curau mashed sweet-corn cooked in coconut milk with sugar and cinnamon
damasco apricot
dióspiro persimmon
dobrada, dobradinha tripe
doce 1) sweet 2) jam
~ **de laranja** marmalade
dourada guilt-head (fish)
eiró eel
eiroses fritas fried eel
ementa 1) menu 2) set menu
empada small type of pie
empadão large type of pie
~ **de batata** shepherd's pie (with minced meat and mashed potato topping)
enchidos assorted pork products made into sausages
endívia chicory (US endive)
enguia eel
ensopado meat or fish casserole served on (or with) slices of bread
entrecosto sparerib
ervilha green pea
escabeche sauce of fried onions, garlic, olive-oil and vinegar
escalfado poached
escalope de vitela escalope of veal, thin, flattened breaded slice of veal
espadarte swordfish
espargo asparagus
ponta de ~ tip
esparregado purée of assorted greens in cream
especiaria spice
espetada kebab
(no) espeto spit-roasted
espinafre spinach
estragão tarragon
estufado braised
esturjão sturgeon
farofa cassava-root meal browned in oil or butter
farófias floating island
fatias slices
~ **da China** cold, baked egg yolks topped with syrup flavoured with lemon and cinnamon
~ **douradas** slices of bread dipped into milk and egg yolk, fried and sprinkled with sugar (US french toast)
favas broad beans
~ **guisadas com chouriço** stewed with *chouriço* and coriander leaves
febras de porco à alentejana pieces of pork fillet grilled with onions, *chouriço* and bacon
feijão bean
~ **branco** navy
~ **catarino** pink
~ **encarnado** red
~ **frade** black-eyed
~ **guisado** stewed with bacon in a tomato sauce
~ **preto** black
~ **tropeiro** black beans fried with chopped *carne de sol* and served with *farofa*
~ **verde** runner (US green)
feijoada dish of dried beans stewed with pig's head and trotters (US feet) bacon, sausages and sometimes vegetables; served in Brazil with *farofa,* rice, sliced oranges and a hot-pepper sauce
fiambre cooked (US boiled) ham
fígado liver
~ **de aves** chicken
figo fig
filete fillet of fish

filhó fritter
~ **de abóbora** of pumpkin purée
fios de ovos dessert of fine golden strands made from beaten egg yolk and melted sugar
folhado sweet puff-pastry delicacy
(no) forno baked
framboesa raspberry
frango chicken
~ **com farofa** served with *farofa* mixed with olives, hard-boiled eggs and giblets
~ **na púcara** chicken cassserole flavoured with port wine, prepared in a special earthenware pot
fresco fresh
fressura de porco guisada casserole of pork offal (US variety meat), sometimes with navy beans
fricassé casserole, usually of lamb or veal in a cream sauce
(na) frigideira sautéed
frio cold
fritada de peixe deep-fried fish
frito 1) fried 2) fritter
fruta fruit
~ **em calda** in syrup
~ **do conde** variety of tropical fruit
~ **cristalizada** candied
fubá maizeflour (US cornflour)
fumado smoked
galantina pressed meat in gelatine
galinha boiling chicken
galinhola woodcock
ganso goose
garoupa large grouper (fish)
gaspacho chilled soup with diced tomatoes, sweet peppers, onions, cucumber and croutons
gelado 1) ice-cream 2) chilled
geleia 1) jelly 2) jam (Brazil)
gengibre ginger
ginja morello cherry
goiaba guava
goiabada guava paste
gombo okra (GB lady's finger)
grão(-de-bico) chickpeas
~ **com bacalhau** stew made of chickpeas, potatoes and dried cod fillets
gratinado oven-browned
grelhado grilled
grelos turnip greens
groselha red currant
guaraná very sweet tropical fruit
guisado 1) stew 2) stewed
hortaliça fresh vegetables
hortelã mint
incluído included
inhame yam, variety of sweet potato
iscas thinly sliced liver
~ **à portuguesa** marinated in white wine with herbs and garlic then fried
jabuticaba bing cherry
jambu variety of cress
jantar dinner
jardineira mixed vegetables
javali wild boar
lagosta spiny lobster
~ **americana** fried with onions and garlic, flambéed in brand and served in a sauce flavoure with Madeira wine
~ **suada** with onions, garlic, tomatoes and flavoured with port wine
lagostim Norwegian lobster, langoustine
~**-do-rio** fresh-water crayfish
lampreia lamprey

~ **à moda do Minho** marinated in "green" wine, port wine, brandy, blood and spices then poached in the marinade and served with rice
lanche snack
laranja orange
lavagante lobster
lebre hare
legumes vegetables
~ **variados** mixed
leitão suck(l)ing pig
~ **à Bairrada** coated with spicy lard and roasted on a spit in a very hot bread-oven
~ **recheado** stuffed with a spicy, brandy-flavoured mince of bacon, *chouriço* and giblets and then roasted
leite-creme blancmange (US pudding) often sprinkled with caramelised sugar
lentilha lentil
lima lime
limão lemon
~ **verde** lime
língua tongue
linguado sole
~ **à meunière** sautéed in butter, served with parsley and lemon-juice
~ **com recheio de camarão** filled with shrimps in a white sauce
linguíça thin pork sausage flavoured with paprika
lista dos vinhos wine list
lombo loin
louro bay leaf
lulas squid
~ **de caldeirada** simmered with white wine, olive-oil, diced potatoes, tomatoes, onions and parsley
~ **recheadas** braised with a stuffing of eggs, onions and *chouriço*
maçã apple
~ **assada** baked
maçapão, massapão 1) marzipan 2) almond macaroon
macarrão macaroni
macaxeira cassava root
maionese mayonnaise
malagueta hot pepper
mamão papaya
mandioca cassava root
manjar de coco coconut blancmange (US pudding) topped with plum syrup
manjericão basil
manteiga butter
mãozinhas de vitela guisadas calves' trotters (US feet) braised with onions, parsley and vinegar, served with vegetables
maracujá passion fruit
marinado marinated
(à) marinheira with white wine, onions, parsley and sometimes tomatoes
marisco seafood
marmelada quince paste
marmelo quince
massa 1) dough, pastry 2) pasta, all types of noodle
medalhão medallion, small choice cut of meat
medronho arbutus berry
meia desfeita poached pieces of dried cod fried with chickpeas, onions and vinegar, topped with hard-boiled eggs and chopped garlic
mel honey
melancia watermelon
melão melon, usually a honeydew

melon
~ **com vinho do Porto** with port wine
merengue meringue
mero red grouper (fish)
mexilhão mussel
mexerica tangerine
migas meat or fish fried in olive-oil with onions and garlic and thickened with bread
mil-folhas flaky pastry with cream filling (US napoleon)
milho doce sweet-corn
mioleira brains
miolos brains
~ **mexidos com ovos** of lamb fried and served with scrambled eggs
misto mixed
miúdos de galinha chicken giblets
mocotós stewed calves' trotters (US feet), usually served with *farofa* and a hot-pepper sauce
molho sauce
~ **branco** white
~ **de manteiga** with butter and lemon
~ **tártaro** mayonnaise with chopped gherkins, chives, capers, olives
~ **verde** olive-oil and vinegar with chopped spinach, parsley and coriander leaves
com ~ with
sem ~ without
moqueca de peixe fish cooked in an earthenware casserole with coconut milk, palm-oil, coriander leaves, ginger and ground shrimps
morango strawberry
~ **silvestre** wild
morcela black pudding, blood sausage
mortadela mortadella (US Bologna sausage)
mostarda mustard
nabiça turnip greens
nabo turnip
nata(s) fresh cream
~ **batida(s)** whipped
(ao) natural plain, without dressing, sauce, stuffing etc.
nêspera medlar, a small apple-like fruit eaten when over-ripe
noz nut, walnut
~ **moscada** nutmeg
óleo oil
~ **de amendoim** peanut oil
omeleta omelette
~ **simples** plain
osso bone
ostras oysters
~ **recheadas** oystershells stuffed with oysters, onions, garlic, breadcrumbs, egg yolk, lemon juice, spice and then oven-browned
ouriço-do-mar sea-urchin
ovas fish roe
ovos eggs
~ **cozidos** hard-boiled
~ **escalfados** poached
~ **estrelados** fried, sunny side up
~ **mexidos** scrambled
~ **moles** beaten egg yolks cooked in syrup
~ **quentes** soft-boiled
~ **verdes** stuffed with hard-boiled yolks mixed with onions flavoured with vinegar and deep-fried in olive-oil
paçoca 1) roast *carne de sol* ground with cassava root and served with sliced bananas 2) dessert made with roast peanuts crushed with

PORTUGUESE

sweetened cassavaroot meal
paio spicy cured pork fillet presented in a casing
~ **com ervilhas** simmered with peas and chopped onions
palmito palm heart
panado breaded
pão bread
~ **de centeio** rye
~ **de forma** white, for toast
pão-de-ló tea bread (US coffee cake)
pãozinho roll
papos de anjo baked egg yolks topped with syrup
pargo red porgy (fish)
passa (de uva) raisin, sultana
(bem) passado well done
(mal) passado medium
(muito mal) passado rare
pastel usually a type of pie
~ **de bacalhau** deep-fried croquette of dried cod and mashed potatoes flavoured with eggs and parsley
~ **de Belém/de nata** custard pie
~ **folhado** flaky pastry
~ **de massa tenra** soft crust-pastry pie filled with minced meat
~ **de Santa Clara** tartlet with almond-paste filling
~ **de Tentúgal** flaky pastry filled with beaten eggs cooked in syrup
pastelão de palmito e camarão shrimp and palm-heart pie
pato duck
~ **estufado** braised in white wine with onions, parsley and bay leaf
~ **ao tucupi** roasted, braised with carrots and *jambu* in cassava-root juice and served with fruit
pé de moleque peanut brittle
pé de porco pig's trotters (US feet)
peito breast
peixe fish
~**-espada** cutlass fish, scabbard fish
~**-galo** 1) moonfish 2) John Dory
~ **da horta** runner beans deep-fried in batter
pepino cucumber
pequeno almoço breakfast
pêra pear
perca perch
perceve barnacle
perdiz partridge
~ **à caçador(a)** simmered with carrots, onions, white wine, herbs and often tomatoes
~ **com molho de vilão** poached and served with a cold sauce of olive-oil, vinegar, onions, garlic and chopped parsley
perna leg
pernil ham
pêro variety of eating apple
peru turkey
pescada whiting
~ **cozida com todos** poached and served with boiled potatoes and runner beans
pescadinhas de rabo na boca plate of whitings fried whole
pêssego peach
pevide 1) pip (US seed) 2) salted pumpkin pip (US seed)
picado de carne minced meat
picante hot, spicy, highly seasoned
pimenta peppercorn
piment(ã)o sweet pepper
pinhão pine kernel

pinhoada pine-kernel brittle
piripiri tiny hot peppers (preserved in olive-oil)
polvo octopus
pombo pigeon
~ **estufado** braised with bacon, onions and white wine, served with fried bread
porco pork
posta slice of fish or meat
prato 1) plate 2) dish
~ **do dia** speciality of the day
preço price
prego small steak often served in a roll
presunto 1) cured ham 2) cooked (US boiled) ham (Brazil)
~ **cru** dried ham
pudim pudding
~ **de bacalhau** dried-cod loaf, served with tomato sauce
~ **flan** caramel custard
~ **à portuguesa** custard flavoured with brandy and raisins
puré puree
~ **de batata** mashed potatoes
queijada small cottage-cheese tart
~ **de Sintra** flavoured with cinnamon
queijinhos do céu marzipan balls rolled in sugar
queijo cheese
~ **de Azeitão** soft or hard and made with ewe's milk
~ **cabreiro** made with goat's milk
~ **cardiga** made with goat's and ewe's milk
~ **catupiri** small, white cream cheese
~ **flamengo** Dutch type of cheese
~ **da ilha** made in the Azores and not unlike Cheddar
~ **de Minas** plain
~ **Prata** mild and yellow
~ **rabaçal** made with goat's milk
~ **requeijão** type of cottage cheese
~ **São Jorge** not unlike Cheddar
~ **da Serra** made with ewe's milk
quente hot
~ **e frio** chocolate-nut (US hot fudge) sundae
quiabo okra (GB lady's finger)
quindim sweet made with eggs and grated coconut
rabanada slice of bread dipped into egg batter and sprinkled with sugar (US french toast)
rabanete radish
raia skate
rainha-cláudia greengage plum
recheado stuffed
recheio stuffing, forcemeat
refeição meal
~ **ligeira** snack
refogado onions fried in olive-oil (base of a stew)
repolho green cabbage
rins kidneys
rissol fritter with minced meat or fish
robalo sea-bass
rodela round slice
rojões à alentejana pork cubes fried with baby clams, diced potatoes and onions
rojões à moda do Minho pork cubes marinated in dry white wine with garlic and paprika, fried and mixed with boiled blood cubes
rolo de carne picada meatloaf

rolos de couve lombarda savoy-cabbage leaves stuffed with minced or sausage meat
romã pomegranate
rosca ring-shaped white bread
ruivo red gurnard (fish)
sal salt
salada salad
~ **de fruta** fruit
~ **mista** mixed
~ **de pimentos assados** made with grilled sweet peppers
~ **russa** cooked, diced vegetables in mayonnaise
salgado 1), salty 2) salted
salmão salmon
~ **fumado** smoked
salmonete surmullet
~ **grelhado com molho de manteiga** grilled and served with melted butter, chopped parsley and lemon
salsa parsley
salsicha sausage
salva sage
sande, sanduíche sandwich
santola spider-crab
~ **ao natural** boiled in salted water with lemon
~ **recheada** stuffed with its own flesh, generally seasoned with mustard, curry powder, lemon and white wine
sarda mackerel
sardinha sardine
ável shad
seco 1) dry 2) dried
sêmola semolina
sericá alentejano cinnamon soufflé
serviço incluído service included
siri crab
sobremesa dessert
solha plaice
sonho type of doughnut
sopa soup
~ **de agriões** with watercress and potatoes
~ **de coentros** with coriander leaves, bread, poached eggs, olive-oil and garlic
~ **do dia** of the day
~ **de feijão** with kidney beans, cabbage, carrots and rice
~ **de hortaliça** with fresh vegetables
~ **juliana** with shredded vegetables
~ **de rabo de boi** oxtail
~ **de tomate à alentejana** with tomatoes, onions and poached eggs
~ **transmontana** with vegetables, ham, bacon and slices of bread
sorvete ice-cream
~ **com água** water-ice (US sherbet)
sururu type of cockle
suspiro meringue
tainha grey mullet (fish)
tâmara date
tangerina tangerine
tempero seasoning
tenro tender
tigelada dessert of eggs beaten with milk and cinnamon, baked in an earthenware bowl
toranja grapefruit
torrada toast
torrão de ovos marzipan sweet
torta swiss roll
~ **de Viana** filled with lemon curd
tosta mista toasted ham-and-cheese sandwich

toucinho bacon
~ **do céu** kind of marzipan pudding
tornedó round cut of prime beef
tremoço salted lupine seed
tripas tripe (usually minced)
~ **à moda do Porto** cooked with assorted pork products, navy beans and pieces of chicken; served with rice
trouxa de vitela veal olive (US veal bird)
trouxas de ovos egg yolks poached in sweetened water and topped with syrup
trufa truffle
truta trout
tutano marrow
tutu à mineira puree of black beans mixed with cassava-root meal and served with cabbage and fried bacon
uva grape
~ **moscatel** muscat
vaca beef
vagens runner beans (US green beans)
variado assorted
vatapá fish and shrimp puree flavoured with coconut milk and palm-oil and served with a peanut-and-cashew sauce
vieira scallop
vinagre vinegar
vitela veal
ximxim de galinha chicken braised in palm-oil and served with a sauce of ground shrimp, sweet peppers, onions, peanuts and ginger

Drink

adocicado slightly sweet
água water
~ **de coco** coconut milk
~**-pé** weak wine, made from a base of watered-down wine draff
~ **tónica** tonic
água mineral mineral water
~ **com gás/gaseificada** fizzy (US carbonated)
~ **sem gás** still
aguardente spirit distilled from vegetable matter or fruit
~ **bagaceira** spirit distilled from grape husks
~ **de figo** spirit distilled from figs
~ **de medronho** spirit distilled from arbutus berries
~ **velha** well-aged brandy
Antiqua Portuguese grape brandy, aged
aperitivo aperitif
batida long drink (US highball) of rum, sugar and fruit juice, usually lemon juice
batido milk-shake flavoured with a scoop of ice-cream
bebida drink
~ **sem álcool/não alcoólica** soft drink
~ **espirituosa** spirits

bica black coffee
Borges Portuguese grape brandy, aged
branco white
Bucelas region north of Lisbon which produces the famous dry, straw-coloured *Bucelas* wine
cacau cocoa
cachaça white rum
café coffee
~ **sem cafeína** caffeine-free
~ **duplo** large cup of coffee
~ **frio** iced coffee
~ **com leite** white coffee
~ **puro** genuine coffee
cafezinho strong black coffee
caipirinha white rum served with lemon juice, ice cubes and a slice of lime or lemon
caldo de cana sugar-cane juice
caneca pint-size beer mug
Carcavelos region west of Lisbon producing good fortified wines
carioca small weak coffee
(água de) Castelo fizzy (US carbonated) mineral water
cerveja 1) beer 2) lager
~ **em garrafa** bottled
~ **imperial** draught (US draft)
~ **preta** stout
chá tea
~ **com leite** with milk
~ **com limão** with lemon
~ **de limão** made from an infusion of lemon peel
~ **maté** made from an infusion of the maté-tree leaf and usually served chilled with a slice of lemon
clarete light red wine
Colares region to the north-west of Lisbon, producing good quality red and white wine; the reds have good colour and body and are rich in tanning; the whites have a strong aromatic flavour
conhaque cognac, French brandy
~ **espanhol** Spanish brandy
Constantino Portuguese brandy, aged
copo glass
Cuba livre rum and Coke
Dão some of the best wines of Portugal, normally drunk quite young, come from this region, in the south-east of Oporto; the reds are strong and of good flavour, the whites dry and fruity
doce sweet
meio- ~ medium-sweet (usually in reference to sparkling wine)
Douro the upper part of this valley, east of Oporto produces the renowned port wine (see *Porto*) and pleasant table wines
espumante 1) sparkling 2) sparkling wine
Favaios dessert wine similar to muscatel
fino draught (US draft) beer
fresco fresh, chilled
frio cold
galão white coffee served in a big glass
garoto white coffee served in a small cup
garrafa bottle
meia-~ half bottle
gasosa fizzy (US carbonated) soft drink
gelado iced
gelo ice, ice cubes
com ~ with ice
sem ~ without ice

genebra Dutch gin, usually produced under licence

gim gin

ginjinha spirit distilled from morello cherries

girafa draught (US draft) beer served in a fluted glass

guaraná soft drink flavoured with *guaraná,* a very sweet tropical fruit

jarro carafe

jeropiga locally made fortified wine (see also *vinho abafado*)

laranjada orangeade

leite milk

~ **com chocolate** chocolate drink

licor liqueur

limonada type of lemon squash (US lemon drink)

Madeira excellent red and white aperitif and dessert wines are produced on this island; *Sercial* is the driest, and this, with *Verdelho* (medium-dry), can be drunk as an aperitif; *Boal* (or *Bual*) is smoky and less sweet than the rich dark-amber *Malmsey* (or *Malvásia*), which is best served for dessert at room temperature

maduro mature (wine produced from ripe grapes, as opposed to "green wine"; see *Minho*)

(suco/sumo de) maracujá passion-fruit (juice)

Mateus rosé famous rosé wine from the district of Trás-os-Montes

mazagrã chilled black coffee served on the rocks with sugar and a slice of lemon

Minho area in the north-west of Portugal where the famous young *vinho verde,* or "green wine", is produced; it is made from unripened grapes; faintly sparkling and acid in taste, very refreshing and with low alcohol content; the whites are more popular than the reds, both should be drunk young and chilled

moscatel 1) muscat grape 2) muscatel, a rich, aromatic dessert wine

pinga 1) wine 2) crude white rum (Brazil)

(vinho do) Porto this famous fortified wine from the upper Douro valley, east of Oporto, is classified by *vintage* and *blend;* the *vintage* ports, only made in exceptional years (indicated on the label), are bottled at least two years after harvesting and then stored to age for 10 to 20 years or more, while the *blended* ports, a subtle mixture of the harvests of different years, are kept in barrels for a minimum of 5 years; there are two types of *blended* ports: the younger *Ruby* variety is full-coloured, full-bodied, and the *Tawny* amber-coloured and delicate; moreover, less sweet, aromatic white ports are also available and are suitable as an aperitif

quente hot

região demarcada controlled and classified wine-producing area, e.g. *Bucelas, Colares, Dão, Douro, Minho,* etc.

seco dry

extra-~ extra-dry

meio-~ medium-dry

Setubal region south of Lisbon noted for its famous dessert wines *(moscatel)* and some good red and rosé table wines
sidra cider
simples neat (US straight)
suco/sumo fruit or vegetable juice
taça long-stemmed glass, cup
tinto red
uísque whisky
vermute vermouth
vinho wine
~ **abafado** locally made fortified wine (see also *jeropiga*)
~ **adamado** sweet wine
~ **da casa** house or carafe wine
~ **espumante natural** sparkling wine produced in a similar fashion to French champagne and available in extra-dry, dry and medium-dry blends
~ **generoso** well-aged and fortified wine, high in alcohol content
~ **licoroso** naturally sweet wine, high in alcohol content e.g. *Moscatel de Setúbal*
~ **da Madeira** Madeira wine (see *Madeira*)
~ **do Porto** port wine (see *Porto*)
~ **da região** local wine
~ **verde** "green wine" (see *Minho*)
xerez sherry

Russian

Guide to pronunciation

Each Russian word in the following menu reader is followed by a simplified transliteration in our own alphabet to help you to recognize and pronounce the word. However, if you're even more interested in speaking the language, you'll want to obtain a copy of RUSSIAN phrase book from your favourite bookshop. This Berlitz phrase book uses imitated pronunciation which is read as if it were English.

Letter	Approximate pronunciation	Symbol
Vowels		
а	between the **a** in c**a**t and the **ar** in c**ar**t	a
е	like **ye** in **ye**t	ye
ё	like **yo** in **yo**nder	yo
и	like **ee** in s**ee**	i
й	like **y** in ga**y** or bo**y**	y
о	like **o** in h**o**t	o
у	like **oo** in b**oo**t	u
ы	similar to **i** in h**i**t	i

э	like **e** in m**e**t	e
ю	like **u** in d**u**ke	yu
я	like **ya** in **ya**rd	ya

Consonants

б	like **b** in **b**it	b
в	like **v** in **v**ine	v
г	like **g** in **g**o	g
д	like **d** in **d**o	d
ж	like **s** in plea**s**ure	zh
з	like **z** in **z**oo	z
к	like **k** in **k**itten	k
л	like **l** in **l**ose	l
м	like **m** in **m**y	m
н	like **n** in **n**ot	n
п	like **p** in **p**ot	p
р	like **r** in **r**un	r
с	like **s** in **s**ee	s
т	like **t** in **t**ip	t
ф	like **f** in **f**ace	f
х	like **ch** in Scottish lo**ch**	kh
ц	like **ts** in si**ts**	ts
ч	like **ch** in **ch**ip	ch
ш	like **sh** in **sh**ut	sh
щ	like **sh** followed by **ch**	shch

Other letters

ь gives a "soft" pronunciation to the preceding consonant. A similar effect can be produced by pronouncing **y** as in **y**et—but very, very short—after the consonant. In our transliteration we'll show this with an apostrophe (') after the soft consonant.

ъ is sometimes used between two parts of a compound word when the second part begins with **я, ю** or **е** to show that the pronunciation of the word should incorporate a clear separation of the two parts.

The alphabet

Here are the characters which comprise the Russian alphabet. The column at left shows the printed capital and small letters, while written letters are shown in the center column. At right you'll find the corresponding letters in our simplified transliteration.

А а	*А а*	a
Б б	*Б б*	b
В в	*В в*	v
Г г	*Г г*	g
Д д	*Д д*	d
Е е	*Е е*	ye
Ё ё	*Ё ё*	yo
Ж ж	*Ж ж*	zh
З з	*З з*	z
И и	*И и*	i
Й й	*Й й*	y
К к	*К к*	k
Л л	*Л л*	l
М м	*М м*	m
Н н	*Н н*	n
О о	*О о*	o
П п	*П п*	p
Р р	*Р р*	r
С с	*С с*	s
Т т	*Т т*	t
У у	*У у*	u
Ф ф	*Ф ф*	f
Х х	*Х х*	kh
Ц ц	*Ц ц*	ts
Ч ч	*Ч ч*	ch
Ш ш	*Ш ш*	sh
Щ щ	*Щ щ*	shch
Ъ ъ	*ъ*	(mute)
Ы ы	*ы*	i
Ь ь	*ь*	'
Э э	*Э э*	e
Ю ю	*Ю ю*	yu
Я я	*Я я*	ya

Some useful expressions

Hungry

I'm hungry/I'm thirsty.	**Я голоден/ Я хочу пить.**	ya golodyen/ ya khochu pit'
Can you recommend a good restaurant?	**Не можете ли порекомендовать, хороший ресторан?**	nye mozhetye li poryekomyendovat' khoroshiy ryestoran
Are there any good, cheap restaurants around here?	**Нет ли хорошего и недорогого ресторана поблизости?**	nyet li khoroshego i nyedorogogo ryestorana poblizosti
I'd like to reserve a table for ... people.	**Я хотел бы заказать столик на...**	ya khotyel bi zakazat' stolik na...
We'll come at ... o'clock.	**Мы придём в...**	mi pridyom v...

Asking

Good evening. I'd like a table for ... people.	**Добрый вечер. Будьте добры, столик на...**	dobriy vyechyer. bud'tye dobri stolik na...
Could we have a table...?	**Пожалуйста столик...**	pozhaluysta stolik
in the corner	**в углу**	v uglu
by the window	**у окна**	u okna
outside	**снаружи**	snaruzhi
on the terrace	**на террасе**	na tyerrasye
May I please have the menu?	**Будьте добры, меню.**	bud'tye dobri myenyu
What's this?	**Что это такое?**	chto eto takoye
Do you have...?	**Есть ли у вас...?**	yest' li u vas
a set menu	**комплексные обеды**	komplyeksniye obyedi
local dishes	**местные блюда**	myestniye blyuda
a children's menu	**детское меню**	dyetskoye myenyu
Waiter/Waitress!	**Официант/ Официантка!**	ofitsiant/ofitsiantka
What do you recommend?	**Что вы посоветуете?**	chto vi posovyetuyetye
Could I have (a/an)... please?	**Принесите мне, пожалуйста...**	prinyesitye mnye pozhaluysta
ashtray	**пепельницу**	pyepyel'nitsu
another chair	**ещё один стул**	yeshchyo odin stul

finger bowl	**воды сполоснуть пальцы**	vodi spolosnut' pal'tsi
fork	**вилку**	vilku
glass	**стакан**	stakan
knife	**нож**	nozh
napkin	**салфетку**	salfyetku
plate	**тарелку**	taryelku
serviette	**салфетку**	salfyetky
spoon	**ложку**	lozhku
toothpick	**зубочистку**	zubochistku

Ordering

I'd like a/an/some…	**Принесите, пожалуйста…**	prinyesitye pozhaluysta
aperitif	**аперитив**	apyeritiv
appetizer	**закуску**	zakusku
beer	**пива**	piva
bread	**хлеба**	khlyeba
butter	**масла**	masla
cheese	**сыру**	siru
chips	**картофель «фри»**	kartofyel' fri
coffee	**кофе**	kofye
dessert	**третье**	tryet'ye
fish	**рыбу**	ribu
french fries	**картофель «фри»**	kartofyel' fri
fruit	**фруктов**	fruktov
game	**дичи**	dichi
green salad	**салат**	salat
ice-cream	**мороженого**	morozhenogo
ketchup	**томатный соус**	tomatniy sous
lemon	**лимон**	limon
meat	**мясо**	myaso
mineral water	**минеральной воды**	minyeral'noy vodi
milk	**молока**	moloka
mustard	**горчицы**	gorchitsi
noodles	**лапшу**	lapshu
oil	**растительного масла**	rastityel'nogo masla
olive oil	**прованского масла**	provanskogo masla
pepper	**перцу**	pyertsu
potatoes	**картошки**	kartoshki
poultry	**птицу**	ptitsu
rice	**рису**	risu
rolls	**булочек**	bulochyek
saccharin	**сахарин**	sakharin
salad	**салат**	salat
salt	**соли**	soli

sandwich	**бутерброд**	butyerbrod
seasoning	**приправу**	pripravu
soup	**супу**	supu
sugar	**сахару**	sakharu
tea	**чаю**	chayu
vegetables	**овощей**	ovoshchyey
vinegar	**уксусу**	uksusu
(iced) water	**воды (со льдом)**	vodi (so l'dom)
wine	**вина**	vina

ПРИЯТНОГО АППЕТИТА!
(priyatnogo apyetita)
ENJOY YOUR MEAL!

baked (of fish)	**печёную**	pyechyonuyu
baked (of meat)	**жареное**	zharyenoye
baked in parchment	**запеченное**	zapyechyennoye
boiled	**варёное**	varyonoye
braised	**тушёное**	tushonoye
cured	**копчёное/солёное/ сушёное**	kopchyonoye/solyonoye/ sushonoye
fried (of fish)	**жареную**	zharyenuyu
fried (of meat)	**жареное**	zharyenoye
grilled (of fish)	**жареное на рашпере**	zharyenoye na rashpyerye
grilled (of meat)	**жареное на рашпере**	zharyenoye na rashpyerye
marinated	**маринованое**	marinovanoye
poached	**отварное**	otvarnoye
roasted	**жареное**	zharyenoye
sautéed	**зажаренное в малом количестве жира**	zazharyennoye v malom kolichyestvye zhira
smoked	**копчёный**	kopchyoniy
steamed	**паровой**	parovoy
stewed (of fish)	**тушёную**	tushonuyu
stewed (of meat)	**тушёное**	tushonoye
underdone (rare)	**слегка поджаренное**	slyegka podzharyennoye
medium	**средне прожаренное**	sryednye prozharyennoye
well-done	**хорошо прожаренное**	khorosho prozharyennoye

ЗА ВАШЕ ЗДОРОВЬЕ!
(za vashe zdorov'ye)
CHEERS!

RUSSIAN

glass	**стакан**	stakan
bottle	**бутылка**	butilka
red	**красное**	krasnoye
white	**белое**	byeloye
rosé	**розовое**	rozovoye
very dry	**очень сухое**	ochyen' sukhoye
dry	**сухое**	sukhoye
sweet	**сладкое**	sladkoye
light	**лёгкое**	lyogkoye
full-bodied	**крепкое**	kryepkoye
sparkling	**шипучее**	shipuchyeye
neat (straight)	**неразбавленное**	nyerazbavlyennoye
on the rocks	**со льдом**	so l'dom

The bill

I'd like to pay.	**Счёт, пожалуйста.**	schyot, pozhaluysta
We'd like to pay separately.	**Мы будем платить порознь.**	mi budyem platit' porozn'
You've made a mistake in this bill, I think.	**Мне кажется, вы ошиблись в счёте.**	mnye kazhetsya vi oshiblis' v schyotye
What's this amount for?	**А это за что?**	a eto za chto
Is service included?	**Чаевые включены?**	chayeviye vklyuchyeni
Is everything included?	**Всё включено?**	vsyo vklyuchyeno
Do you accept traveller's cheques?	**Берёте ли вы дорожные чеки?**	byeryotye li vi dorozhniye chyeki
Thank you. This is for you.	**Спасибо, это вам.**	spasibo eto vam
Keep the change.	**Сдачу оставьте себе.**	sdachu ostav'tye syebye
That was a very good meal.	**Было очень вкусно.**	bilo ochyen' vkusno
We enjoyed it, thank you.	**Нам понравилось, спасибо.**	nam ponravilos' spasibo

Complaints

That's not what I ordered. I asked for…	**Я не это заказывал. Я заказал…**	ya nye eto zakazival ya zakazal
May I change this?	**Дайте мне, пожалуйста, что-нибудь другое.**	daytye mnye pozhaluysta chto nibud' drugoye

The meat is...	**Мясо...**	myaso
overdone underdone too rare too tough	**пережарено** **недожарено** **сырое** **жёсткое**	pyeryezharyeno nyedozharyeno siroye zhostkoye
This is too...	**Это слишком...**	eto slishkom
bitter/salty/sweet	**горько/солоно/сладко**	gor'ko/solono/sladko
The food is cold.	**Еда холодная.**	yeda kholodnaya
This isn't fresh.	**Это не свежее.**	eto nye svyezheye
What's taking you so long?	**Почему вы так долго не подаёте?**	pochyemu vi tak dolgo nye podayotye
Where are our drinks?	**А напитки?**	a napitki
This isn't clean.	**Это грязно.**	eto gryazno
Would you ask the head waiter to come over?	**Позовите, пожалуйста-мэтр д'отеля.**	pozovitye pozhaluysta metr dotyelya

RUSSIAN

Numbers

1	**один**	odin
2	**два**	dva
3	**три**	tri
4	**четыре**	chyetirye
5	**пять**	pyat'
6	**шесть**	shest'
7	**семь**	syem'
8	**восемь**	vosyem'
9	**девять**	dyevyat'
10	**десять**	dyesyat'
11	**одиннадцать**	odinnadtsat'
12	**двенадцать**	dvyenadtsat'
13	**тринадцать**	trinadtsat'
14	**четырнадцать**	chyetirnadtsat'
15	**пятнадцать**	pyatnadtsat'
16	**шестнадцать**	shestnadtsat'
17	**семнадцать**	syemnadtsat'
18	**восемнадцать**	vosyemnadtsat'
19	**девятнадцать**	dyevyatnadtsat'
20	**двадцать**	dvadtsat'

Food

абрикосы *(abrikosi)* apricots
азу *(azu)* slivered beef braised with tomatoes, onions and gherkins (Tartar Republic)
айва *(ayva)* quince
ананас *(ananas)* pineapple
антоновка *(antonovka)* one of the best varieties of winter apples; very sour, strong aroma
антрекот *(antryekot)* rib steak
анчоусы *(anchousi)* anchovies
 ~ **в масле** *(v maslye)* in oil
арбуз *(arbuz)* watermelon
ассорти *(assorti)* assorted appetizers
 ~ **рыбное** *(ribnoye)* assorted fish appetizers
 ~ **мясное** *(myasnoye)* cold cuts
баба *(baba)* tall moulded cake with hole in centre
 ~ **ромовая** *(romovaya)* sponge cake steeped in rum
баклажанная икра *(baklazhannaya ikra)* "eggplant caviar"; purée of cooked aubergines (eggplants), onions, tomatoes, olive oil and lemon juice
баклажаны *(baklazhani)* aubergine (eggplant)
 ~ **фаршированные** *(farshirovanyie)* stuffed with meat, vegetables and/or rice
 ~ **тушёные в сметане** *(tushonyie v smyetanye)* stewed in sour cream
балык *(balik)* dried back of sturgeon or similar fish
банан *(banan)* banana
баранина *(baranina)* mutton
 ~ **жареная** *(zharyenaya)* fried
 ~ **отварная в томатном соусе с яблоками** *(otvarnaya v tomatnom sousye s yablokami)* casserole of mutton, tomatoes and apples
 ~ **тушёная** *(tushonaya)* braised
 плов из ~ы *(plov iz ~i)* rice and mutton casserole
 поджарка из ~ы *(podzharka iz ~i)* minced mutton fried with onions and braised with sour cream
 рагу из ~ы *(ragu iz ~i)*

RUSSIAN

stew with vegetables

бастурма *(basturma)* marinated and grilled chunks of mutton or beef (Armenia, Georgia)

безе *(byezye)* meringue

бекас *(byekas)* snipe

белуга *(byeluga)* white sturgeon; largest type of sturgeon; caviar from this sturgeon is considered fine; generally a greyish fish

беляши *(byelyashi)* fried meat pasties

беф-строганов *(byef-stroganov)* beef Stroganoff: sautéed beef with mushrooms and onions in sour cream sauce

~ **с картофелем фри** *(s kartofyelyem fri)* with chips (US french fries)

бешбармак *(byeshbarmak)* "five fingers"; thinly sliced meat with noodles, served with a bowl of the meat broth (Kazakstan)

бисквит *(biskvit)* cake, biscuits (US cookies)

бифштекс *(bifshtyeks)* beefsteak

~ **натуральный** *(natural'niy)* grilled

~ **рубленый** *(rublyeniy)* beefburger

~ **с яйцом** *(s yaytsom)* grilled, topped with a fried egg

блинчики *(blinchiki)* thin, unleavened pancakes

~ **с вареньем** *(s varyen'yem)* filled with jam

~ **с мясом** *(s myasom)* filled with minced meat

~ **со сметаной** *(so smyetanoy)* filled with sour cream

~ **с творогом** *(s tvorogom)* filled with cottage cheese

блины *(blini)* yeast buckwheat pancakes

~ **с икрой** *(s ikroy)* with caviar

~ **со сметаной** *(so smyetanoy)* served with sour cream

~ **с сёмгой** *(s syomgoy)* served with smoked salmon

блюдо *(blyudo)* dish, course

второе ~ *(vtoroye)* main course

первое ~ *(pyervoye)* first course

сладкое ~ *(sladkoye)* dessert

фирменное ~ *(firmyennoye)* speciality of the restaurant

бобы *(bobi)* butter beans (US navy beans)

турецкие ~ *(turyetskiye)* kidney beans

бозбаш *(bozbash)* mutton soup with peas (Azerbaijan)

борщ *(borshch)* borscht; beetroot soup to which other vegetables and meat can be added, served with sour cream

~ **зелёный** *(zyelyoniy)* with pork, sorrel, eggs, seasoning

~ **киевский** *(kiyevskiy)*

with beef, mutton, vegetables and herbs
~ **московский** *(moskovskiy)* with beef, vegetables, tomato purée, bacon
~ **полтавский** *(poltavskiy)* with goose or chicken, vegetables, dill
~ **флотский** *(flotskiy)* with bacon or ham bones, vegetables, tomato purée
~ **украинский** *(ukrainskiy)* with beef, cabbage, potato, carrot, tomato, red and green pepper, herbs

ботвинья *(botvin'ya)* chilled soup made with *kvass*, beet greens, onions and fish

брынза *(brinza)* matured cheese made from ewe's milk

брюква *(bryukva)* rutabaga

бублики *(bubliki)* bagel; a hard, glazed doughnut-shaped roll topped with poppy seeds

буженина *(buzhenina)* boiled pork, sliced and served cold

булочка *(bulochka)* roll, bun
~ **ванильная** *(vanil'naya)* vanilla-flavoured
~ **с изюмом** *(s izyumom)* raisin bun
~ **с маком** *(s makom)* poppy-seed roll
~ **с марципаном** *(s martsipanom)* with marzipan
~ **с повидлом** *(s povidlom)* jam doughnut
~ **сдобная** *(sdobnaya)* butter roll

бульон *(bul'on)* broth, consommé
~ **из говядины с макаронами** *(iz govyadini s makaronami)* beef and noodle soup
~ **куриный с гренками** *(kuriniy s gryenkami)* chicken consommé with sippets (croutons)
~ **с пирожком** *(s pirozhkom)* served with meat pasties
~ **с фрикадельками** *(s frikadyel'kami)* with meat dumplings

бутерброд *(butyerbrod)* sandwich
~ **с ветчиной** *(s vyetchinoy)* ham
~ **с икрой** *(s ikroy)* caviar
~ **с кильками** *(s kil'kami)* Norwegian sardines
~ **с колбасой** *(s kolbasoy)* sausage
~ **с маслом и сыром** *(s maslom i sirom)* cheese and butter
~ **с огурцами, помидорами и яйцом** *(s ogurtsami, pomidorami i yaytsom)* cucumber, tomato and egg
~ **с паштетом** *(s pashtyetom)* liver pâté
~ **с сардинами** *(s sardinami)* sardine
~ **с сельдью** *(s syel'd'yu)* herring
~ **с сёмгой** *(s syomgoy)* salmon
~ **со шпротами** *(so shpro-*

tami) sprats, small herring
ваниль *(vanil')* vanilla
вареники *(varyeniki)* poached pasties, made out of flour and cottage cheese thickened with egg yolk
~ **с квашеной капустой и грибами** *(s kvashenoy kapustoy i gribami)* with sauerkraut and mushroom filling
~ **ленивые** *(lyenivyie)* "lazy"; no filling
~ **с мясом** *(s myasom)* with meat filling
~ **с творогом** *(s tvorogom)* with cottage cheese filling
~ **с ягодами** *(s yagodami)* with berry filling
варёный *(varyoniy)* boiled
варенье *(varyen'ye)* jam
~ **вишнёвое** *(vishnyovoye)* cherry
~ **малиновое** *(malinovoye)* raspberry
ватрушка *(vatruchka)* cottage-cheese tartlets
~ **с повидлом** *(s povidlom)* with jam topping
вафля *(vaflya)* waffle
вермишель *(vyermishel')* thin noodles
(на) вертел(е) *([na] vyertyel [ye])* cooked on a skewer
ветчина *(vyechina)* ham
~ **жареная с горчицей и луком** *(zharyenaya s gorchitsey i lukom)* fried with onions, served with mustard
~ **с хреном** *(s khryenom)* served cold with horse-radish sauce
винегрет *(vinyegryet)* vegetable salad (of potato, beetroot, etc.) served with an oil and vinegar dressing
виноград *(vinograd)* grapes
вишня *(vishnya)* morello cherries
вобла *(vobla)* roach (a variety of freshwater sunfish)
~ **вяленая** *(vyalyenaya)* dried in the open air
~ **сушёная** *(sushonaya)* dried
второе (блюдо) *(vtoroye [blyudo])* main course with vegetables
вымя отварное *(vimya otvarnoye)* cow's udder, boiled and served with onions and tomato sauce
вяленый *(vyalyeniy)* dried in the open air
галушки *(galushki)* fluffy dumpling served with sour cream and onions (Ukraine)
гарнир *(garnir)* garnish
с ~ом *(s ~om)* garnished
глазировка *(glazirovka)* icing
говядина *(govyadina)* beef
~ **отварная с молочным соусом** *(otvarnaya s molochnim sousom)* boiled, served with a white sauce
~ **тушёная с кореньями** *(tushonaya s koryen'yami)* braised with aromatic vegetables
~ **тушёная со сметаной** *(tushonaya so smyetanoy)*

braised with sour cream

~ **тушёная с грибами** *(tushonaya s gribami)* braised with mushrooms

~ **тушёная с черносливом** *(tushonaya s chernoslivom)* braised with prunes

головизна *(golovizna)* heads of sturgeon and similar fish, used in making soup or gelatine

голубцы *(golubtsi)* stuffed cabbage roll

горошек *(goroshek)* peas

~ **зелёный** *(zyelyoniy)* green peas

горчица *(gorchitsa)* mustard

горячий *(goryachiy)* hot

грибы *(gribi)* mushrooms

~ **белые** *(byeliye)* boletus

~ **маринованные** *(marinovanniye)* marinated

~ **в сметане** *(v smyetanye)* sliced mushrooms fried with onions, served with sour cream

~ **солёные** *(solyoniye)* salted

~ **сушёные** *(sushoniye)* dried

грудинка *(grudinka)* brisket

~ **баранья** *(baran'ya)* of mutton

~ **свиная** *(svinaya)* of pork

груша *(grusha)* pear

гуляш *(gulyash)* goulash

гусь *(gus')* goose

~ **жареный с яблоками** *(zharyeniy s yablokami)* stuffed with apples, roasted

десерт *(dyesyert)* dessert

дичь *(dich')* game, venison

долма *(dolma)* grape leaves stuffed with minced mutton (Caucasia)

домашний *(domashniy)* home-made

домашняя птица *(domashnyaya ptitsa)* fowl

дрожжи *(drozhzhi)* yeast

дыня *(dinya)* melon

ежевика *(yezhevika)* blackberries

жареный *(zharyeniy)* fried, roasted

жаркое *(zharkoye)* casserole of beef with tomatoes, potatoes and carrots

~ **из свинины со сливами** *(iz svinini so slivami)* roast pork with plums

желе *(zhelye)* fruit jam

~ **лимонное** *(limonnoye)* lemon

~ **из чёрной и красной смородины** *(iz chyornoy i krasnoy smorodini)* black- and redcurrant

~ **яблочное** *(yablochnoye)* apple

жир *(zhir)* fat, lard

жирный *(zhirniy)* fat (adj)

завтрак *(zavtrak)* breakfast

закуски *(zakuski)* appetizers, often very abundant and varied, usually accompanied by vodka

~ **горячие** *(goryachiye)* hot

~ **мясные** *(myasniye)* meat

~ **рыбные** *(ribniye)* fish

~ **холодные** *(kholodniye)*

cold appetizers

заяц *(zayats)* hare

~ **тушёный в сметане** *(tushoniy v smyetanye)* jugged and braised in sour cream

~ **шпигованный** *(shpigovanniy)* jugged, larded and roasted

зразы *(zrazi)* beef rolls made of slices of beef stuffed with a mixture of breadcrumbs, mushrooms, parsley and dill

изюм *(izyum)* raisins

икра *(ikra)*

1) caviar (sturgeon or salmon roe); three varieties of sturgeon give caviar: *osetr*, *beluga*, which can weigh up to 2000 lbs. and gives a large-grained caviar, and *sevryuga*, yielding small-grained caviar

~ **зернистая** *(zyernistaya)* soft grained, fresh or lightly salted

~ **кетовая** *(kyetovaya)* red, prepared from eggs of *kyeta*, a Siberian salmon

~ **красная** *(krasnaya)* red, prepared from salmon eggs

~ **малосольная** *(malosol'naya)* lightly salted

~ **паюсная** *(payusnaya)* coarsely grained, pressed, heavily salted

~ **чёрная** *(chyornaya)* black

2) "vegetable caviar"; mashed or puréed vegetables

~ **баклажанная** *(baklazhannaya)* "eggplant caviar"; mashed aubergine (eggplant) stewed with onions and tomatoes

~ **грибная** *(gribnaya)* "mushroom caviar"; minced mushrooms stewed in tomato sauce, oil and seasoning

~ **кабачковая** *(kabachkovaya)* "vegetable-marrow (US zucchini) caviar"; mashed vegetable marrow (US zucchini) stewed with carrots, onions and tomatoes

имбирь *(imbir')* ginger

индейка *(indyeyka)* turkey

~ **жареная с яблоками** *(zharyenaya s yablokami)* stuffed with apples, roasted

~ **фаршированная белым хлебом и печёнкой** *(farshirovannaya byelim khlyebom i pyechyonkoy)* stuffed with a bread and kidney dressing

~ **по-болгарски** *(po-bolgarski)* turkey casserole with carrots, onions, tomatoes and wine

кабачки *(kabachki)* vegetable marrow (US zucchini)

~ **жареные** *(zharyeniye)* fried

~ **по-русски** *(po-russki)* stuffed with mushrooms and vegetable-marrow (US zucchini) pulp, served with sour cream and eggs

~ **в томатном соусе** *(v*

tomatnom sousye) fried and served with tomato sauce

какао с мороженым *(kakao s morozhenim)* chilled cocoa sauce poured over ice-cream

калач *(kalach)* padlock-shaped bread

камбала *(kambala)* flounder

~ **в белом соусе** *(v byelom sousye)* poached, served with a white sauce

~ **в томатном соусе** *(v tomatnom sousye)* poached, served in tomato sauce

капуста *(kapusta)* cabbage

~ **белокочанная** *(byelokochannaya)* white

~ **квашеная** *(kvashenaya)* sauerkraut

~ **красная** *(krasnaya)* red

~ **цветная** *(tsvyetnaya)* cauliflower

карп *(karp)* carp

~ **фаршированный по-украински** *(farshirovanniy po-ukrainski)* stuffed with a seasoned mixture of ham and carp

картофель *(kartofyel')* potatoes

~ **жареный** *(zharyeniy)* sautéed in butter

~ **молодой** *(molodoy)* new

~ **в молоке** *(v molokye)* mashed

~ **в «мундире»** *(v mundirye)* boiled in their jackets

~ **отварной** *(otvarnoy)* boiled

~ **печёный** *(pyechyoniy)* baked

~ **сваренный на пару** *(svaryenniy na paru)* steamed

~ **в сметане** *(v smyetanye)* boiled and sautéed, served with sour cream

~ **тушёный со свежими грибами** *(tushoniy so svyezhimi gribami)* stewed with fresh mushrooms

~ **с сельдью** *(s syel'dyu)* served with herring

~ **«фри»** *(fri)* chips (US french fries)

~**ное пюре** *(~noye pyurye)* mashed

каша *(kasha)* gruel, porridge

~ **гречневая с грибами и луком** *(gryechnyevaya s gribami i lukom)* buckwheat, cooked with mushrooms and onions

~ **гречневая с маслом/молоком** *(gryechnyevaya s maslom/molokom)* buckwheat, served with butter or milk

~ **манная** *(mannaya)* semolina (farina)

~ **перловая** *(pyerlovaya)* pearl barley

~ **пшённая** *(pshonnaja)* millet gruel

~ **рисовая с маслом/молоком** *(risovaya s maslom/molokom)* rice, served with butter or milk

кебаб *(kyebab)* kebab; chunks of mutton marinated in lemon juice, cooked on a skewer with onions, toma-

toes and other vegetables
люля ~ *(lyulya)* minced mutton patties, seasoned and cooked on a skewer
тава ~ *(tava)* mutton pies
кекс *(kyeks)* plum cake
кета *(kyeta)* Siberian salmon
клёцки *(klyotski)* dumplings, for soup
~ из курицы *(iz kuritsi)* dumplings made of minced chicken mixed with bread-crumbs soaked in milk or water
~ из печёнки *(iz pyechyonki)* liver minced with bacon and mixed with breadcrumbs
кильки *(kil'ki)* pilchard
~ маринованные *(marinovanniye)* marinated
кисель *(kisyel')* a sourish, thickened fruit-juice dessert
~ вишнёвый *(vichnyoviy)* cherry
~ клюквенный *(klyukvyenniy)* cranberry
~ смородиновый *(smorodinoviy)* redcurrant
~ яблочный *(yablotchniy)* apple
кисло-сладкий *(kislo-sladkiy)* bitter-sweet
кислый *(kisliy)* sour
клубника *(klubnika)* strawberry
клюква *(klyukva)* cranberry
коврижка *(kovrizhka)* honey cake
коктейль с фруктами *(koktyeyl' s fruktami)* fruit cocktail steeped in liqueur, sparkling wine or wine
колбаса *(kolbasa)* cold cuts, sausages
~ ветчинно-рубленная *(vyechinno-rublyennaya)* boiled fat pork sausage
~ докторская *(doktorskaya)* type of meatloaf
~ домашняя *(domashnyaya)* highly seasoned pork sausage
~ копчёная *(kopchyonaya)* smoked salami
~ ливерная *(livyernaya)* liver sausage
~ любительская *(lyubityel'skaya)* bologna
~ языковая *(yazikovaya)* sausage made from beef or pork tongue
компот *(kompot)* stewed fruit
~ из слив *(iz sliv)* prunes
~ из сушёных фруктов *(iz sushonikh fruktov)* mixed fruit, served in syrup
консервированный *(konsyervirovanniy)* tinned (US canned)
конфеты *(konfyeti)* sweets (US candy)
копчёный *(kopchyoniy)* smoked
корейка *(koryeyka)* smoked and salted spare ribs
кость *(kost')* bone
котлеты (рубленые) *(kotlyeti [rublyeniye])* fried pies or breaded meat in the shape of a meat pie
~ капустные *(kapustniye)*

RUSSIAN

filled with cabbage
~ **морковные** *(morkovniye)* filled with carrot
~ **пожарские** *(pozharskiye)* chicken pie
~ **по-киевски** *(po-kiyevski)* breaded breast of chicken filled with butter, Kiev style
~ **рыбные** *(ribniye)* fish pie
котлеты натуральные *(kotlyeti natural'niye)* chops, cutlets
~ **бараньи** *(baran'i)* mutton chops
~ **куриные** *(kuriniye)* breast of chicken
~ **отбивные** *(otbivniye)* lamb, mutton, pork chops, pounded
~ **свиные** *(sviniye)* pork chops
кофе-«Гляссе» *(kofyeglyasse)* iced coffee topped with ice-cream
краб *(krab)* crab
креветки *(kryevyetki)* shrimp
крем *(kryem)* a frothy, creamy dessert
~ **апельсиновый** *(apyel'sinoviy)* orange
~ **ванильный** *(vanil'niy)* vanilla
~ **кофейный** *(kofyeyniy)* mocha
~ **лимонный** *(limonniy)* lemon
~ **миндальный** *(mindal'niy)* almond
~ **ромовый** *(romoviy)* rum
~ **сливочный с ягодами** *(slivochniy s yagodami)* berry
~ **шоколадный** *(shokoladniy)* chocolate
крендель *(kryendyel')* tea bread (US coffee cake) shaped in a figure "8"
кролик *(krolik)* rabbit
~ **тушёный с гарниром из овощей** *(tushoniy s garnirom iz ovoshchyej)* stewed, garnished with vegetables
крупа *(krupa)* grits, porridge
крыжовник *(krizhovnik)* gooseberries
кукуруза *(kukuruza)* maize (US corn)
кулебяка *(kulyebyaka)* loaf, may be made of meat, fish or vegetables
кулич *(kulich)* tall Easter cake containing raisins and often iced with marzipan
купаты *(kupati)* grilled, spicy sausage, served with hot sauce (Georgia)
курага *(kuraga)* dried apricots
курица *(kuritsa)* chicken
~ **жареная с грибами** *(zharyenaya s gribami)* chicken and mushroom casserole
~ **отварная с рисом** *(otvarnaya s risom)* boiled, served with rice
~ **тушёная под белым соусом** *(tushonaya pod byelim sousom)* braised, served with a white sauce
~ **фаршированная потро-**

хами *(farshirovannaya potrokhami)* stuffed with giblets
куропатка *(kuropatka)* partridge
~ **жареная с вареньем** *(zharyenaya s varyen'yem)* roasted, served with jam
кусок *(kusok)* piece, slice
лаваш *(lavash)* unleavened white bread
лавровый лист *(lavroviy list)* bay leaf
лагман *(lagman)* meat soup made with spaghetti (Central Asia)
лангет *(langyet)* rib steak
лапша *(lapsha)* noodles, noodle soup
лещ *(lyeshch)* bream
лимон *(limon)* lemon
лисички *(lisichki)* chanterelle mushrooms
лобио *(lobio)* kidney beans with walnut purée and herb dressing (Georgia)
лососина *(lososina)* salmon, lightly salted and pinkish in colour
лук *(luk)* onion
~ **зелёный** *(zyelyoniy)* chives
майонез *(mayonyez)* mayonnaise
мак *(mak)* poppy seeds
макароны *(makaroni)* macaroni
макрель *(makryel')* mackerel
малина *(malina)* raspberries
мандарин *(mandarin)* tangerine
маринованный *(marinovanniy)* marinated
маслины *(maslini)* olives
масло *(maslo)* oil, butter
~ **оливковое** *(olivkovoye)* olive oil
~ **подсолнечное** *(podsolnyechnoye)* sunflower oil
мастава *(mastava)* rice soup with mutton and sour milk
мёд *(myod)* honey
медвежатина *(myedvyezhatina)* bear meat, usually marinated and stewed
меню *(myenyu)* menu
миндаль *(mindal')* almond
минога *(minoga)* lamprey eel
~ **маринованная** *(marinovannaya)* marinated
~ **жареная** *(zharyenaya)* fried
мозги *(mozgi)* brains
морковь *(morkov')* carrot
мороженое *(morozhenoye)* ice-cream
~ **ванильное** *(vanil'noye)* vanilla
~ **миндальное** *(mindal'noye)* almond
~ **молочное** *(molochnoye)* ice, sherbet
~ **ореховое** *(oryekhovoye)* walnut
~ **сливочное** *(slivochnoye)* ice-cream, enriched
~ **фруктово-ягодное** *(fruktovo-yagodnoye)* fruit ice
~ **шоколадное** *(shokoladnoye)* chocolate
~ **«эскимо»** *(eskimo)* chocolate-coated ice-cream bar

RUSSIAN

мука *(muka)* flour
мусака *(musaka)* stew of aubergine (eggplant), tomatoes, green peppers, carrots, vegetable marrows (US zucchini) and garlic
мусс *(muss)* dessert made from beaten egg whites folded into a fruit purée or honey
~ **клюквенный** *(klyukvyennyj)* cranberry
~ **медовый** *(myedovyj)* honey
~ **яблочный** *(yablochnyj)* apple
~ **ягодный** *(yagodnyj)* berry
мясо *(myaso)* meat
~ **варёное** *(varyonoye)* boiled
~ **жареное** *(zharyenoye)* fried
~ **жаренное на рашпере** *(zharyennoye na rashpyerye)* grilled
~ **на вертеле** *(na vyertyelye)* spit-roasted
~ **не прожаренное** *(nye prozharyennoye)* underdone (US rare)
~ **сильно прожаренное** *(sil'no prozharyennoye)* well done
~ **средне прожаренное** *(sryednye prozharyennoye)* medium
~ **тушёное** *(tushonoye)* braised, stewed
~ **фаршированное** *(farshirovannoye)* stuffed
мясной сок *(myasnoy sok)* drippings
мята *(myata)* mint
~ **перечная** *(pyeryechnaya)* peppermint
~ **зелёная** *(zyelyonaya)* spearmint
навага *(navaga)* cod
налистники *(nalistniki)* fried cabbage leaves
~ **с творогом** *(s tvorogom)* stuffed with cottage cheese
~ **с яблоками** *(s yablokami)* stuffed with apples
~ **с мясом** *(s myasom)* stuffed with forcemeat
начинка *(nachinka)* filling, stuffing
обед *(obyed)* lunch
овдух *(ovdukh)* chilled meat and cucumber soup with yoghurt (Azerbaijan)
овощи *(ovoshchi)* vegetables
~ **консервированные** *(konsyervirovanniye)* tinned (US canned)
~ **свежие** *(svyezhie)* fresh
огурец *(oguryets)* cucumber
малосольный ~ *(malosol'niy)* lightly salted
маринованный ~ *(marinovanniy)* pickled
свежий ~ *(svyezhiy)* fresh
солёный ~ *(solyoniy)* salted
салат из свежих огурцов *(salat iz svyezhikh ogurtsov)* cucumber salad
окорок *(okorok)* ham
окрошка *(okroshka)* chilled soup made with *kvass*

~ **овощная** *(ovoshchnaya)* with cucumbers and other vegetables
~ **сборная мясная** *(sbornaya myasnaya)* with meat
окунь *(okun')* perch
оладьи *(olad'i)* yeast fritter
~ **с вареньем** *(s varyen'yem)* served with jam
~ **с мёдом** *(s myodom)* served with honey
~ **со сметаной** *(so smyetanoy)* served with sour cream
оленина *(olyenina)* venison
омлет *(omlyet)* omelet
~ **с зелёным луком** *(s zyelyonim lukom)* chive
~ **с картофелем** *(s kartofyelyem)* potato
~ **натуральный** *(natural'niy)* plain
~ **с яблоками** *(s yablokami)* apple
орех *(oryekh)* nut
~ **грецкий** *(gretskiy)* walnut
~ **лесной** *(lyesnoy)* hazelnut
осетрина *(osyetrina)* sturgeon
~ **на вертеле** *(na vyertyelye)* grilled on a spit
~ **заливная** *(zalivnaya)* in gelatine
~ **под маринадом** *(pod marinadom)* marinated
~ **паровая** *(parovaya)* steamed
~ **по-русски** *(po-russki)* poached with tomato sauce and vegetables
~ **в томате** *(v tomatye)* in tomato sauce
~ **«фри»** *(fri)* fried
отварной *(otvarnoy)* poached
палтус *(paltus)* halibut
~ **жареный** *(zharyeniy)* fried
паровой *(parovoy)* steamed
пастила *(pastila)* fruit-flavoured sweets (US candy)
паштет *(pashtyet)* meat pie
~ **из домашней птицы** *(iz domashnyej ptitsi)* chicken
~ **из зайца** *(iz zaytsa)* hare
~ **из кролика** *(iz krolika)* rabbit
~ **из печёнки** *(iz pyechyonki)* chopped liver
пельмени *(pyel'myeni)* dough envelope (like ravioli), poached in broth, served with melted butter and sour cream or with vinegar
~ **с капустой** *(s kapustoy)* with a cabbage filling
~ **сибирские** *(sibirskiye)* with a meat filling
первое (блюдо) *(pyervoye [blyudo])* first course (soup)
перепел *(pyeryepyel)* quail
~ **жаренный на решётке** *(zharyennyj na ryeshotkye)* grilled
перец *(pyeryets)* pepper
~ **горький** *(gor'kiy)* pimento
~ **сладкий болгарский** *(sladkiy bolgarskiy)* sweet green pepper

~ **фаршированный овощами в томатном соусе** *(farshirovanniy ovoshchami v tomatnom sousye)* green pepper stuffed with vegetables

персик *(pyersik)* peach

петрушка *(pyetrushka)* parsley

печёнка куриная *(pyechyonka kurinaya)* chicken livers

~ **в сметанном соусе** *(v smyetannom sousye)* in sour cream sauce

~ **в соусе с мадерой** *(v sousye s madyeroy)* in madeira-type wine

печёный *(pyechyonyj)* baked

печень *(pyechyen')* liver

~ **варёная с гарниром** *(varyonaya s garnirom)* boiled, garnished with vegetables

~ **в сметане** *(v smyetanye)* braised with sour cream

~ **телячья жареная** *(tyelyach'ya zharyenaya)* fried calf's liver

~ **тресковая в масле** *(tryeskovaya v maslye)* cod liver in oil

печенье *(pyechyen'ye)* biscuits (cookies)

пирог *(pirog)* pie, flan, tart

~ **с капустой** *(s kapustoy)* cabbage tart

~ **рисовый с яйцами** *(risoviy s yaytsami)* rice and egg pie

~ **сибирский с рыбой** *(sibirskiy s riboy)* fish and onion pie

~ **сладкий с яблоками** *(sladkiy s yablokami)* apple pie

пирожки *(pirozhki)* turnover

~ **с капустой** *(s kapustoy)* cabbage

~ **с мясом** *(s myasom)* meat

~ **с повидлом** *(s povidlom)* jam

~ **с творогом** *(s tvorogom)* cottage cheese

пирожное *(pirozhnoye)* a rich, cream pastry; often like a napoleon

пити *(piti)* mutton soup with beans, potatoes and sour prunes (Azerbaijan)

плавленый *(plavlyeniy)* melted

плов *(plov)* rice casserole

~ **с бараниной** *(s baraninoy)* with minced mutton

~ **с грибами** *(s gribami)* with mushrooms

~ **с изюмом** *(s izyumom)* with raisins

~ **по-казахски** *(po-kazakhski)* with minced mutton, onions, dried apricots, apples and carrots

~ **по-узбекски** *(po-uzbyekski)* with mutton, carrots, peppers, onions

пломбир *(plombir)* ice-cream, enriched

повидло *(povidlo)* jam

~ **сливовое** *(slivovoye)* plum

~ **яблочное** *(yablochnoye)* apple

полуфабрикаты *(polufabrikati)* instant food

половина *(polovina)* half

помидоры *(pomidori)* tomatoes

~ **свежие** *(svyezhiye)* fresh

~ **фаршированные мясом и рисом** *(farshirovanniye myasom i risom)* stuffed with meat and rice

салат из свежих ~ов *(salat iz svyezhikh ~ov)* tomato salad

пончики *(ponchiki)* fritter

поросёнок *(porosyonok)* sucking pig

~ **жареный** *(zharyeniy)* roast

~ **заливной** *(zalivnoy)* in gelatine

~ **с начинкой** *(s nachinkoy)* stuffed

порция *(portsiya)* ration

потроха *(potrokha)* giblets, offal (US variety meat)

почки *(pochki)* kidneys

~ **тушёные в луковом соусе** *(tushoniye v lukovom sousye)* braised in onion sauce

~ **тушёные с вином** *(tushoniye s vinom)* braised in wine sauce

провансаль *(provansal')* garnish of sauerkraut and grated apples and other fruits

простокваша *(prostokvasha)* yoghurt

пряники *(pryaniki)* gingerbread

~ **медовые** *(myedoviye)* made with honey

~ **мятные** *(myatniye)* mint-flavoured

пряность *(pryanost')* spice

пудинг *(puding)* casserole

~ **с изюмом** *(s izyumom)* rice casserole with raisins

~ **с мясом** *(s myasom)* potato and meat casserole

~ **ореховый** *(oryekhoviy)* nutmeat casserole

~ **рисовый** *(risoviy)* rice casserole

~ **творожный** *(tvorozhniy)* cottage-cheese casserole

рагу *(ragu)* stew

~ **из овощей** *(iz ovoshchyey)* vegetable stew, containing potatoes, carrots, turnips, onions and tomato purée

раки *(raki)* crayfish

~ **натуральные** *(natural'niye)* poached with carrots, onions and parsley

~ **в пиве** *(v pivye)* poached in beer

рассольник *(rassol'nik)* gherkin soup, containing other vegetables and meat (often giblets)

~ **с курицей** *(s kuritsyey)* chicken, carrots, potatoes, sour cream

~ **«Ленинградский»** *(lyeningradskiy)* rice, potatoes, tomatoes, carrots and sour cream

~ **с почками** *(s pochkami)* kidneys, sorrel, potatoes
~ **с рыбой** *(s riboy)* fish, rice and vegetables
расстегай *(rasstyegay)* fish pies
рашпер *(rashpyer)* grill
ревень *(ryevyen')* rhubarb
редис, редиска *(ryedis, ryediska)* radishes
~ **тёртый со сметаной** *(tyortiy so smyetanoy)* grated, served with sour cream
репа *(ryepa)* turnip
рис *(ris)* rice
рожок *(rozhok)* horn-shaped bread
рокфор *(rokfor)* blue cheese, made from ewe's milk
рольмопс *(rol'mops)* marinated, rolled herring
ромштекс *(romshtyeks)* rump steak
ростбиф *(rostbif)* roast beef
рулет *(rulyet)* pasty stuffed with meat or other filling
рыба *(riba)* fish
~ **заливная** *(zalivnaya)* in gelatine
~ **по-запорожски** *(po-zaporozhski)* casserole of fish, carrots, parsley, onions, tomatoes
~ **жареная** *(zharyenaya)* fried
~ **жаренная на вертеле/рашпере** *(zharyenaya na vyertyelye/rashpyerye)* spit-roasted/grilled
~ **копчёная** *(kopchyonaya)* smoked, as an appetizer
~ **маринованная** *(marinovannaya)* marinated
~ **отварная** *(otvarnaya)* poached
~ **прожаренная** *(prozharyennaya)* deep-fried
~ **паровая** *(parovaya)* steamed
~ **печёная** *(pyechyonaya)* baked
~ **тушёная** *(tushonaya)* stewed
~ **фаршированная** *(farshirovannaya)* stuffed
рябчики *(ryabchiki)* hazel grouse
~ **жареные с вареньем** *(zharyeniye s varyen'yem)* broiled and served with jam
~ **тушёные в сметане** *(tushoniye v smyetanye)* braised in sour cream
ряженка *(ryazhenka)* milk, pasteurized in the oven and soured naturally
салат *(salat)* salad
~ **из картофеля с творогом** *(iz kartofyelya s tvorogom)* potatoes, cottage cheese, onion, eggs in sour cream
~ **из крабов** *(iz krabov)* crab
~ **из креветок** *(iz kryevyetok)* shrimp
~ **из моркови и яблок** *(iz morkovi i yablok)* grated sour apples and carrots, served in oil and vinegar
~ **Московский** *(Moskov-*

skiy) beef, potatoes, eggs, carrots, apples

~ **из огурцов** *(iz ogurtsov)* mayonnaise or sour cream, cucumber

~ **из помидоров** *(iz pomidorov)* tomato

~ **из редиса** *(iz ryedisa)* finely sliced radishes with sour cream and salt

~ **русский зелёный** *(russkiy zyelyoniy)* cabbage, spinach, lettuce, green pepper, onions and cucumbers served in oil and vinegar or sour cream

~ **Провансаль** *(provansal')* sauerkraut, apples, raisins, marinated plums and cherries

~ **из свежей капусты** *(iz svyezhyey kapusti)* cabbage, spring onions, apples, mixed with sugar and vegetable oil

~ **из сельди** *(iz syel'di)* herring, potatoes, apples, cucumbers, eggs

сало *(salo)* bacon fat

сарделька *(sardyel'ka)* frankfurter-type sausage

сардины *(sardini)* sardines

сахар *(sakhar)* sugar

~ **рафинад** *(rafinad)* refined

~ **ная пудра** *(~naya pudra)* castor (US powdered)

~ **ный песок** *(~niy pyesok)* granulated

сациви *(satsivi)* sauce with walnuts, onions and spices (Georgia)

свежий *(svyezhiy)* fresh

свёкла *(svyokla)* beetroot

~ **в соусе с укропом** *(v sousye s ukropom)* in dill sauce

~ **в сметане** *(v smyetanye)* in sour-cream sauce

свекольник *(svyekol'nik)* chilled soup based on beetroot, with eggs, cucumber, dill, parsley, served with sour cream

свинина *(svinina)* pork

~ **жареная с грибным соусом** *(zharyenaya s gribnim sousom)* braised in mushroom sauce

~ **тушённая в пиве** *(tushonnaya v pivye)* chops braised in beer

~ **тушёная с яблоками** *(tushonaya s yablokami)* braised and served with apple slices

севрюга *(syevryuga)* smaller type of sturgeon giving smaller and generally darker roe

сельдерей *(syel'dyeryey)* celery

сельдь *(syel'd')* herring

~ **с гарниром** *(s garnirom)* with a garnish of sliced onions, sliced hard-boiled eggs, salted cucumbers, salted mushrooms and beetroot strips

~ **с луком** *(s lukom)* with onions

~ **маринованная** *(marinovannaya)* marinated

~ **натуральная с отвар-**

ным картофелем *(natural'naya s otvarnim kartofyelyem)* with boiled potatoes

~ **в сметане** *(v smyetanye)* served with sour cream

~ **солёная** *(solyonaya)* pickled

сёмга *(syomga)* salmon

скумбрия *(skumbriya)* mackerel

сладкий *(sladkiy)* sweet

слива *(sliva)* plum

сливки *(slivki)* cream

сметана *(smyetana)* sour cream

смородина *(smorodina)* currant

~ **красная** *(krasnaya)* red

~ **чёрная** *(tchyornaya)* black

солёный *(solyoniy)* salted

соломка *(solomka)* salted or sugared biscuits (US crackers or cookies), may be 2 ft. long

соль *(sol')* salt

солянка *(solyanka)* soup of gherkins and capers

~ **грибная** *(gribnaya)* with cabbage, mushrooms, and chunks of meat or fish

~ **по-грузински** *(po-gruzinski)* stew of beef or mutton, tomatoes, cucumbers and wine (Georgia)

~ **из курицы** *(iz kuritsi)* chicken casserole with tomato purée, cucumbers and sour cream

~ **мясная сборная** *(myasnaya sbornaya)* stew containing chunks of meat or kidneys, sausages, gherkins, olives

~ **рыбная** *(ribnaya)* fish chowder

сом *(som)* catfish

сосиски *(sosiski)* frankfurters

соус *(sous)* sauce

~ **белый** *(byeliy)* white bechamel

~ **кисло-сладкий** *(kislosladkiy)* sweet and sour; tomato, prunes, raisins, red wine

~ **«Кубанский»** *(kubanskiy)* sweet-and-sour tomato sauce

~ **молочный** *(molochniy)* white, bechamel

~ **сметанный** *(smyetanniy)* cream

~ **томатный** *(tomatniy)* tomato

~ **Ткемали** *(tkyemali)* plum and coriander

~ **с хреном** *(s khryenom)* horseradish

сочный *(sochniy)* juicy

стерлядь *(styerlyad')* sterlet, a small sturgeon

студень *(studen')* brawn (US headcheese)

~ **говяжий** *(govyazhiy)* beef

~ **из головизны** *(iz golovizni)* sturgeon head

~ **рыбный** *(ribniy)* fish

~ **из свиных ножек** *(iz svinikh nozhek)* pig's trot-

ters (US pig's feet)
~ **телячий** *(tyelyachiy)* veal
судак *(sudak)* pike-perch
~ **заливной** *(zalivnoy)* in gelatine
~ **запечённый с шампиньонами в сметанном соусе** *(zapyechyonniy s champin'onami v smyetannom sousye)* baked with mushrooms in sour-cream sauce
~ **отварной в яичном соусе** *(otvarnoy v yaichnom sousye)* poached in egg sauce
~ **в томатном соусе** *(v tomatnom sousye)* in tomato sauce
сулгуни *(sulguni)* matured cheese, made from ewe's milk (Georgia)
суп *(sup)* soup
~ **грибной** *(gribnoy)* mushroom
~ **картофельный** *(kartofyel'niy)* potato
~ **крестьянский** *(kryest'yanskiy)* cabbage, potato, carrot, parsley, tomato and sour cream
~ **лапша с курицей** *(lapsha s kuritsyey)* chicken-noodle
~ **овощной** *(ovoshchnoy)* vegetable
~ **рыбный** *(ribniy)* fish
~ **из фасоли** *(iz fasoli)* butter beans (US navy beans)
~ **харчо** *(kharcho)* mutton with vegetables (Georgia)
суп молочный *(sup molochniy)* milk-based soup
~ **с вермишелью** *(s vyermishel'yu)* with noodles
~ **перловый** *(pyerloviy)* with pearl barley
~ **рисовый** *(risoviy)* with rice
суп-пюре *(sup-pyurye)* cream soup, cream of ... soup
~ **из гороха** *(iz gorokha)* pea
~ **грибной** *(gribnoy)* mushroom
~ **из курицы** *(iz kuritsi)* chicken
~ **из моркови** *(iz morkovi)* carrot
~ **из помидоров** *(iz pomidorov)* tomato
суп сладкий *(sup sladkiy)* fruit soup served chilled or hot, containing noodles, rice or dumplings
~ **из вишен** *(iz vishen)* cherries, cinnamon, cream
~ **из кураги с рисом** *(iz kuragi s risom)* dried apricots, rice, cream
~ **из ревеня с манными клёцками** *(iz ryevyenya s mannimi klyotskami)* rhubarb, served with dumplings
~ **из чёрной смородины с творожными клёцками** *(iz chyornoy smorodini s tvorozhnimi klyotskami)* blackcurrants, served with cottage-cheese dumplings
~ **из яблок** *(iz yablok)*

apples, cinnamon, cream

суфле *(suflye)* soufflé; a savoury sauce into which beaten egg whites are folded; mixture is baked until browned and puffed up

сухарь *(sukhar')* rusks (US zwieback)

сухой *(sukhoy)* dry

сыворотка *(sivorotka)* buttermilk

сыр *(sir)* cheese

голландский ~ *(gollandskiy)* imitation Dutch edam cheese, yellow, mild and firm

швейцарский ~ *(chvyeytsarskiy)* imitation swiss cheese, like gruyère; pale yellow, nutty flavour, with small holes

сырники со сметаной *(sirniki so smyetanoy)* cottage-cheese fritters served with sour cream

сырой *(siroy)* raw, cured

творог *(tvorog)* cottage cheese

телятина *(tyelyatina)* veal

~ духовая с кабачками *(dukhovaya s kabachkami)* braised with vegetable marrow (US zucchini)

~ жаренная с грибами и помидорами *(zharyennaya s gribami i pomidorami)* fried with mushrooms and tomatoes

~ отварная с белым соусом *(otvarnaya s byelim sousom)* poached and served with white sauce

~ тушённая с черносливом *(tushonnaya s chyernoslivom)* braised in white wine and prunes

тёртый *(tyortiy)* grated

тесто *(tyesto)* dough, batter

~ бездрожжевое *(byezdrozhzhevoye)* unleavened

~ дрожжевое *(drozhzhevoye)* leavened

~ сдобное *(sdobnoe)* made with butter

~ слоёное *(sloyonoye)* puff pastry

тетерев *(tyetyeryev)* black grouse

тефтели *(tyeftyeli)* meatballs, fried then braised in seasoned broth, served in tomato sauce

тмин *(tmin)* cumin

торт *(tort)* creamy layer cake

толстый *(tolstiy)* thick

треска *(tryeska)* cod

~ в белом соусе *(v byelom sousye)* in white sauce

~ под маринадом *(pod marinadom)* marinated

~ со сметаной и помидорами *(so smyetanoy i pomidorami)* in sour cream with tomatoes

тунец *(tunyets)* tunny (US tuna fish)

тушёный *(tushoniy)* stewed, braised

тыква *(tikva)* pumpkin

угорь *(ugor')* eel

копчёный ~ *(kopchyoniy)* smoked

угро *(ugro)* soup of beef, potato and sour milk (Kirgiz Republic)
ужин *(uzhin)* dinner
укроп *(ukrop)* dill
уксус *(uksus)* vinegar
утка *(utka)* duck
~ **дикая** *(dikaya)* wild
~ **жареная с вишнями** *(zharyenaya s vishnyami)* roasted, served with cherry sauce
~ **жареная с яблоками** *(zharyenaya s yablokami)* roasted with baked apples
~ **тушённая с грибами** *(tushonnaya s gribami)* braised with mushrooms
уха *(ukha)* soup of fresh-water fish
~ **рыбацкая** *(ribatskaya)* a chowder of smelt-like fish
фазан *(fazan)* pheasant
~ **по-грузински** *(po-gruzinski)* braised in orange juice and green tea with walnuts and raisins
~ **жаренный с луком и грибами** *(zharyenniy s lukom i gribami)* fried with onions and mushrooms
~ **с яблоками** *(s yablokami)* browned with bacon, braised in a sauce with blackcurrant jelly, garnished with baked apples
фарш *(farsh)* stuffing
фаршированный *(farshirovanniy)* stuffed
фасоль *(fasol')* beans
филе *(filye)* fillet
форель *(foryel')* trout
форшмак *(forshmak)* mixture of herring and apples
фрикадельки *(frikadyel'ki)* meatballs
фрукт(ы) *(frukt[i])* fruit
~**овый коктейль** *(~oviy koktyeyl')* fruit cocktail steeped in liqueur, Russian champagne or wine
халва *(khalva)* a sugary-loaf confection; may be made in one of several varieties, e.g., with pistachios
хамраши *(khamrashi)* mutton soup, with butter (US navy) beans, noodles, chives and parsley
харчо *(kharcho)* mutton, onion, rice and tomato soup (Georgia)
хачапури *(khachapuri)* cheese tarts (Georgia)
хворост *(khvorost)* crisp and flaky deep-fried pastry
хлеб *(khlyeb)* bread
~ **белый** *(byeliy)* white
~ **бородинский** *(borodinskiy)* coriander-flavoured black bread (US pumpernickel)
~ **с изюмом** *(s izyumom)* raisin
~ **с маком** *(s makom)* poppyseed
~ **ржаной** *(rzhanoj)* black (pumpernickel)
~ **чёрный** *(tchyorniy)* black (pumpernickel)
холодец *(kholodyets)* brawn (US headcheese)

хрен *(khryen)* horseradish
цесарка *(tsesarka)* guinea fowl
цукат *(tsukat)* candied fruit
цыплята *(tsiplyata)* chicken
~ **жареные с картофелем** *(zharyeniye s kartofyelyem)* broiled with potatoes
~ **жареные со сметанным соусом** *(zharyeniye so smyetannim sousom)* roasted, served with a sour-cream sauce
~ **отварные с рисом** *(otvarniye s risom)* cooked with rice
~ **Табака** *(tabaka)* boned, pounded, flavoured with garlic and fried under a weight (Georgia)
чанахи *(chanakhi)* casserole of mutton, potatoes, tomatoes, aubergine (eggplant) and green beans (Georgia)
чахохбили *(chakhokhbili)* spicy chicken and tomato casserole (Georgia)
чебуреки *(chyeburyeki)* deep-fried meat pies (Tartar Republic)
черешня *(chyeryeshnya)* cherries
черника *(chyernika)* bilberries
чернослив *(chyernosliv)* prunes
чеснок *(chyesnok)* garlic
чечевица *(chyechyevitsa)* lentils
чихиртма из баранины *(chikhirtma iz baranini)* mutton and egg soup with saffron (Caucasia)
чурек *(churyek)* unleavened bread with sesame seeds (Georgia)
шафран *(shafran)* saffron
шашлык *(shashlik)* shashlik; chunks of meat grilled on a skewer; may be served in a hot tomato sauce (Caucasia)
~ **из баранины** *(iz baranini)* mutton
~ **из говядины** *(iz govyadini)* beef
шницель *(shnitsel')* cutlet
~ **из телятины в сметанном соусе** *(iz tyelyatini v smyetannom sousye)* veal cutlet served with sour cream
шоколад *(shokolad)* chocolate
шпигованный *(shpigovanniy)* larded
шпик *(shpik)* bacon
шпинат *(shpinat)* spinach
шпроты *(shproty)* sprats
шурпа *(shurpa)* mutton soup and tomatoes (Central Asia)
щавель *(shchavyel')* sorrel
щи *(shchi)* cabbage or sauerkraut soup to which other vegetables can be added; served with sour cream
~ **зелёные с яйцом и сметаной** *(zyelyoniye s yaytsom i smyetanoy)* spinach or sorrel soup
~ **с квашеной капустой и грибами** *(s kvashenoy kapustoy i gribami)* sauer-

RUSSIAN

kraut, vegetables, mushrooms

~ **крапивные** *(krapivniye)* nettle soup

~ **ленивые** *(lyeniviye)* "lazy soup"; cabbage cut into chunks

~ **невские** *(nyevskiye)* sauerkraut, sautéed meat added before serving

~ **со свежей капустой и рыбой** *(so svyezhey kapustoy i riboy)* sturgeon or pike perch, fresh cabbage, carrots, parsley

~ **суточные** *(sutochniye)* "24 hours"; sauerkraut, carrot, tomato; served the day after its preparation

щука *(shchyuka)* pike

~ **тушёная с хреном** *(tushyonaya s khryenom)* stewed with horseradish and sour cream

эскалоп *(eskalop)* cutlet

яблоки *(yabloki)* apples

~ **маринованные** *(marinovanniye)* marinated in vinegar

~ **мочёные** *(mochyoniye)* pickled in a mixture of water, *kvass*, honey and sugar

~ **печёные** *(pyechyoniye)* baked

~ **сушёные** *(sushoniye)* dried

язык *(yazik)* tongue

~ **заливной** *(zalivnoy)* in gelatine

~ **отварной под белым соусом** *(otvarnoy pod byelim sousom)* boiled and served with white sauce

~ **под соусом с изюмом** *(pod sousom s izyumom)* boiled and served with a sauce made from tongue stock and raisins

яичница *(yaichnitsa)* fried eggs

~ **взбитая** *(vzbitaya)* scrambled eggs

~ **глазунья** *(glazun'ya)* fried, sunny-side up

~ **с сельдью** *(s syel'd'yu)* fried herring with eggs

~ **с сыром** *(s sirom)* cheese and bacon omelet

яйни *(yayni)* soup of beef, tomato and potato

яйца *(yaytsa)* eggs

~ **вкрутую** *(vkrutuyu)* hard-boiled

~ **всмятку** *(vsmyatku)* soft-boiled

~ **с икрой** *(s ikroy)* hard-boiled eggs filled with soft caviar and garnished with lettuce

~ **крутые с хреном** *(krutiye s khryenom)* hard-boiled eggs with horseradish, mayonnaise and sour cream

~ **под майонезом** *(pod mayonyezom)* egg salad

~ **в мешочек** *(v myeshochyek)* medium-boiled

Drink

Азербайджан Azerbaijan; particularly noted for its cordial wine like *Shemakha* **(Шемаха)**; its *Kiurdamir* **(Кюрдамир)** is a velvety wine having the exotic aftertaste of chocolate

Армения Armenia; produces mainly dessert wine like the well-known *Artashat* **(Арташат)**

Боржоми *(borzhomi)* mineral water from the famous Georgian spa of the same name

вино *(vino)* wine
- ~ **белое** *(byeloye)* white
- ~ **десертное** *(dyesyertnoye)* dessert
- ~ **красное** *(krasnoye)* red
- ~ **полусухое** *(polusukhoye)* slightly sweet
- ~ **сладкое** *(sladkoye)* sweet
- ~ **столовое** *(stolovoye)* table
- ~ **сухое** *(sukhoye)* dry

вода *(voda)* water
- ~ **газированная** *(gazirovannaya)* soda water
- ~ **минеральная** *(minyeral'naya)* mineral water

водка *(vodka)* vodka
- ~ **Горилка** *(gorilka)* a Ukrainian peper-flavoured vodka
- ~ **Зубровка** *(zubrovka)* flavoured with wild buffalo-grass
- ~ **крепкая** *(kryepkaya)* strong
- ~ **Московская** *(moskovskaya)* ordinary
- ~ **перцовая** *(pyertsovaya)* pepper-flavoured
- ~ **рябиновая** *(ryabinovaya)* mountain-ashberry-flavoured
- ~ **Столичная** *(stolichnaya)* considered the best among non-flavoured vodkas
- ~ **Старка** *(starka)* aged, a brownish colour

Грузия Georgia; this republic's wines have always been renowned; produces slightly sweet wine of superior quality, e.g., *Khvanchkara* **(Хванчкара)**, *Kindzmarauli* **(Киндзмараули)**,

Odzhaleshi **(Оджалеши)**, *Chkhaveri* **(Чхавери)**, *Tvishi* **(Твиши)**; *Salkhino* **(Салхино)** is a favourite coffee-coloured dessert wine

какао *(kakao)* cocoa

квас *(kvas)* kvass, unalcoholic rye beer, often home-made from stale dark bread steeped in hot water and allowed to ferment for a few hours; sugar, fruit or honey usually added as a sweetener

кефир *(kyefir)* sour milk

коктейль *(koktyeyl')* cocktail, usually much sweeter than western-type cocktails

~ **Десертный** *(dyesyertniy)* liqueur, sweet wine, sparkling wine

~ **Игристый** *(igristiy)* sparkling cocktail; made with soda water or champagne base

~ **Крепкий** *(kryepkiy)* strong cocktail; vodka or brandy with fruit juice

~ **Коньячный** *(kon'yachniy)* brandy base

~ **Лимонный** *(limonniy)* lemon liqueur and juice

коньяк *(kon'yak)* brandy; excellent brandies are produced in Armenia and Georgia; those from Azerbaidjan, Moldavia and the northern slopes of the Caucasus are also considered of superior quality; the finest brandies are produced by Ararat in Armenia under such labels as **Юбилейный** *(Yubilejnij)*, **Армения** *(Armenia)*, **Ереван** *(Erevan)*, as well as by **Самтрест** *(Samtrest)* in Georgia; the stars on the label indicate the number of years the brandy has been aged: 1-5 years for one star, 6-10 years for two, etc.; initials also indicate age and quality: **ОС**, very old; **ОВ**, well aged; **ВК**, of exceptional quality; **ОВВК**, well aged, of exceptional quality

кофе *(kofye)* coffee

~ **по-восточному/по-турецки** *(po-vostochnomu/po-turyetski)* Turkish-style; boiled with sugar; poured in a demi-tasse with grounds

~ **с молоком** *(s molokom)* with milk

~ **чёрный** *(chyorniy)* black

Красный Камень *(krasniy kamen')* rosé muscat wine (Crimea, Ukraine)

крюшон *(kryushon)* sparkling punch (champagne or soda water added before being served)

кумыс *(kumis)* fermented mare's milk

ликёр *(likyor)* liqueur

~ **клубничный** *(klubnichniy)* strawberry

~ **лимонный** *(limonniy)* lemon

~ **сливовый** *(slivoviy)* plum

лимонад *(limonad)* lemonade
мадера *(madyera)* imitation madeira wine; dessert wine
Массандра *(massandra)* a vineyard in Crimea famed for its muscat wine, e.g., **Красный Камень** *(Krasniy Kamen')* and **Таврида** *(Tavrida)*
Молдавия Moldavia; this republic produces one third of the nation's wine though most of it is table wine
молоко *(moloko)* milk
~ **пастеризованное** *(pastyerizovannoye)* pasteurized
~ **сгущённое** *(sgushchyonnoye)* condensed
~ **топлёное** *(toplyonoye)* baked milk
морс *(mors)* fruit water; liquid remaining from cooked fruit
~ **клюквенный** *(klyukvyenniy)* cranberry
мускат *(muskat)* muscat wine, produced mainly in Crimea, Ukraine
наливка *(nalivka)* alcoholic beverage made from macerated fruit
напиток *(napitok)* drink
Нарзан *(narzan)* a mineral water from northern Caucasus
настойка *(nastoyka)* liqueur
портвейн *(portvyeyn)* imitation port wine
пиво *(pivo)* beer; best brands are **«Жигулёвское»** *(Zhigulyovskoye)*, **«Рижское»** *(Rizhskoye)*, **«Московское»** *(Moskovskoye)*
~ **светлое** *(svyetloye)* light
~ **тёмное** *(tyomnoye)* dark
пунш *(punsh)* punch
~ **молочный** *(molochniy)* milk, brandy or liqueur and sugar
~ **ягодный с шампанским** *(yagodniy s shampanskim)* berry syrup and sparkling wine
~ **яичный** *(yaichniy)* egg yolks, milk, brandy, sugar
ром *(rom)* rum
рислинг *(risling)* a dry white wine, imitation riesling
РСФСР Russian Soviet Federated Socialist Republic; representing over three quarters of the USSR's area, the **РСФСР** sprawls over the heartland of the Soviet Union, with Moscow also serving as its administrative capital; some wine is produced in this vast region though principally table wine like the wine of the Abrow-Durso and Anapa vineyards
сладкий *(sladkiy)* sweet
сок *(sok)* juice
~ **апельсиновый** *(apyel'sinoviy)* orange
~ **виноградный** *(vinogradniy)* grape
~ **вишнёвый** *(vishnyoviy)* cherry
~ **мандариновый** *(mandarinoviy)* tangerine

~ **сливовый** *(slivoviy)* plum

~ **томатный** *(tomatniy)* tomato

~ **фруктовый** *(fruktoviy)* fruit

~ **яблочный** *(yablochniy)* apple

Средняя Азия Central Asia; wine from this region has a high sugar content; some examples: *Shirini* **(Ширини)** from Tadjikistan and *Yasman Salik* **(Ясман Салик)** and *Ter Bash* **(Тер Баш)** from Turkmenistan

сухой *(sukhoy)* dry

токай *(tokay)* tokay wine, dessert wine

херес *(khyeryes)* imitation sherry

Цимлянское *(tsimlyanskoye)* sparkling rosé wine, imitation pink champagne; produced in the Don area

чай *(chay)* tea

~ **с вареньем** *(s varyen'yem)* served with jam

~ **с лимоном** *(s limonom)* with lemon

~ **с молоком** *(s molokom)* with milk

~ **с мёдом** *(s myodom)* served with honey

Чёрный Камень *(chyorniy kamyen')* red, sweet Crimean wine

Украина Ukraine; with Crimea, this republic furnishes nearly all of the country's sparkling wine, referred to as *Shampanskoye* **(Шампанское)**; the Soviet product is often a good imitation of French champagne; *Shato-Ikyem* **(Шато-Икем)** and *Barsak* **(Барсак)** are also imitations of white Bordeaux wines; muscat wine is a speciality, particularly from the vineyards around Massandra, e.g., *Krasniy Kamen'* **(Красный Камень)** and *Tavrida* **(Таврида)**; tokay wine is produced, especially around Ay-Danil and Magaratch; favourite dessert wines are *Portvyeyn Yuzhnobyeryezhniy* **(Портвейн Южнобережный)** and *Pino gri* **(Пино Гри)**

шампанское *(shampanskoye)* sparkling wine, imitation *champagne;* can be of fine quality; nearly all produced in the Ukraine, particularly Crimea

~ **полусладкое** *(polusladkoye)* slightly sweet (7 per cent sugar content)

~ **полусухое** *(polusukhoye)* slightly dry (5 per cent sugar content)

~ **сладкое** *(sladkoye)* sweet (10 per cent sugar content)

~ **сухое** *(sukhoye)* dry (less than 5 per cent sugar content)

RUSSIAN

Spanish

Guide to pronunciation

Letter	Approximate pronunciation
Consonants	
ch, f, k, l, m, n, p, t, y	as in English
b	generally as in English but sometimes more like **v**
c	1) before **e** and **i**, like **th** in **th**in 2) otherwise, like **k** in **k**it
d	1) generally as in **d**og, although less decisive 2) between vowels and at the end of a word, like **th** in **th**is
g	1) before **e** and **i**, like **ch** in Scottish lo**ch** 2) otherwise, like **g** in **g**o
h	always silent
j	like **ch** in Scottish lo**ch**
ll	like **lli** in mi**lli**on
ñ	like **ni** in o**ni**on
qu	like **k** in **k**it

r	more strongly trilled (like a Scottish **r**), especially at the beginning of a word
rr	strongly trilled
s	always like the **s** in **s**it, often with a slight lisp
v	tends to be like **b** in **b**ad, but less tense; within a word, more like English **v**
z	like **th** in **th**in

Vowels

a	like **a** in c**a**r, but fairly short
e	1) sometimes like **a** in l**a**te 2) less often, like **e** in g**e**t
i	like **ee** in f**ee**t
o	1) sometimes fairly like **o** in r**o**pe 2) sometimes like **o** in g**o**t
u	like **oo** in l**oo**t
y	only a vowel when alone or at the end of a word; like **ee** in f**ee**t

Note

1) In forming diphthongs, **a, e** and **o** are strong vowels, and **i** and **u** are weak vowels. This means that in diphthongs the strong vowels are pronounced more strongly than the weak ones. If two weak vowels form a diphthong, the second one is pronounced more strongly.
2) In words ending with a consonant (except **n** and **s**), the last syllable is stressed.
3) In words ending with a vowel (and in those ending with **n** and **s**), the next to the last syllable is stressed.
4) Words not stressed in accordance with these rules have an acute accent (ʹ) over the vowel of the stressed syllable.

Some useful expressions

Hungry

I'm hungry/I'm thirsty.	**Tengo hambre/Tengo sed.**
Can you recommend a good restaurant?	**¿Puede recomendarme un buen restaurante?**
Are there any good, cheap restaurants around here?	**¿Hay algún restaurante bueno y barato cerca de aquí?**
I'd like to reserve a table for … people.	**Quiero reservar una mesa para ...**
We'll come at … o'clock.	**Vendremos a las ...**

Asking

Good evening. I'd like a table for … people.	**Buenas tardes, quisiera una mesa para ...**
Could we have a table…?	**¿Nos puede dar una mesa... ?**
in the corner	**en el rincón**
by the window	**al lado de la ventana**
outside	**fuera**
on the terrace	**en el patio**
May I please have the menu?	**¿Puedo ver la carta, por favor ?**
What's this?	**¿Qué es esto ?**
Do you have…?	**¿Tienen... ?**
a set menu	**platos combinados**
local dishes	**especialidades locales**
a children's menu	**un menú para niños**
Waiter/Waitress!	**¡Camarero/Señorita!**
What do you recommend?	**¿Qué me aconseja ?**
Could I have (a/an)… please?	**¿Puede darme..., por favor ?**
ashtray	**un cenicero**
another chair	**otra silla**
finger bowl	**un enjuagatorio [un lavadedos]**
fork	**un tenedor**
glass	**un vaso**

(Latin American usage is shown in brackets)

knife	**un cuchillo**
napkin	**una servilleta**
plate	**un plato**
serviette	**una servilleta**
spoon	**una cuchara**
toothpick	**un palillo**

Ordering

I'd like a/an/some…	**Quisiera...**
aperitif	**un aperitivo**
appetizer	**unas tapas [unos saladitos]**
beer	**una cerveza**
bread	**pan**
butter	**mantequilla [manteca]**
cheese	**queso**
chips	**patatas fritas [papas fritas]**
coffee	**un café**
dessert	**un postre**
fish	**pescado**
french fries	**patatas fritas [papas fritas]**
fruit	**frutas**
game	**carne de caza**
ice-cream	**un helado**
ketchup	**salsa de tomate**
lemon	**limón**
lettuce	**lechuga**
meat	**carne**
mineral water	**agua mineral**
milk	**leche**
mustard	**mostaza**
noodles	**tallarines**
oil	**aceite**
olive oil	**aceite de oliva**
pepper	**pimienta**
potatoes	**patatas [papas]**
poultry	**aves**
rice	**arroz**
rolls	**panecillos [pancitos]**
saccharin	**sacarina**
salad	**una ensalada**
salt	**sal**

sandwich	**un bocadillo [un sandwich/un emparedado]**
seafood	**mariscos**
seasoning	**condimentos**
soup	**una sopa**
starter	**unas tapas [unos saladitos]**
sugar	**azúcar**
tea	**un té**
vegetables	**legumbres**
vinegar	**vinagre**
(iced) water	**agua (helada)**
wine	**vino**

¡QUE APROVECHE!
ENJOY YOUR MEAL!

baked	**al horno**
baked in parchment	**cocido envuelto**
boiled	**hervido**
braised	**estofado**
cured	**en salazón**
fried	**frito**
grilled	**a la parrilla**
marinated	**en escabeche**
poached	**hervido**
roasted	**asado**
sautéed	**salteado [sofreído/sofrito]**
smoked	**ahumado**
steamed	**cocido al vapor**
stewed	**estofado**
underdone (rare)	**poco hecho**
medium	**regular**
well-done	**muy hecho**

¡SALUD!
CHEERS!

glass	**un vaso**
bottle	**una botella**

red	**tinto**
white	**blanco**
rosé	**clarete [rosado, rosé]**
very dry	**muy seco**
dry	**seco**
sweet	**dulce**
light	**liviano**
full-bodied	**de cuerpo**
sparkling	**espumoso**
neat (straight)	**solo**
on the rocks	**con hielo**

The bill

I'd like to pay.	**Quisiera pagar.**
We'd like to pay separately.	**Quisiéramos pagar separadamente.**
You've made a mistake in this bill, I think.	**Me parece que se ha equivocado en esta cuenta.**
What's this amount for?	**¿A qué corresponde esta cantidad?**
Is service included?	**¿Está el servicio incluido?**
Is everything included?	**¿Está todo incluido?**
Do you accept traveller's cheques?	**¿Acepta cheques de viajero?**
Thank you. This is for you.	**Gracias, esto es para usted.**
Keep the change.	**Quédese con el cambio.**
That was a very good meal.	**Ha sido una comida excelente.**
We enjoyed it, thank you.	**Nos ha gustado, gracias.**

Complaints

That's not what I ordered.	**Esto no es lo que he pedido.**
I asked for...	**He pedido...**
May I change this?	**¿Puede cambiarme esto?**

The meat is...	**La carne está...**
overdone	**demasiado hecha**
underdone	**poco hecha**
too rare	**demasiado cruda**
too tough	**demasiado dura**
This is too...	**Esto está demasiado...**
bitter/salty/sweet	**amargo/salado/dulce**
The food is cold.	**La comida está fría.**
This isn't fresh.	**Esto no está fresco.**
What's taking you so long?	**¿Por qué se demora tanto?**
Where are our drinks?	**¿Dónde están nuestras bebidas?**
This isn't clean.	**Esto no está limpio.**
Would you ask the head waiter to come over?	**¿Quiere decirle al jefe que venga?**

Numbers

1	**uno**	11	**once**
2	**dos**	12	**doce**
3	**tres**	13	**trece**
4	**cuatro**	14	**catorce**
5	**cinco**	15	**quince**
6	**seis**	16	**dieciséis**
7	**siete**	17	**diecisiete**
8	**ocho**	18	**dieciocho**
9	**nueve**	19	**diecinueve**
10	**diez**	20	**veinte**

SPANISH

Food

Please note that **ch, ll,** and **ñ** are treated as separate letters in Spanish alphabetical order.

a caballo steak topped with two eggs
acedera sorrel
aceite oil
aceituna olive
achicoria endive (US chicory)
(al) adobo marinated
aguacate avocado (pear)
ahumado smoked
ajiaceite garlic mayonnaise
ajiaco bogotano chicken soup with potatoes
(al) ajillo cooked in garlic and oil
ajo garlic
al, a la in the style of, with
albahaca basil
albaricoque apricot
albóndiga spiced meat- or fishball
alcachofa artichoke
alcaparra caper
aliñado seasoned
alioli garlic mayonnaise
almeja clam, cockle
almejas a la marinera cooked in hot, pimento sauce
almendra almond
~ **garrapiñada** sugared almond
almíbar syrup
almuerzo lunch
alubia bean
anchoa anchovy
anguila eel
angula baby eel
anticucho beef heart grilled on a skewer with green peppers
apio celery
a punto medium (done)
arenque herring
~ **en escabeche** marinated, pickled herring
arepa flapjack made of maize (corn)
arroz rice
~ **blanco** boiled, steamed
~ **escarlata** with tomatoes and prawns
~ **a la española** with chicken liver, pork, tomatoes, fish stock
~ **con leche** rice pudding
~ **primavera** with spring vegetables
~ **a la valenciana** with vegetables, chicken, shellfish (and sometimes eel)
asado roast
~ **antiguo a la venezolana mechado** roast beef stuffed with capers
asturias a strong, fermented cheese with a sharp flavour

atún tunny (US tuna)
avellana hazelnut
azafrán saffron
azúcar sugar
bacalao cod
~ **a la vizcaína** with green peppers, potatoes, tomato sauce
barbo barbel (fish)
batata sweet potato, yam
becada woodcock
berberecho cockle
berenjena aubergine (US eggplant)
berraza parsnip
berro cress
berza cabbage
besugo sea bream
bien hecho well-done
biftec, bistec beef steak
bizcocho sponge cake, sponge finger (US ladyfinger)
~ **borracho** cake steeped in rum (or wine) and syrup
bizcotela glazed biscuit (US cookie)
blando soft
bocadillo 1) sandwich 2) sweet (Colombia)
bollito, bollo roll, bun
bonito a kind of tunny (US tuna)
boquerón 1) anchovy 2) whitebait
(en) brocheta (on a) skewer
budín blancmange, custard
buey ox
buñuelo 1) doughnut 2) fritter with ham, mussels and prawns (sometimes flavoured with brandy)
burgos a popular soft, creamy cheese named after the Spanish province of its origin
butifarra spiced sausage
caballa fish of the mackerel family
cabeza de ternera calf's head
cabra goat
cabrales blue-veined goat's-milk cheese
cabrito kid
cacahuete peanut
cachelos diced potatoes boiled with cabbage, paprika, garlic, bacon, *chorizo* sausage
calabacín vegetable marrow, courgette (US zucchini)
calabaza pumpkin
calamar squid
calamares a la romana squids fried in batter
caldereta de cabrito kid stew (often cooked in red wine)
caldillo de congrio conger-eel soup with tomatoes and potatoes
caldo consommé
~ **gallego** meat and vegetable broth
callos tripe (often served in pimento sauce)
~ **a la madrileña** in piquant sauce with *chorizo* sausage and tomatoes
camarón shrimp
canela cinnamon
cangrejo de mar crab
cangrejo de río crayfish
cantarela chanterelle mushroom
caracol snail
carbonada criolla baked pumpkin stuffed with diced beef
carne meat
~ **asada al horno** roast meat
~ **molida** minced beef
~ **a la parrilla** charcoal-grilled steak
~ **picada** minced beef
carnero mutton
carpa carp
casero home made

castaña chestnut
castañola sea perch
(a la) catalana with onions, parsley, tomatoes and herbs
caza game
(a la) cazadora with mushrooms, spring onions, herbs in wine
cazuela de cordero lamb stew with vegetables
cebolla onion
cebolleta chive
cebrero blue-veined cheese of creamy texture with a pale, yellow rind; sharp taste
cena dinner, supper
centolla spider-crab, served cold
cerdo pork
cereza cherry
ceviche fish marinated in lemon and lime juice
cigala Dublin Bay prawn
cincho a hard cheese made from sheep's milk
ciruela plum
~ **pasa** prune
cocido 1) cooked, boiled 2) stew of beef with ham, fowl, chick peas, potatoes and vegetables (the broth is eaten first)
cochifrito de cordero highly seasoned stew of lamb or kid
codorniz quail
col cabbage
~ **de Bruselas** brussels sprout
coliflor cauliflower
comida meal
compota stewed fruit
conejo rabbit
confitura jam
congrio conger eel
consomé al jerez chicken broth with sherry
copa nuria egg-yolk and egg-white, whipped and served with jam
corazón de alcachofa artichoke heart
corazonada heart stewed in sauce
cordero lamb
~ **recental** spring lamb
cortadillo small pancake with lemon
corzo deer
costilla chop
crema 1) cream or mousse
~ **batida** whipped cream
~ **española** dessert of milk, eggs, fruit jelly
~ **nieve** frothy egg-yolk, sugar, rum (or wine)
crema 2) soup
criadillas (de toro) glands (of bull)
(a la) criolla with green peppers, spices and tomatoes
croqueta croquette, fish or meat dumpling
crudo raw
cubierto cover charge
cuenta bill (US check)
curanto dish consisting of seafood, vegetables and suck(l)ing pig, all cooked in an earthen well, lined with charcoal
chabacano apricot
chalote shallot
champiñón mushroom
chancho adobado pork braised with sweet potatoes, orange and lemon juice
chanfaina goat's liver and kidney stew, served in a thick sauce
chanquete whitebait
chile chili pepper
chiles en nogada green peppers stuffed with whipped cream and nut sauce
chimichurri hot parsley sauce
chipirón small squid

hopa a kind of sea bream
horizo pork sausage, highly seasoned with garlic and paprika
huleta cutlet
hupe de mariscos scallops served with a creamy sauce and gratinéed with cheese
hurro sugared tubular fritter
amasco variety of apricot
átil date
esayuno breakfast
orada gilt-head
ulce sweet
~ **de naranja** marmalade
urazno peach
mbuchado stuffed with meat
mbutido spicy sausage
mpanada pie or tart with meat or fish filling
~ **de horno** dough filled with minced meat, similar to ravioli
mpanadilla small patty stuffed with seasoned meat or fish
mpanado breaded
mperador swordfish
ncurtido pickle
nchilada a maizeflour (US cornmeal) pancake *(tortilla)* stuffed and usually served with vegetable garnish and sauce
~ **roja** sausage-filled maizeflour pancake dipped into a red sweet-pepper sauce
~ **verde** maizeflour pancake stuffed with meat or fowl and braised in a green-tomato sauce
ndibia chicory (US endive)
neldo dill
nsalada salad
~ **común** green
~ **de frutas** fruit salad
~ **(a la) primavera** spring
~ **valenciana** with green peppers, lettuce and oranges
ensaladilla rusa diced cold vegetables with mayonnaise
entremés appetizer, hors-d'oeuvre
erizo de mar sea urchin
(en) escabeche marinated, pickled
~ **de gallina** chicken marinated in vinegar
escarcho red gurnard (fish)
escarola endive (US chicory)
espalda shoulder
(a la) española with tomatoes
espárrago asparagus
especia spice
especialidad de la casa chef's speciality
espinaca spinach
esqueixada mixed fish salad
(al) estilo de in the style of
estofado stew(ed)
estragón tarragon
fabada (asturiana) stew of pork, beans, bacon and sausage
faisán pheasant
fiambres cold meat (US cold cuts)
fideo thin noodle
filete steak
~ **de lomo** fillet steak (US tenderloin)
~ **de res** beef steak
~ **de lenguado empanado** breaded fillet of sole
(a la) flamenca with onions, peas, green peppers, tomatoes and spiced sausage
flan caramel mould, custard
frambuesa raspberry
(a la) francesa sautéed in butter
fresa strawberry
~ **de bosque** wild
fresco fresh, chilled
fresón large strawberry
fricandó veal bird, thin slice of meat rolled in bacon and braised

frijol bean
frijoles refritos fried mashed beans
frío cold
frito 1) fried 2) fry
~ **de patata** deep-fried potato croquette
fritura fry
~ **mixta** meat, fish or vegetables deep-fried in batter
fruta fruit
~ **escarchada** crystallized (US candied) fruit
galleta salted or sweet biscuit (US cracker or cookie)
~ **de nata** cream biscuit (US sandwich cookie)
gallina hen
~ **de Guinea** guinea fowl
gallo cockerel
gamba shrimp
~ **grande** prawn
gambas con mayonesa shrimp cocktail
ganso goose
garbanzo chick pea
gazpacho seasoned broth made of raw onions, garlic, tomatoes, cucumber and green pepper; served chilled
(a la) gitanilla with garlic
gordo fatty, rich (of food)
granada pomegranate
grande large
(al) gratín gratinéed
gratinado gratinéed
grelo turnip greens
grosella currant
~ **espinosa** gooseberry
~ **negra** blackcurrant
~ **roja** redcurrant
guacamole a purée of avocado and spices used as a dip, in a salad, for a *tortilla* filling or as a garnish
guarnición garnish, trimming
guayaba guava (fruit)
guinda sour cherry
guindilla chili pepper
guisado stew(ed)
guisante green pea
haba broad bean
habichuela verde French bean (US green bean)
hamburguesa hamburger
hayaca central maizeflour (US cornmeal) pancake, usually with a minced-meat filling
helado ice-cream, ice
hervido 1) boiled 2) stew of beef and vegetables (Latin America)
hielo ice
hierba herb
hierbas finas finely chopped mixture of herbs
hígado liver
higo fig
hinojo fennel
hongo mushroom
(al) horno baked
hortaliza greens
hueso bone
huevo egg
~ **cocido** boiled
~ **duro** hard-boiled
~ **escalfado** poached
~ **a la española** stuffed with tomatoes and served with cheese sauce
~ **a la flamenca** baked with asparagus, peas, peppers, onions, tomatoes and sausage
~ **frito** fried
~ **al nido** egg-yolk placed into small, soft roll, fried, then covered with egg-white
~ **pasado por agua** soft-boiled
~ **revuelto** scrambled

~ **con tocino** bacon and egg
umita boiled maize (US corn) with tomatoes, green peppers, onions and cheese
a la) inglesa 1) underdone (of meat) 2) boiled 3) served with boiled vegetables
abalí wild boar
alea jelly
amón ham
~ **cocido** boiled (often referred to as *jamón de York*)
~ **en dulce** boiled and served cold
~ **gallego** smoked and cut thinly
~ **serrano** cured and cut thinly
a la) jardinera with carrots, peas and other vegetables
engibre ginger
al) jerez braised in sherry
udía bean
~ **verde** French bean (US green bean)
ugo gravy, meat juice
en su ~ in its own juice
uliana with shredded vegetables
urel variety of mackerel
acón shoulder of pork
~ **curado** salted pork
amprea lamprey
angosta spiny lobster
angostino Norway lobster, Dublin Bay prawn
aurel bay leaf
echón suck(l)ing pig
echuga lettuce
egumbre vegetable
engua tongue
enguado sole, flounder
~ **frito** fried fillet of sole on bed of vegetables
enteja lentil
iebre hare
~ **estofada** jugged hare
lima 1) lime 2) sweet lime (Latin America)
limón lemon
lista de platos menu
lista de vinos wine list
lobarro a variety of bass
lombarda red cabbage
lomo loin
longaniza long, highly seasoned sausage
lonja slice of meat
lubina bass
macarrones macaroni
(a la) madrileña with *chorizo* sausage, tomatoes and paprika
magras al estilo de Aragón cured ham in tomato sauce
maíz maize (US corn)
(a la) mallorquina usually refers to highly seasoned fish and shellfish
manchego hard cheese from La Mancha, made from sheep's milk, white or golden-yellow in colour
maní peanut
mantecado 1) small butter cake 2) custard ice-cream
mantequilla butter
manzana apple
~ **en dulce** in honey
(a la) marinera usually with mussels, onions, tomatoes, herbs and wine
marisco seafood
matambre rolled beef stuffed with vegetables
mayonesa mayonnaise
mazapán marzipan, almond paste
mejillón mussel
mejorana marjoram
melaza treacle, molasses
melocotón peach

SPANISH

membrillo quince
menestra boiled green vegetable soup
~ **de pollo** chicken and vegetable soup
menta mint
menú menu
~ **del día** set menu
~ **turístico** tourist menu
menudillos giblets
merengue meringue
merienda snack
merluza hake
mermelada jam
mezclado mixed
miel honey
(a la) milanesa with cheese, generally baked
minuta menu
mixto mixed
mole poblano chicken served with a sauce of chili peppers, spices and chocolate
molusco mollusc (snail, mussel, clam)
molleja sweetbread
mora mulberry
morcilla black pudding (US blood sausage)
morilla morel mushroom
moros y cristianos rice and black beans with diced ham, garlic, green peppers and herbs
mostaza mustard
mújol mullet
nabo turnip
naranja orange
nata cream
~ **batida** whipped cream
natillas custard
~ **al limón** lemon cream
níspola medlar (fruit)
nopalito young cactus leaf served with salad dressing
nuez nut
~ **moscada** nutmeg
olla stew
~ **gitana** vegetable stew
~ **podrida** stew made of vegetables, meat, fowl and ham
ostra oyster
oveja ewe
pabellón criollo beef in tomato sauce garnished with beans, rice and bananas
paella consists basically of saffron rice with assorted seafood and sometimes meat
~ **alicantina** with green peppers, onions, tomatoes, artichokes and fish
~ **catalana** with sausages, pork, squid, tomatoes, red sweet peppers and peas
~ **marinera** with fish, shellfish and meat
~ **(a la) valenciana** with chicken, shrimps, peas, tomatoes, mussels and garlic
palmito palm heart
palta avocado (pear)
pan bread
panecillo roll
papa potato
papas a la huancaína with cheese and green peppers
(a la) parrilla grilled
parrillada mixta mixed grill
pasado done, cooked
bien ~ well-done
poco ~ underdone (US rare)
pastas noodles, macaroni, spaghetti
pastel cake, pie
~ **de choclo** maize with minced beef, chicken, raisins and olives
pastelillo small tart
pata trotter (US foot)

SPANISH

patatas potatoes
~ **fritas** fried; usually chips (US french fries)
~ **(a la) leonesa** with onions
~ **nuevas** new
pato duck, duckling
pavo turkey
pechuga breast (of fowl)
pepinillo gherkin (US pickle)
pepino cucumber
(en) pepitoria stewed with onions, green peppers and tomatoes
pera pear
perca perch
percebe barnacle (shellfish)
perdiz partridge
~ **en escabeche** cooked in oil with vinegar, onions, parsley, carrots and green pepper; served cold
~ **estofada** stewed and served with a white-wine sauce
perejil parsley
perifollo chervil
perilla a firm, bland cheese
pescadilla whiting
pescado fish
pez espada swordfish
picadillo minced meat, hash
picado minced
picante sharp, spicy, highly seasoned
picatoste deep-fried slice of bread
pichoncillo young pigeon (US squab)
pierna leg
pimentón chili pepper
pimienta pepper
pimiento sweet pepper
~ **morrón** red (sweet) pepper
pincho moruno grilled meat (often kidneys) on a skewer, sometimes served with spicy sauces
pintada guinea fowl
piña pineapple
pisto diced and sautéed vegetables: mainly aubergines, green peppers and tomatoes; served cold
(a la) plancha grilled on a girdle
plátano banana
plato plate, dish, portion
~ **típico de la región** regional speciality
pollito spring chicken
pollo chicken
~ **pibil** simmered in fruit juice and spices
polvorón hazelnut biscuit (US cookie)
pomelo grapefruit
porción portion
porotos granados shelled beans served with pumpkin and maize (US corn)
postre dessert, sweet
potaje vegetable soup
puchero stew
puerro leek
pulpo octopus
punta de espárrago asparagus tip
punto de nieve dessert of whipped cream with beaten egg-whites
puré de patatas mashed potatoes
queso cheese
quisquilla shrimp
rábano radish
~ **picante** horse-radish
raja slice or portion
rallado grated
rape angler fish
ravioles ravioli
raya skate, ray
rebanada slice
rebozado breaded or fried in batter
recargo extra charge
rehogada sautéed

SPANISH

relleno stuffed
remolacha beetroot
repollo cabbage
requesón a fresh-curd cheese
riñón kidney
róbalo haddock
rodaballo turbot, flounder
(a la) romana dipped in batter and fried
romero rosemary
roncal cheese made from sheep's milk; close grained and hard in texture with a few small holes; piquant flavour
ropa vieja cooked, left-over meat and vegetables, covered with tomatoes and green peppers
rosbif roast beef
rosquilla doughnut
rubio red mullet
ruibarbo rhubarb
sal salt
salado salted, salty
salchicha small pork sausage for frying
salchichón salami
salmón salmon
salmonete red mullet
salsa sauce
~ **blanca** white
~ **española** brown sauce with herbs, spices and wine
~ **mayordoma** butter and parsley
~ **picante** hot pepper
~ **romana** bacon or ham, egg, cream (sometimes flavoured with nutmeg)
~ **tártara** tartar
~ **verde** parsley
salsifí salsify
salteado sauté(ed)
salvia sage
san simón a firm, bland cheese resembling *perilla*; shiny yellow rind
sandía watermelon
sardina sardine, pilchard
sémola semolina
sencillo plain
sepia cuttlefish
servicio service
~ **(no) incluido** (not) included
sesos brains
seta mushroom
sobrasada salami
solomillo fillet steak (US tenderloin)
sopa soup
~ **(de) cola de buey** oxtail
~ **sevillana** a highly spiced fish soup
suave soft
suflé soufflé
suizo bun
surtido assorted
taco wheat or maizeflour (US cornmeal) pancake usually with a meat filling and garnished with a spicy sauce
tajada slice
tallarín noodle
tamal a pastry dough of coarsely ground maizeflour with meat or fruit filling, steamed in maizehusks (US corn husks)
tapa appetizer, snack
tarta cake, tart
~ **helada** ice-cream tart
ternera veal
tocino bacon
~ **de cielo** 1) caramel mould 2) custard-filled cake
tomate tomato
tomillo thyme
tordo thrush
toronja variety of grapefruit
tortilla 1) omelet 2) a type of

SPANISH

pancake made with maizeflour (US cornmeal)
~ **de chorizo** with pieces of a spicy sausage
~ **a la española** with onions, potatoes and seasoning
~ **a la francesa** plain
~ **gallega** potatoes with ham, red sweet peppers and peas
~ **a la jardinera** with mixed, diced vegetables
~ **al ron** rum
tortita waffle
tortuga turtle
tostada toast
tripas tripe
trucha trout
~ **frita a la asturiana** floured and fried in butter, garnished with lemon
trufa truffle
turrón nougat
ulloa a soft cheese from Galicia, rather like a mature camembert
uva grape
~ **pasa** raisin
vaca salada corned beef
vainilla vanilla
(a la) valenciana with rice, tomatoes and garlic
variado varied, assorted
varios sundries
venado venison
venera scallop, coquille St. Jacques
verdura greens
vieira scallop
villalón a cheese from sheep's milk
vinagre vinegar
vinagreta a piquant vinegar dressing (vinaigrette) to accompany salads
(a la) ~ marinated in oil and vinegar or lemon juice with mixed herbs
(a la) vizcaína with green peppers, tomatoes, garlic and paprika
yema egg-yolk
yemas a dessert of whipped egg-yolks and sugar
zanahoria carrot
zarzamora blackberry
zarzuela savoury stew of assorted fish and shellfish
~ **de mariscos** seafood stew
~ **de pescado** selection of fish served with a highly seasoned sauce
~ **de verduras** vegetable stew

Drink

abocado sherry made from a blend of sweet and dry wines
agua water
aguardiente spirits
Alicante this region to the south of Valencia produces a large quantity of red table wine and some good rosé, particularly from Yecla
Amontillado medium-dry sherry,

light amber in colour, with a nutty flavour
Andalucía a drink of dry sherry and orange juice
Angélica a Basque herb liqueur similar to yellow Chartreuse
anís aniseed liqueur
Anís del Mono a Calatonian aniseed liqueur
anís seco aniseed brandy
anisado an aniseed-based soft drink which may be slightly alcoholic
batido milk shake
bebida drink
Bobadilla Gran Reserva a wine-distilled brandy
botella bottle
 media ~ half bottle
café coffee
 ~ **cortado** small cup of strong coffee with a dash of milk or cream
 ~ **descafeinado** coffeine-free
 ~ **exprés** espresso
 ~ **granizado** iced (white)
 ~ **con leche** white
 ~ **negro/solo** black
Calisay a quinine-flavoured liqueur
Carlos I a wine-distilled brandy
Cataluña Catalonia; this region southwest of Barcelona is known for its *xampañ*, bearing little resemblance to the famed French sparkling wine
Cazalla an aniseed liqueur
cerveza beer
 ~ **de barril** draught (US draft)
 ~ **dorada** light
 ~ **negra** dark
cola de mono a blend of coffee, milk, rum and *pisco*
coñac 1) French Cognac 2) term applied to any Spanish wine-distilled brandy
Cordoníu a brand-name of Catalonian sparkling wine locally referred to as *xampañ* (champagne)
cosecha harvest; indicates the vintage of wine
crema de cacao cocoa liqueur, crème de cacao
Cuarenta y Tres an egg liqueur
Cuba libre rum and Coke
champán, champaña 1) French Champagne 2) term applied to any Spanish sparkling wine
chicha de manzana apple brandy
Chinchón an aniseed liqueur
chocolate chocolate drink
 ~ **con leche** hot chocolate with milk
Dulce dessert wine
Fino dry sherry wine, very pale and straw-coloured
Fundador a wine-distilled brandy
Galicia this Atlantic coastal region has good table wines
gaseosa fizzy (US carbonated) water
ginebra gin
gran vino term found on Chilean wine labels to indicate a wine of exceptional quality
granadina pomegranate syrup mixed with wine or brandy
horchata de almendra (or **de chufa)** drink made from ground almonds (or Jerusalem artichoke
Jerez 1) sherry 2) the Spanish region near the Portuguese border, internationally renowned for its *Jerez*
jugo fruit juice
leche milk
limonada lemonade, lemon

squash
Málaga 1) dessert wine 2) the region in the south of Spain, is particularly noted for its dessert wine
Manzanilla dry sherry, very pale and straw-coloured
margarita *tequila* with lime juice
Montilla a dessert wine from near Cordoba, often drunk as an aperitif
Moscatel fruity dessert wine
naranjada orangeade
Oloroso sweet, dark sherry, drunk as dessert wine, resembles brown cream sherry
Oporto port (wine)
pisco grape brandy
ponche crema egg-nog liquor
Priorato the region south of Barcelona produces good quality red and white wine but also a dessert wine, usually called *Priorato* but renamed *Tarragona* when it is exported
refresco a soft drink
reservado term found on Chilean wine labels to indicate a wine of exceptional quality
Rioja the northern region near the French border is considered to produce Spain's best wines—especially red; some of the finest Rioja wines resemble good Bordeaux wines
ron rum
sangría a mixture of red wine, ice, orange, lemon, brandy and sugar
sangrita *tequila* with tomato, orange and lime juices
sidra cider
sol y sombra a blend of wine-distilled brandy and aniseed liqueur
sorbete (iced) fruit drink
té tea
tequila brandy made from agave (US aloe)
tinto 1) red wine 2) black coffee with sugar (Colombia)
Tío Pepe a brand-name sherry
Triple Seco an orange liqueur
Valdepeñas the region south of Madrid is an important wine-producing area
vermú vermouth
Veterano Osborne a wine-distilled brandy
vino wine
~ **blanco** white
~ **clarete** rosé
~ **común** table wine
~ **dulce** dessert
~ **espumoso** sparkling
~ **de mesa** table wine
~ **del país** local wine
~ **rosado** rosé
~ **seco** dry
~ **suave** sweet
~ **tinto** red
xampañ Catalonian sparkling wine
Yerba mate South American holly tea
zumo juice

SPANISH

Swedish

Guide to pronunciation

Letter	Approximate pronunciation
Consonants	
b, c, d, f, h, l, m, n, p, v, w, x	as in English
ch	at the beginning of words borrowed from French, like **sh** in **sh**ut
g	1) before stressed **i, e, y, ä, ö** and sometimes after **l** or **r**, like **y** in **y**et 2) before **e** and **i** in many words of French origin, like **sh** in **sh**ut 3) elsewhere, generally like **g** in **g**o
j, dj, gj, lj	like **y** in **y**et
k	1) before stressed **i, e, y, ä, ö,** generally like **ch** in Scottish lo**ch**, but pronounced in the front of the mouth 2) elsewhere, like **k** in **k**it
kj	like **ch** in Scottish lo**ch**, but pronounced in the front of the mouth

qu	like **k** in **k**it followed by **v** in **v**at
r	slightly rolled near the front of the mouth
s	1) in the ending **-sion** like **sh** in **sh**ut 2) elsewhere, like **s** in **s**o 3) the groups **sch, skj, stj** are pronounced like **sh** in **sh**ut
sk	1) before stressed **e, i, y, ä, ö,** like **sh** in **sh**ut 2) elsewhere, like **sk** in **sk**ip
t	1) **ti** in the ending **-tion** is pronounced like **sh** in **sh**ut or like **ch** in **ch**at 2) elsewhere, like **t** in **t**op
tj	like **ch** in Scottish lo**ch;** but pronounced in the front of the mouth; sometimes with a **t** sound at the beginning
z	like **s** in **s**o

Notice that in the groups **rd, rl, rn, rs** and **rt,** the letter **r** is generally not pronounced but influences the pronunciation of the **d, l, n, s** or **t** which is then pronounced with the end of the tongue, *not* on the upper front teeth, but behind the gums of the upper teeth.

SWEDISH

Vowels

A vowel is generally long in stressed syllables when it's the final letter or followed by only one consonant. If followed by two or more consonants or in unstressed syllables, the vowel is generally short.

a	1) when long, like **a** in c**a**r 2) when short, something like the **u** in c**u**t
e	1) when long, like **ay** in s**ay,** but a *pure* vowel, not a diphthong 2) in the stressed prefix **er-,** like **a** in m**a**n, but longer 3) when short, like **e** in g**e**t 4) when unstressed, like **a** in **a**bout
ej	like **a** in m**a**te
i	1) when long, like **ee** in b**ee** 2) when short, between **ee** in m**ee**t and **i** in h**i**t
o	1) when long, often like **oo** in s**oo**n, but with the lips more tightly rounded and with a puff of breath at the end 2) the same sound can be short 3) when long, it's also sometimes pronounced like **oa** in m**oa**n 4) when short, sometimes like **o** in h**o**t
u	1) when long, like Swedish **y,** but with the tongue a little lower in the mouth and with a puff of breath at the end

	2) when short, a little more like the **u** of **pu**t; a very difficult sound
y	pronounce the **ee** of b**ee** and then round your lips without moving your tongue; the sound can be long or short
å	1) when long, like **aw** in r**aw**, but with the tongue a little higher in the mouth 2) when short, like **o** in h**o**t
ä	1) when followed by **r**, like **a** in m**a**n; either long or short 2) elsewhere, like **e** in g**e**t; either long or short
ö	like **u** in f**u**r; either long or short; when followed by **r**, it's pronounced with the mouth a little more open

Note

The principal stress is generally on the *first* syllable of a word unless it comes from Latin or French.

Some useful expressions

Hungry

I'm hungry/I'm thirsty.	**Jag är hungrig/Jag är törstig.**
Can you recommend a good restaurant?	**Kan Ni rekommendera en bra restaurang?**
Are there any good, cheap restaurants around here?	**Finns det några bra och billiga restauranger i närheten?**
I'd like to reserve a table for ... people.	**Jag skulle vilja beställa ett bord för ...**
We'll come at ... o'clock.	**Vi kommer kl. ...**

Asking

Good evening. I'd like a table for ... people.	**God afton, jag skulle vilja ha ett bord för ...**
Could we have a table...?	**Kan vi få ett...?**
in the corner	**hörnbord**
by the window	**fönsterbord**
outside	**bord utomhus**
on the terrace	**bord på terrassen**

May I please have the menu?	**Kan jag få se på matsedeln?**
What's this?	**Vad är detta?**
Do you have...?	**Har Ni...?**
a set menu	**en "dagens meny"**
local dishes	**specialiteter från trakten**
a children's menu	**en barnmatsedel**
Waiter/Waitress!	**Hovmästaren/Fröken!**
What do you recommend?	**Vad föreslår Ni?**
Could I have (a/an)... please?	**Kan jag få...**
ashtray	**en askkopp**
another chair	**en stol till**
finger bowl	**en sköljkopp**
fork	**en gaffel**
glass	**ett glas**
knife	**en kniv**
napkin	**en servett**
plate	**en tallrik**
pepper mill	**en pepparkvarn**
serviette	**en servett**
spoon	**en sked**
toothpick	**en tandpetare**

Ordering

I'd like a/an/some...	**Jag skulle vilja ha...**
aperitif	**en aperitif**
appetizer	**en förrätt**
beer	**en öl**
bread	**bröd**
butter	**smör**
cheese	**ost**
chips	**pommes frites**
coffee	**kaffe**
dessert	**en efterrätt**
fish	**fisk**
french fries	**pommes frites**
fruit	**frukt**
game	**vilt**
ice-cream	**glass**

lemon	**citron**
lettuce	**grönsallad**
meat	**kött**
mineral water	**mineralvatten**
milk	**mjölk**
mustard	**senap**
noodles	**nudlar**
oil	**olja**
olive oil	**olivolja**
pepper	**peppar**
potatoes	**potatis**
poultry	**fågel**
rice	**ris**
rolls	**kuvertbröd**
saccharin	**sackarin**
salad	**en sallad**
salt	**salt**
sandwich	**en smörgås**
seafood	**skaldjur**
seasoning	**kryddor**
soup	**en soppa**
starter	**en förrätt**
sugar	**socker**
tea	**te**
vegetables	**grönsaker**
vinegar	**vinäger**
(iced) water	**(is)vatten**
wine	**vin**

SMAKLIG MÅLTID!
ENJOY YOUR MEAL!

baked	**ugnsbakad**
baked in parchment	**ugnsbakad i smörgåspapper**
boiled	**kokt**
braised	**bräserad**
cured	**saltad**
fried	**stekt**
grilled	**grillad**
marinated	**marinerad**

poached	**pocherad**
poached (of eggs)	**förlorat**
roasted	**ugnstekt**
sautéed	**brynt**
smoked	**rökt**
steamed	**ångkokt**
stewed	**kokt på svag värme**
underdone (rare)	**blodig**
medium	**lagom**
well-done	**välstekt**

SKÅL!
CHEERS!

glass	**glas**
bottle	**flaska**
red	**rött**
white	**vitt**
rosé	**rosé**
very dry	**mycket torrt**
dry	**torrt**
sweet	**sött**
light	**lätt**
full-bodied	**fylligt**
sparkling	**mousserande**
neat (straight)	**ren**
on the rocks	**med isbitar**

The bill

I'd like to pay.	**Kan jag få notan, tack?**
We'd like to pay separately.	**Vi vill betala var och en för sig.**
You've made a mistake in this bill, I think.	**Jag tror Ni har gjort ett litet fel på notan.**
What's this amount for?	**Vad står den här summan för?**
Is service included?	**Är dricksen inräknad?**
Is everything included?	**Är allt inräknat?**

SWEDISH

Do you accept traveller's cheques?	**Tar Ni emot resechecker?**
Thank you. This is for you.	**Tack så mycket, det här är för Er.**
Keep the change.	**Behåll växeln.**
That was a very good meal.	**Det var mycket gott.**
We enjoyed it, thank you.	**Vi tyckte mycket om det.**

Complaints

That's not what I ordered.	**Jag har inte beställt det här.**
I asked for...	**Jag bad om...**
May I change this?	**Kan jag få byta ut det här?**
The meat is...	**Köttet är...**
overdone	**för hårt stekt**
underdone	**inte tillräckligt stekt**
too rare	**för rått**
too tough	**för segt**
This is too...	**Det här är alltför...**
bitter/salty/sweet	**beskt/salt/sött**
The food is cold.	**Maten är kall.**
This isn't fresh.	**Det här är inte färskt.**
What's taking you so long?	**Varför tar det så lång tid?**
Where are our drinks?	**Vad händer med vår beställning?**
This isn't clean.	**Det här är inte rent.**
Would you ask the head waiter to come over?	**Kan Ni be hovmästaren komma hit?**

Numbers

1	**en, ett**	11	**elva**
2	**två**	12	**tolv**
3	**tre**	13	**tretton**
4	**fyra**	14	**fjorton**
5	**fem**	15	**femton**
6	**sex**	16	**sexton**
7	**sju**	17	**sjutton**
8	**åtta**	18	**arton**
9	**nio**	19	**nitton**
10	**tio**	20	**tjugo**

Food

Please note that Swedish alphabetical order is **a-z, å, ä, ö.**

abborre perch
aladåb aspic
ananas pineapple
and wild duck
anka duck
ansjovis marinated sprats
apelsin orange
aprikos apricot
aromsmör herb butter
bakad baked
bakelse pastry, fancy cake
banan banana
barnmatsedel children's menu
betjäningsavgift service charge
biff beef steak
~ **à la Lindström** minced beef mixed with pickled beetroot, capers and onions, shaped into patties and fried
~ **Rydberg** fried diced beef and potatoes, served with a light mustard sauce
bit piece
björnbär blackberry
bladspenat spinach
blandad mixed, assorted
blini buckwheat pancake
blodpudding black pudding (US blood sausage)
blomkål cauliflower
blåbär bilberry (US blueberry)
bondbönor broad beans
bruna bönor baked brown beans flavoured with vinegar and syrup
brylépudding caramel blanc-mange (US caramel custard)
brynt browned
brysselkål brussels sprout
bräckkorv smoked pork sausage
bräckt sautéed, fried
bräserad braised
bröd bread
~ **och smör** bread and butter
bröst breast (of fowl)
buljong consommé
bär berry
böckling smoked herring
böna bean
camembert soft, runny cheese with pungent flavour
champinjon button mushroom
choklad chocolate
citron lemon
dagens rätt dish of the day
dietmat diet food
dill dill
~ **kött** stewed lamb or veal served with a sour-sweet dill sauce

dricks tip
duva pigeon (US squab)
efterrätt dessert
enbär juniper berry
endiv chicory (US endive)
enrisrökt smoked over juniper embers
entrecote sirloin steak, rib-eye steak
falukorv lightly smoked pork sausage
fasan pheasant
fastlagsbulle bun filled with almond paste and cream, eaten during Lent
fattiga riddare French toast; bread dipped in batter and fried, served with sugar and jam
femöring med ägg small steak topped with fried egg and served with onions
filbunke junket
filé fillet (US tenderloin)
~ **Oscar** fillets of veal served with bearnaise sauce (vinegar, egg-yolks, butter, shallots and tarragon), asparagus tips and lobster
filmjölk sour milk, type of thin junket
fisk fish
~**bullar** codfish-balls
~**färs** loaf, mousse
~**gratäng** baked casserole
~**pinnar** sticks
flamberad flamed (with liquor)
flundra flounder
fläsk pork
~ **med löksås** slices of thick bacon served with onion sauce
~**filé** fillet (US tenderloin)
~**karré** loin
~**korv** boiled sausage
~**kotlett** chop
~**lägg** boiled, pickled knuckle
~**pannkaka** pancake with diced bacon
~**stek** roast
forell trout
franskbröd white bread
frasvåffla warm (crisp) waffle
frikadell boiled veal meat ball
friterad deep-fried
~ **camembert** deep-fried pieces of *camembert* served with Arctic cloudberry jam
fromage mousse, blancmange
frukost breakfast
~**flingor** dry breakfast cereal, cornflakes
frukt fruit
frusen grädde frozen whipped cream
fylld stuffed, filled
fyllning stuffing, forcemeat
fågel fowl, game bird
får mutton
~ **i kål** Irish stew; mutton (more usually lamb) and cabbage stew
fänkål fennel
färsk fresh, new
färska räkor unshelled fresh shrimps
färskrökt lax slightly smoked salmon
förrätt starter, first course
gelé jelly, aspic
getost a soft, rather sweet whey cheese made from goat's milk
glace au four sponge cake filled with ice-cream, covered with meringue, quickly browned in oven and served flaming (US baked Alaska)
glass ice-cream
~**tårta** ice-cream cake

grapefrukt grapefruit
gratinerad oven-browned
gratäng (au) gratin
gravad lax (gravlax) fresh salmon cured with sugar, sea salt, pepper and dill; served with mustard sauce
gravad strömming marinated Baltic herring
grillad grilled, broiled
grillkorv grilled sausage
gris pork
~**fötter** pigs' trotters (US pigs' feet)
~**hals** scrag
grodlår frogs' legs
grytstek pot roast
grädde cream
gräddfil sour cream
gräddmjölk light cream (half and half)
gräddtårta sponge layer cake with cream and jam filling
gräslök chive
grönkål kale
grönpeppar green peppercorn
grönsak vegetable
grönsakssoppa vegetable soup
grönsallad lettuce
gröt porridge
gurka cucumber, gherkin
gås goose
~**lever** 1) goose liver 2) goose-liver pâté
gädda pike
gäddfärsbullar pike dumplings
gös pike-perch (US walleyed pike)
hackad minced, chopped
~ **biff med lök** hamburger steak with fried onions
hallon raspberry
halstrad grilled over open fire
haricots verts French beans (US green beans)
harstek roast hare
hasselbackspotatis sliced potatoes covered with melted butter, then roasted
hasselnöt hazelnut
havregryn oats
havregrynsgröt oatmeal (porridge)
havskräfta seawater crayfish, Dublin Bay prawn
helgeflundra halibut
helstekt roasted whole
hemlagad home-made
herrgårdsost hard cheese with a mild to slightly strong flavour
hjortron Arctic cloudberry
honung honey
hovdessert meringue with whipped cream and chocolate sauce
hummer lobster
husmanskost home cooking, plain food
hälleflundra halibut
hälsokost organic health food
hökarpanna kidney stew with bacon, potatoes and onions, braised in beer
höna boiling fowl
höns med ris och curry boiled chicken, curry sauce and rice
ingefära ginger
inkokt boiled and served cold
inlagd marinated in vinegar, sugar and spices
is ice
~**glass** water ice (US sherbet)
~**kyld** iced
islandssill Iceland herring
isterband coarse, very tasty pork sausage
Janssons frestelse layers of sliced

potatoes, onions and marinated sprats, baked with cream
jordgubbe strawberry
jordgubbstårta sponge cake with whipped cream and strawberries
jordnöt peanut
jordärtskocka Jerusalem artichoke
jordärtskockspuré purée of Jerusalem artichoke
julbord buffet of Christmas specialities
julskinka baked ham
jultallrik plate of specialities taken from the *julbord*
jägarschnitzel veal cutlet with mushrooms
järpe hazelhen
kaka cake, biscuit (US cookie)
kalkon turkey
kall cold
kallskuret cold meat (US cold cuts)
kalops beef stew flavoured with bay leaves
kalorifattig low calorie
kalv veal, calf
~**bräss** sweetbread
~**filé** fillet (US tenderloin)
~**frikassé** stew
~**järpe** meatball made of minced veal
~**kotlett** chop
~**lever** liver
~**njure** kidney
~**schnitzel** cutlet
~**stek** roast
~**sylta** potted veal
~**tunga** tongue
kanel cinnamon
~**bulle** cinnamon roll
kanin rabbit
kantarell chanterelle mushroom
kapris caper
karljohanssvamp boletus mushroom
kassler lightly smoked loin of pork
kastanj chestnut
kastanjepuré chestnut purée
katrinplommon prune
kaviar caviar
röd ~ cod's roe (red, salted)
svart ~ black caviar, roe from lumpfish
keso a type of cottage cheese
kex biscuit (US cookie)
knyte filled puff pastry (US turnover)
knäckebröd crisp bread (US hardtack)
kokad boiled, cooked
kokos grated coconut
~**kaka** coconut macaroon
kokt boiled, cooked
kolasås caramel sauce
kolja haddock
kompott stewed fruit
korv sausage
krabba crab
krasse cress
kronärtskocka artichoke
kronärtskocksbotten artichoke bottom
kroppkakor potato dumplings stuffed with minced bacon and onions, served with melted butter
krusbär gooseberry
krusbärspaj gooseberry tart/pie
krydda spice
kryddnejlika clove
kryddost hard semi-fat cheese with cumin seeds
kryddpeppar allspice
kryddsmör herb butter
kräftor freshwater crayfish boiled with salt and dill, served cold

(Swedish speciality available only during August and September)
kräm 1) cream, custard 2) stewed fruit or syrup thickened with potato flour
kummin cumin
kuvertavgift cover charge
kuvertbröd French roll
kyckling chicken
~**bröst** breast
~**lever** liver
~**lår** leg
kål cabbage
~**dolmar** cabbage leaves stuffed with minced meat and rice
~**pudding** layers of cabbage leaves and minced meat
~**rot** turnip
käx biscuit (US cookie)
körsbär cherry
körvel chervil
kött meat
~**bullar** meat balls
köttfärs minced meat
~**limpa** meat loaf
~**sås** meat sauce for spaghetti
lagerblad bay leaf
lake burbot (freshwater fish)
lamm lamb
~**bog** shoulder
~**bringa** brisket
~**kotlett** chop
~**sadel** saddle
~**stek** roast
landgång a long, open sandwich with different garnishes
lapskojs lobscouse; casserole of potatoes, meat and vegetables
lax salmon
~**pudding** layers of flaked salmon, potatoes, onions and eggs, baked
laxöring salmon trout
legymsallad blanched vegetables, served in a mayonnaise sauce
lever liver
~**korv** sausage
~**pastej** paste
limpa rye bread; loaf
lingon lingonberry, small cranberry
~**sylt** lingonberry jam
lutfisk specially treated, poached stockfish, served with white sauce (Christmas speciality)
låda casserole
lättstekt underdone (US rare)
löjrom vendace roe often served on toast with onions and sour cream
lök onion
lövbiff thinly sliced beef
majonnäs mayonnaise
majs maize (US corn)
~**kolv** corn on the cob
makaroner macaroni
makrill mackerel
mandel almond
~**biskvi** almond biscuit (US cookie)
marinerad marinated
marmelad marmalade
marsipan marzipan, almond paste
maräng meringue
marängsviss meringue with whipped cream and chocolate sauce
matjessill marinated herring fillets, served with sour cream and chives
matsedel bill of fare
mejram marjoram
meny menu, bill of fare
mesost whey cheese
messmör soft whey cheese
middag dinner

mixed grill pieces of meat, onions, tomatoes and green peppers grilled on a skewer
mjukost soft white cheese
morkulla woodcock
morot (pl **morötter**) carrot
mullbär mulberry
munk doughnut
murkelstuvning creamed morel mushrooms
murkelsås morel mushroom sauce
murkla morel mushroom
muskot nutmeg
mussla mussel, clam
märg marrow
~**ben** marrow bone
njure kidney
nota bill (US check)
nypon rose-hip
~**soppa** rose-hip soup (dessert)
nässelsoppa nettle soup
oliv olive
olja oil
orre black grouse
ost cheese
~**bricka** cheese board
~**gratinerad** oven-browned, with cheese topping
~**kaka** kind of curd cake served with jam
~**stänger** cheese straws
ostron oyster
oxbringa brisket of beef
oxfilé fillet of beef (US tenderloin)
oxjärpe meatball of minced beef
oxkött beef
oxrulad beef olive; slice of beef rolled and braised in gravy
oxstek roast beef
oxsvanssoppa oxtail soup
oxtunga beef tongue
paj pie, tart
palsternacka parsnip
panerad breaded
pannbiff hamburger steak with fried onions
pannkaka pancake
paprika (grön) (green) pepper
parisare minced beef with capers, beetroot and onions served on toast, topped with a fried egg
pastej pie, patty, pâté
peppar pepper
~**kaka** ginger biscuit (US ginger snap)
~**rot** horseradish
~**rotskött** boiled beef with horseradish sauce
persika peach
persilja parsley
persiljesmör parsley butter
piggvar turbot
pilgrimsmussla scallop, coquille St. Jacques
pirog Russian pasty; stuffed pasty (caviar, cheese, fish or vegetables)
plankstek a thin steak served on a wooden platter (US plank steak)
plommon plum
~**späckad fläskkarré** roast loin of pork flavoured with prunes
plättar small, thin pancakes
pommes frites chips (US French fries)
potatis potato
färsk ~ new potatoes
~**mos** mashed potatoes
pressgurka marinated sliced, fresh cucumber
pressylta brawn (US head cheese)
prinsesstårta sponge cake with vanilla custard and whipped cream, covered with green almond paste
prinskorv cocktail sausage, small frankfurter

pudding mould, baked casserole
purjolök leek
pyttipanna kind of bubble and squeak; fried pieces of meat, sausage, onions and potatoes, served with an egg-yolk or a fried egg and pickled beetroot
päron pear
pölsa hash made of boiled pork and barley
rabarber rhubarb
raggmunk med fläsk potato pancake with bacon
rapphöna partridge
ren reindeer
~**sadel** saddle
~**skav** in thin slices
~**stek** roast
revbensspjäll spare-rib
rimmad, rimsaltad slightly salted
ris rice
risgrynsgröt rice pudding served with milk and cinnamon
riven, rivna grated
rom roe
rosmarin rosemary
rostat bröd toast
rostbiff roast beef
rotmos mashed turnips
russin raisin
rysk kaviar caviar
rå raw
~**biff** steak tartare: finely chopped raw beef with egg-yolks, capers, onions, pickled beetroot and seasoning
rådjur venison
rådjurssadel saddle of venison
rådjursstek roast venison
råkost uncooked shredded vegetables
rån small wafer
rårörda lingon lingonberry (small cranberry) jam preserved without cooking
rädisa radish
räka shrimp
räkcocktail shrimp cocktail
rättika black radish
rödbeta beetroot
rödbetssallad beetroot salad
röding char (fish)
rödkål red cabbage
rödspätta plaice
rökt smoked
rönnbär rowanberry (mountain ashberry)
rönnbärsgelé rowanberry jelly
rött (pl **röda**) **vinbär** redcurrant
saffran saffron
saffransbröd sweet saffron loaf or rolls
sallad salad
salta biten salted boiled beef
saltad salted
saltgurka salt-pickled gherkin
sardell anchovy
~**smör** anchovy butter
sardin sardine
schalottenlök shallot
schweizerost Swiss cheese
schweizerschnitzel cordon bleu; veal scallop stuffed with ham and cheese
selleri celery
~**rot** celery root
senap mustard
serveringsavgift service charge
sik whitefish
~**löja** vendace (small white-fish)
~**rom** whitefish roe
sill herring
~**bricka** board of assorted herring
~**bullar** herring dumplings
~**gratäng** baked casserole of herring, onions and potatoes

~**sallad** herring salad with pickled beetroot and gherkins, apples, boiled potatoes, onions and whipped cream
~**tallrik** portion of assorted herring
sirap treacle, molasses
sjömansbiff beef casserole with carrots, onions and potatoes, braised in beer
sjötunga sole
sjötungsfilé fillet of sole
skaldjur shellfish
skarpsås mayonnaise enriched with mustard and herbs
skinka ham
skinklåda ham-and-egg casserole
skinkomelett ham omelet
skiva slice
sky dripping, gravy
sköldpaddssoppa turtle soup
slottsstek pot roast flavoured with brandy, molasses and marinated sprats
slätvar brill
smultron wild strawberry
småfranska French roll
småkaka fancy biscuit (US fancy cookie)
småvarmt small hot dishes (on *smörgåsbord*)
smör butter
smörgås open sandwich
~**bord** a buffet offering a wide variety of appetizers, hot and cold meats, smoked and pickled fish, cheese, salads, relishes, vegetables and desserts
sniglar snails
snöripa ptarmigan
socker sugar
~**kaka** sponge cake
~**ärter** sugar peas
solöga marinated sprats, onions, capers, pickled beetroot and raw egg-yolk
soppa soup
sotare grilled Baltic herring
sparris asparagus
~**knopp** asparagus tip
spenat spinach
spettekaka tall, cone-shaped cake made on a spit
spicken sill salted herring
spritärter green peas
spädgris suck(l)ing pig
stekt fried, roasted
~ **(salt) sill** fried (salt) herring
stenbitssoppa lumpfish soup
strömming fresh Baltic herring
strömmingsflundra fried double fillets of Baltic herring stuffed with dill or parsley
strömmingslåda baked casserole of Baltic herring and potatoes
stuvad cooked in white sauce, creamed
~ **spenat** creamed spinach
sufflé soufflé
supé (late) supper
sur sour
~**kål** sauerkraut
~**stek** marinated roast beef
~**strömming** specially processed, cured and fermented Baltic herring
svamp mushroom
~**stuvning** creamed mushrooms
~**sås** mushroom sauce
svart (pl **svarta**) **vinbär** blackcurrant
svartsoppa soup made of goose blood
svartvinbärsgelé blackcurrant jelly
sveciaost hard cheese with pungent flavour

sylt jam
syltad 1) preserved (fruit) 2) pickled (vegetables)
syltlök pickled pearl onion
sås sauce, dressing, gravy
söt sweet
T-benstek T-bone steak
timjan thyme
tjäder wood-grouse, capercaillie
tomat tomato
tonfisk tunny (US tuna)
torkad frukt dried fruit
torr dry
torsk cod
~**rom** cod's roe
tranbär cranberry
tryffel truffle
tunga tongue
tunnbröd unleavened barley bread
tårta cake
ugnsbakad baked
ugnspannkaka kind of batter pudding
ugnstekt roasted
vaktel quail
valnöt walnut
vanilj vanilla
~**glass** vanilla ice-cream
~**sås** vanilla custard sauce
varm warm
~**rätt** hot dish, main dish
vattenmelon watermelon
vaxbönor butter beans (US wax beans)
vilt game
vinbär currant (black, red or white)
vindruva grape
vinlista wine list
vintersallad salad of grated carrots, apples and cabbage
vinäger vinegar
vinägrettsås vinegar-and-oil dressing
vispgrädde whipped cream
vitkål cabbage
vitling whiting
vitlök garlic
våffla waffle
välling soup made of cereal, gruel
välstekt well-done
västerbottenost pungent, hard cheese, strong when mature
västkustsallad seafood salad
Wallenbergare steak made of minced veal, egg-yolks and cream
wienerbröd Danish pastry
wienerkorv wiener, frankfurter
wienerschnitzel breaded veal cutlet
ål eel
inkokt ~ jellied
ägg egg
förlorat ~ poached
hårdkokt ~ hard-boiled
kokt ~ boiled
löskokt ~ soft-boiled
stekt ~ fried
~**röra** scrambled
~**stanning** baked egg custard
äggplanta aubergine (US egg-plant)
älg elk
~**filé** fillet (US tenderloin)
~**stek** roast
äppelkaka apple charlotte, apple pudding
äppelmos apple sauce
äpple apple
ärter peas
~ **och fläsk** yellow pea soup with diced pork
ättika white vinegar
ättiksgurka pickled gherkin (US pickle)

SWEDISH

Drink

akvavit aquavit, spirits distilled from potatoes or grain, often flavoured with aromatic seeds and spices
alkoholfri(tt) non-alcoholic
apelsinjuice orange juice
apelsinsaft orange squash (US orange drink)
brännvin aquavit
1) **Absolut rent brännvin (Renat)** unflavoured
2) **Bäska droppar** bitter and flavoured with a leaf of wormwood
3) **Herrgårds Aquavit** flavoured with herbs and slightly sweet
4) **O.P. Anderson Aquavit** flavoured with aniseed, caraway and fennel seeds
5) **Skåne Akvavit** less spicy than *O. P. Anderson*
6) **Svart-Vinbärs-Brännvin** flavoured with blackcurrants
choklad chocolate drink
kall ~ cold
varm ~ hot
exportöl beer with high alcoholic content
fatöl draught (US draft) beer
folköl light beer
fruktjuice fruit juice
glögg similar to mulled wine, served with raisins and almonds
grädde cream
Grönstedts French cognac bottled in Sweden
husets vin open wine
härtappning imported wine bottled in Sweden
julmust a foamy, malted drink served at Christmas
julöl beer specially brewed at Christmas
kaffe coffee
~ **med grädde och socker** with cream and sugar
~ **utan grädde och socker** black
koffeinfri(tt) ~ caffeine-free
Kaptenlöjtnant liqueur and brandy
karaffvin wine served in a carafe
Klosterlikör herb liqueur
konjak brandy, cognac
kärnmjölk buttermilk
likör liqueur
lingondricka cranberry drink
läskedryck soft drink, lemonade
~ **med kolsyra** fizzy (US carbonated)
~ **utan kolsyra** flat (US non-carbonated)
lättmjölk skim milk
lättöl beer with low alcoholic content
mjölk milk
kall ~ cold
varm ~ hot
portvin port (wine)
punsch a yellow liqueur on a base of arrack (spirit distilled from rice and sugar) served hot with pea soup or ice-cold as an after-dinner drink with coffee
rom rum
saft squash (US fruit drink)
slottstappning produced and bottled at the château
snaps glass of aquavit

sodavatten soda water
spritdrycker spirits
starksprit spirits
starköl beer with high alcoholic content
te tea
~ **med citron** with lemon
~ **med mjölk** with milk
~ **med socker** with sugar
vatten water
is~ iced
mineral~ mineral
vin wine
mousserande ~ sparkling
röd~ red
stark~ fortified
sött ~ sweet
torrt ~ dry
vitt ~ white
vindrinkar wine cobblers, long drinks on a wine base
äppelmust apple juice
öl beer
ljust ~ light
mörkt ~ dark
örtte infusion of herbs

Tipping guide

The figures below are shown either as a percentage of the bill or in local currency. They indicate a suggested tip for the service described. Even where service is included, additional gratuities are expected by some employees; it's also customary to round off a bill or payment, and leave the small change.

Obviously, tipping is an individual matter, and the correct amount to leave varies enormously with category of restaurant, size of city and so on. The sums we suggest represent normal tips for average middle-grade establishments in big cities.

Austria

Service charge, bill	10–15% included
Waiter	optional
Cloakroom attendant	5–10 shillings
Lavatory attendant	5–10 shillings

Belgium

Service charge, bill	15% included
Waiter	optional
Cloakroom attendant	50 francs
Lavatory attendant	10 francs

Czech Republic

Service charge, bill	generally included
Waiter	10–15%
Cloakroom attendant	2 Kčs
Lavatory attendant	1–2 Kčs

Finland

Service charge, bill	14–15% included
Waiter	optional
Cloakroom attendant	3–5 marks
Lavatory attendant	charges posted or 2.50 marks

France

Service charge, bill	12–15% generally included
Waiter	optional
Cloakroom attendant	3–5 francs
Lavatory attendant	2 francs

Germany

Service charge, bill	15% generally included
Waiter	optional
Cloakroom attendant	1–2 marks
Lavatory attendant	50 pfennigs – 1 mark

Great Britain

Service charge, bill	15% generally included
Waiter	10–15% (if not included)
Cloakroom attendant	20 pence
Lavatory attendant	20 pence

Greece

Service charge, bill	15% included
Waiter	optional
Cloakroom attendant	20 drachmas
Lavatory attendant	20 drachmas

Netherlands

Service charge, bill	included
Waiter	optional
Cloakroom attendant	1–2 florins
Lavatory attendant	50 cents

Ireland

Service charge, bill	generally included
Waiter	optional
Cloakroom attendant	20 pence
Lavatory attendant	20 pence

Italy

Service charge, bill	12–15% included
Waiter	10%
Cloakroom attendant	500 lire
Lavatory attendant	300 lire

Norway

Service charge, bill	10–15% included
Waiter	optional
Cloakroom attendant	charges posted or 3–5 kroner
Lavatory attendant	charges posted or 3 kroner

Poland

Service charge, bill	10% included
Waiter	round off upwards
Cloakroom attendant	charges posted or 2,000 zlotys
Lavatory attendant	2,000 zlotys

Portugal

Service charge, bill	15% included
Waiter	10% optional
Cloakroom attendant	25–40 escudos
Lavatory attendant	25 escudos

Russia

Service charge, bill	10–15% included
Waiter	optional
Cloakroom attendant	15 roubles
Lavatory attendant	10–15 roubles

Spain

Service charge, bill	15% generally included
Waiter	10%
Cloakroom attendant	25–50 pesetas
Lavatory attendant	25–50 pesetas

Sweden

Service charge, bill	13½% included
Waiter	round up (optional)
Cloakroom attendant	charges posted or 3.50 kronor
Lavatory attendant	3–5 kroner

Switzerland

Service charge, bill	15% included
Waiter	optional
Cloakroom attendant	1 franc
Lavatory attendant	50 centimes